EARLY DEVELOPMENTS IN
MATHEMATICAL ECONOMICS

EARLY DEVELOPMENTS IN MATHEMATICAL ECONOMICS

REGHINOS D. THEOCHARIS

FOREWORD BY
LORD ROBBINS

SECOND EDITION

PORCUPINE PRESS

Philadelphia

First edition 1961
Second edition 1983

Published in the United States of America 1983 by
PORCUPINE PRESS
Philadelphia, Pennsylvania

Library of Congress Cataloging in Publication Data

Theocharis, Reghinos D. 1929
  Early developments in mathematical economics.
  Bibliography: p.
  Includes index.
  I. Economics, Mathematical—History. I. Title.
  HB99.T47 1982   330.15′43   80-16638
  ISBN 0-87991-808-X

Printed in Hong Kong

Contents

Contents

Preface to the Second Edition

The present edition includes a major addition. This is the section on Cournot and his contribution to the development of mathematical economics. Since the appearance of the first edition, I have been feeling that the book was incomplete. A process in the development of mathematical economics was described which was shown to be gathering momentum and which was bound to lead to a major development but the book just stopped at the threshold of this. This is why a section on Cournot is now included. He marks the end of the era of the 'protohistory' of mathematical economics and the beginning of its new era of rapid developments.

What I have just said does not mean, however, that I would now wish to belittle the importance of the contributions to mathematical economics of the authors before Cournot. For, as Professor G.L.S. Shackle has said in his review in the *Economica* of the first edition of this book, one of its major purposes was, apart from describing the essentials of the early contributions to mathematical economics, to point out:

> their often charming directness and incisive power, their frequently astonishing anticipations of what we think of as the discoveries of our own generation, the tale they so plainly tell, in many cases, of a mind of true genius struggling, alone, in an utterly untrodden country, enjoying, of course, by that very fact the exquisite freedom of the first explorer:

> Libera per vacuum posui vestigia princeps

The present work springs from a thesis approved by the University of London in 1958 for a Ph.D. under the title 'Augustin Cournot and his Contribution to Economic Analysis with special reference to the General Theory of Monopoly'.

The work was originally undertaken at the London School of

Economics under the guidance of Lord Robbins and, partly, of Dr G. Morton and Professor M. Peston.

I wish to express my sincere thanks to Dr Morton and Professor Peston for the help so generously given, especially in the mathematical sections. The responsibility for any mistakes is, of course, entirely mine.

My major debt is, however, to Lord Robbins who, with his unequalled knowledge of the literature of economics, supervised the work at all its stages and guided my steps towards discovering sources which would have remained unknown to me. Lord Robbins's keen interest in seeing that the work is published as well as his kindness and generous encouragement will never be forgotten.

There is another debt that I wish to acknowledge towards Lord Robbins. Throughout these years his warm-hearted friendship has been one of the main-stays of my work and life.

I also wish to thank Professor K. Okuguchi, who has done so much to revitalise Cournot's thinking in a dynamic setting, for his keen interest in my work and his appreciation.

Lastly, but not least, I wish to thank my wife; without her devotion, love and help this work and its revision would have never been completed.

Athens School of Economics
  and Business Science
Athens, December 1978   REGHINOS D. THEOCHARIS

Foreword

The history of mathematical economics before Cournot must in some respects be regarded as consisting of antiquarian *curiosa*. For it cannot be claimed that anything that was done during this period has survived in immediately recognisable form to the present day. It was not until Cournot, that great original mind, presented, with the simplicity of genius, the idea of demand as a function of price, that a contribution which has proved to be of permanent value and influence was forthcoming from this quarter.

Nevertheless, all such beginnings must have a profound significance for those who are interested in the struggles of the mind to understand the universe about it: and these early attempts to enlist the most powerful method of logical reasoning in the service of economic thought have an interest and a fascination of their own. Nor should it be imagined that their authors belonged chiefly to an underworld of the neglected and obscure. There were indeed such to whom perhaps for the first time this book does full justice. But many were outstanding in the general history of thought. The names of Bernoulli, Hutcheson, Beccaria, Du Pont de Nemours, for instance, have an importance far transcending their place in this history. And this perhaps is an added justification for this kind of study.

I must confess, however, that when Dr Theocharis, who has since had the great distinction to become the first Finance Minister of the Republic of Cyprus, first told me that he was planning the earlier chapters of his doctor's thesis on Cournot so as to cover this period, I had certain qualms and hesitations, although I did not communicate them to him. I knew my Jevons and Irving Fisher, I had read the copious opening chapters of the *epigoni* of the School of Lausanne, I knew at first hand a few of the authors whose work he proposed to investigate; and I had doubts whether the field would repay further intensive study on this scale. But it is one of the privileges of being a supervisor in a graduate school that if you are at all lucky with your pupils, you learn much more than you teach; and I am sure that all readers of this book will agree that Dr Theocharis has triumphantly proved the baselessness of my initial reserves and has produced in these chapters a monograph of lasting value and interest. Not only has he succeeded in providing for the first time a systematic survey of the literature; he has also made discoveries of authors not previously recognised and compelled the revaluation of contributions already known. His discovery of Joseph Lang and his re-examination of Canard are outstanding cases in point. I am confident that historians of economic thought will join with me in gratitude and admiration for the results of Dr Theocharis' researches.

There is another circumstance connected with this book which I hope Dr Theocharis will not mind my mentioning. These chapters, and indeed the whole thesis of which they are part, were written at the London School of Economics when relations between his country and ours were at their worst. I like to think of them as a testimony to the fact that, in these disturbed times, there is at least one spot on earth where, as in the Temple of Isis and Osiris in the *Magic Flute*, 'Kennt man die Rache nicht', and where the pursuit of knowledge and truth can proceed, as it proceeded in less troubled days, unimpeded by political divisions.

ROBBINS

London School of Economics
10 October 1960

1 Introduction

The aim of the present work is to examine the early development of mathematical economics. No attempt has so far been made to examine systematically the literature of mathematical economics before 1838. Occasional attempts[1] have been made, however, to evaluate the work of certain of the authors of that period and the interesting fact about these attempts is that they practically all agree that the authors of that period 'stand now as more or less isolated figures, who cannot be said to have contributed to a current of thought because there is no discernible flow'.[2]

We hope to show that, on the contrary, certain currents of thought may be detected, in the sense that not only do we find contributions from people, not in direct connection with one another, who use the same method, but beyond this it will be shown that authors, knowing the work and ideas of their predecessors, have been able to develop further these ideas. So we shall find Ceva leading to Spinelli, Beccaria to Silio, Frisi through Ortes, Ferroni, Venturi and others to Valeriani and Fuoco, Canard to Fuoco, Gioja and Cournot, Kröncke to Thünen, Isnard to Lang. The fact is, however, that having followed the thread up to a point, we suddenly come to an end in most cases. In Italy, especially, mathematical economics flourished during the eighteenth and early nineteenth centuries and it would be very interesting to know what influence these early authors exercised on authors after Cournot, but such a task is outside the scope of this study.

In our treatment we have preferred to divide the authors according to the language they used. We have, however, made some exceptions.

We have preferred to examine the very early contributors to mathematical economics, with the exception of Daniel Bernoulli, separately because they all use the geometric method; they start with certain axioms and the proof of their theorems is made in terms of logic rather than formal mathematical treatment. This is the reason why we have called them 'the logicians'.

The second exception is that we have called the Italian contribution, with the exception of Fuoco who has been considerably influenced by the French, the 'Milanese School'. This has been done in order to stress the importance of the Lombard contribution, with its centre at Milan, to mathematical economics. It is made up of an illustrious conglomeration of men, mostly nobles, as G. Pecchio[3] has observed, who had the widest possible interests from economics to criminology, from poetry to astronomy. As G. Rossi remarks, 'having been educated in a period when mathematical analysis was fashionable and poets wrote poems about science and geometric treatises, they often used eagerly and advantageously reasonings and demonstrations, which, if not always taking the form of, had all the force and character of mathematics'.[4]

NOTES

1. Chiefly (a). A. Montanari, *La matematica applicata all'economia politica* (1892), who deals with Beccaria, Silio, Valeriani and Scialoja. (b) Notes by M. Fasiani to F. Fuoco, *Applicazione dell'algebra all economia politica* (1937). (c) Helmut Reichardt, *A.A. Cournot* (Tübingen, 1954) pp. 67–91. (d) Ross M. Robertson, 'Mathematical Economics before Cournot' in *Journal of Political Economy* (1949) pp. 523–36, who deals with only some of the mathematical economists of the period. (e) G.H. Bousquet, 'Histoire de l' économie mathématique jusqu' à Cournot', *Metro-economica* (1958) pp. 121–35; G.H. Bousquet, 'Le Systéme Mathématique de l' équilibre économique selon Léon Walras et ses origines', *Revue d' Economie Politique* (1963) pp. 948–76.
    A very useful anthology of works in mathematical economics, including early ones, has appeared since the first edition of this Book. This is W.J. Baumol and S.M. Goldfeld, *Precursors in Mathematical Economics: An Anthology* (London School of Economics, 1968).
2. Robertson, op. cit., p. 535; see also Reichardt, op. cit., p. 67.
3. G. Pecchio, *Histoire de l'économie politique en Italie* (1830) pp. 395 and 379.
4. G. Rossi, *La matematica applicata alla teoria della ricchezza sociale* (Reggio Emilia, 1889) p. ix.

2 The Logicians

2.1 ARISTOTLE

The earliest author to use mathematics in an economic argument was Aristotle. In the fifth book of the *Nicomachean Ethics*, in his general examination of Justice, Aristotle deals with two kinds of 'particular justice', justice in the distribution of wealth and justice in the various transactions between men.

In the distribution of wealth the shares of two persons must be proportional to the persons themselves. If the persons are not equal, they must not have equal shares. This he illustrates by assuming that A and B are the persons and C and D the things. 'The ratio between the two pairs of terms is the same, because the persons and the things are divided similarly. It will stand then thus, $A : B :: C : D$, and then permutando $A : C :: B :: D$ and then (supposing C and D to represent the things)

$$A + C : B + D :: A : B$$

The distribution in fact consisting in putting together these terms thus: and if they are put together so as to preserve this ratio, the distribution puts them together justly.'[1]

One kind of transaction, the principles of justice of which Aristotle examines, is exchange. If this is to be just there must be what the Pythagoreans called 'Reciprocation'. He visualises an agriculturist and a shoemaker exchanging their products and explains that 'there will be Reciprocation when the terms have been equalised so as to stand in this proportion; Agriculturist: Shoemaker :: wares of Shoemaker: wares of Agriculturist'.[2] 'Let A represent an agriculturist, C food, B a shoemaker, D his wares equalised with A's. 'Then the proportion will be correct, $A : B :: C : D$; now Reciprocation will be practicable, if it were not, *there would have been no dealing*.'[3] The last phrase seems to be of special interest, as Aristotle appears to be no longer interested in merely defining a just exchange but is attempting to lay down some form of equilibrium conditions of exchange. The value of each product is determined by the quality of labour spent upon it[4] and, in equilibrium, quantities of products exchanged must be proportional to the quality of labour which produced them.

Aristotle was much inspired in his treatment of this subject by geometrical concepts. In his presentation of exchange there occurs a passage[5] which is rendered thus by his translator:[6]

> Now the acts of mutual giving in due proportion may be represented by the diameters of a parallelogram, at the four angles of which the parties and their wares are so placed that the side connecting the parties be opposite to that connecting the wares and each party be connected by one side with his own ware (as in Figure 2.1.)

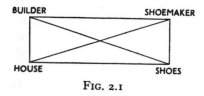

Fig. 2.1

2.2 GIOVANNI CEVA

The period intervening between Aristotle and the early eighteenth century produced no use of mathematics in the economic writings of the scholastics of the Middle Ages or the laical intellectuals.

The first clear attempt after Aristotle to use mathematics in an economic problem was made by Ceva in an Essay published in Mantua in 1711 under the title 'De re numaria, quoad fieri potuit geometrice tractata, ad illustrissimos et excellentissimos dominos praesidem quaestoresque huius arciducalis Caesarei magistratus Mantuae'.[7]

His views on the use of the mathematical method are clear and decided. In the dedication, at the beginning of his book, he points out that commerce is so great and complex that the exploration of its nature cannot be done in any other way except through the use of geometry.[8] This he does in his treatment of money by building up a model through the use of definitions and postulates.

After defining 'monetary material' to include every kind of money circulating in a country, he distinguishes between its intrinsic value (internus valor) which is the quantity of pure metal it contains, and its 'external value', which he defines as the purchasing power of money, adding, however, that it corresponds to the value of the metal plus minting expenses.[9]

Ceva's first postulate is that, other things being equal, the external value of a currency is inversely related to its quantity. The second postulate links changes in the purchasing power of money with changes in the population of a country; other things being equal, the external value of money is directly proportional to the population of a country.[10]

Given these, he proceeds to prove his first theorem that the 'external values' of two currencies are in compound proportion, made up of the direct proportion of their respective populations and inverse proportion of their quantities.

He uses the following illustration which I reproduce.[11]

I	a	b	c
L	a	e	h
K	d	e	f

Ceva assumes that at time I the population of a country is a, the quantity of money b and the external value of money c. At time K the population is d, the quantity of money e and the external value f. To prove his theorem he makes use of an intermediate step, assuming that at time L the population is equal to that at time I, while the quantity of money is equal to that at time K; the external value of money is equal to h.

Now he compares time I with time L. By the first postulate, when other things are equal (and here a is unchanged) value is inversely related to the quantity of money:

$$c : h :: e : b$$

Ceva then proceeds to compare values at times L and K. As the quantities are now the same, by the second postulate, the value of money is directly related to population:

$$h : f :: a : d$$

As, however, $\dfrac{c}{f} = \dfrac{c}{h} \times \dfrac{h}{f}$, we have $\dfrac{c}{f} = \dfrac{e}{b} \times \dfrac{a}{d}$, which demonstrates that the ratio of the two values is equal to a compound ratio made up of the inverse ratio of their respective quantities and the direct ratio of their populations.

Through appropriate postulates, Ceva now proceeds to introduce a situation where gold, silver and copper coins circulate and attempts to prove a second theorem[12] according to which, when the quantity of gold coins circulating remains unchanged, their value is directly related to the quantity of copper money and inversely related to the quantity of silver money. He uses an illustration which we reproduce and argues in the following way:

G	a	b	c
I	d	b	c
H	d	e	c
Time	copper	silver	gold

coins

Let at time G the quantity of copper, silver and gold money respectively be a, b and c; and at time H, d, e and c; and further assume that at an intermediate time I, the quantity of copper coins is d, silver coins b and gold coins c. Ceva starts by comparing times G and I where the quantities of gold and silver are the same; as, however, the quantity of copper coins changes, the value of gold coins will change proportionally. An increase in the quantity of copper coins leads to an increase in the value of gold coins, presumably because people trust gold more than copper, although Ceva does not point this out and had not included it in his postulates.[13] He then compares times I and H where, with unchanged quantities of copper and gold coins, the value of gold is inversely proportional to changes in the quantity of silver coins, i.e. $e : b$. An increase therefore of silver leads to a decrease in the value of gold. Gold and silver are put on the same plane.

But[14]
$$\frac{\text{value of gold coins at time } G}{\text{value of gold coins at time } H}$$

$$= \frac{\text{value of gold coins at } G}{\text{value of gold coins at } I} \times \frac{\text{value of gold coins at } I}{\text{value of gold coins at } H} = \frac{a}{d} \times \frac{e}{b}$$

In the second part of his essay[15] he solves various problems, where there are coins of the same metal but of different intrinsic value or of different metals, and demonstrates that their intrinsic values are proportional to the product of their respective 'titles'[16] by their respective weights;[17] he also discusses various other cases of minting coins when their weights, minting expenses, titles, etc are given. In all these problems he uses extensively algebraic notation, which he stresses can be translated by anyone into numbers.[18]

This is in general outline the work of Ceva. Of interest to us are not so much his results but his method, expressed in his insistence that in the examination of such problems one must proceed from the general to the particular; in his careful use of the 'ceteris paribus' hypothesis; in his illustrations and above all in his bold innovation of applying 'geometry' to an economic argument.[19]

2.3 EDMÉ MARIOTTE AND FRANCIS HUTCHESON

Mariotte is sometimes included among early writers of mathematical economics,[20] but his book, *Éssai de logique*,[21] on which the claim is founded, is a borderline case. He attempts first to advance various propositions which he thinks must be accepted as truthful. Some of these are rules of reasoning and the others principles to establish both the Moral and Physical Sciences. He then attempts to show how these propositions could be applied through the processes of ordinary logic to discover social and natural truths which are not self-evident.[22]

Certain of his principles are of economic interest. Thus:

(a) If two equal future goods are offered, one must choose that which is the most probable.[23]

(b) One 'good' is said to be equal to an 'evil', if, when they are joined together, one is indifferent either to pursue them or to avoid them.[24] If we replace 'good' and 'evil' by the words 'utility' and 'disutility', as Mariotte himself points out in Principle xcvii which we give later, the importance of Mariotte as a precursor of the idea of indifference becomes obvious.

(c) One must choose the greatest among equally possible goods.[25]

(d) When choosing 'goods' or 'evils' we must consider the quantity of pleasure or pain which the things give us and not the size or number of these things.[26]

(e) If there are two equal goods, of which one is present and the other future, the present one must be preferred because of the uncertainty of the future.[27]

In application of these principles he gives an example of a man who is asked to play in one game his whole property of 20,000 écus against a probable gain of 100,000 écus.[28] One would think that this man would have an advantage of 5 to 1; but while 20,000 écus are enough for a man to live comfortably, 100,000 more 'will not increase his happiness more than approximately 3 to 2 or 3 to 1'. If he loses his property, he will find himself in complete poverty, 'and the proportion between having enough to live comfortably and having nothing at all is almost infinite or like 100,000 to 1'.[29] Here is then the idea of diminishing utility of income with infinite utility at the one end and infinitesimal utility at the other.

In a work published in 1728 Francis Hutcheson[30] adopts a similar procedure to that of Mariotte. He gives a set of formal definitions where, among other things, he defines natural good as pleasure and natural evil as pain,[31] and a set of axioms, some of which are:[32]

1. 'The strength either of the private or public desire of any event, is proportioned to the imagined quantity of good, which will arise from it to the agent, or the person for whose sake it is desired.'
2. 'Equal mixtures of good and evil stop all desire or aversion.' This is similar to Mariotte's Principle 95.
3. 'The moment of good in any object is in compound proportion of the duration and intenseness.'
4. 'The ratio of the hazard of acquiring or retaining any good must be multiplied into the moment of the good.' 'Hence it is that the smallest certain good may arise stronger desire than the greatest good, if the uncertainty of the latter surpass that of the former, in a greater proportion than that of the greater to the less.' The similarity of this axiom to Mariotte's Principle 91 is again obvious.[33]

2.4 TROJANO SPINELLI

Spinelli wrote a book most probably about 1750[34] under the title *'Riflessioni politiche sopra alcuni punti della scienza della moneta'* which is clearly an extension of Ceva's work.

Like Ceva he starts with definitions,[35] but the intrinsic value of money for him is the esteem in which money is held by public opinion while the 'external' or nominal value of money (valore estrinseco) is the value imposed by order of the Prince or the State. He also defines, among other things, appreciation of money as the increase of the nominal value by order of the Prince and depreciation (abassamento) as the lowering of the nominal value.

His Definition ix[36] is of interest. This says that currencies whose ratio of intrinsic values, as estimated from the value of pure metal they contain, is greater than the ratio of their nominal values are called *stronger* currencies as opposed to *weaker* currencies, whose ratio of nominal values exceeds that of their intrinsic value. To illustrate this, he gives the following diagram:

$$A$$
$$B \qquad C$$
$$D$$
$$E \qquad F$$

where the currencies are A and D, the nominal value of A is C and its intrinsic value B, while the nominal value of D is F and its intrinsic value E. Then if

$$B : C > E : F \text{ or } B : E > C : F, A \text{ is stronger than } D$$

and consequently

$$C : B < F : E \text{ or } E : B < F : C, D \text{ is weaker than } A.[37]$$

His axioms[38], however, are on a much narrower plane than Ceva's. His main idea is that the weight of the pure metal contained in a coin multiplied by the value of the metal (what he calles the 'specific' value) gives a value ('absolute' value) which determines the intrinsic value of money.

The second part of his book contains an argument against fixing the nominal value of money above its intrinsic value because of the possibility of arbitrage; he also argues that, if there is bimetallism, the two kinds of currency must be of equal strength. His argument is the following:

$$\begin{array}{ccccc} & D{-} & & F{-} & \\ \text{gold} & & & \text{silver} & \\ A & & & B & \\ & E{-} & & G{-} & \\ & & & \text{silver} & \\ & & C & H & \end{array}$$

Let the gold currency A of a country have nominal value D and intrinsic value E and the silver currency B have nominal value F and intrinsic value G; then if gold is weaker than silver, this would mean that the ratio of the nominal values of A to B will be bigger than the ratio of their respective intrinsic values, and also that the ratio of the nominal value D of A to its intrinsic value E will be greater than the ratio of the nominal value F of B to its intrinsic value G.[39] In modern notation we would therefore have written $D : F > E : G$.

If by order of the State the nominal values of both currencies are fixed at parity, while their intrinsic values continue to differ, G being greater than F, since silver is stronger than gold, anyone may export silver, buy gold abroad and exchange it at home, because of the parity of nominal value, for a greater quantity of silver. This would of course mean that the 'stronger' metal would leave the country.

At the conclusion of his book Spinelli presents certain propositions 'geometrically demonstrated'.[40] The first of these,[41] for which he uses Figure 2.2.

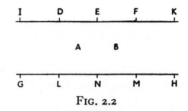

FIG. 2.2

is that the value of two material bodies, where the value per unit of weight of the material from which they are made is the same, is proportional to their weights. If the values of A and B are respectively DE and EF and their weights LN and NM then the ratio of DE to EF is the same as the ratio of LN to NM. If the weights are increased, the values must be increased proportionally so that the ratio of EI now to EK is the same as the ratio of GN to NH.

A second proposition similarly demonstrated is that the value of two bodies of different material, e.g. gold and silver but of equal weight is proportional to the price of the material.[42]

NOTES

1. *The Nicomachean Ethics of Aristotle*, trans. D. P. Chase (London 1949) p. 108. The passage is taken from Book V, 1131 b (Bekker's edn). It must be noted that Aristotle did not use the sign, conventionally accepted today, to indicate proportion; this was expressed literally. Thus $A : B :: B : C$ was expressed as 'ως η του A πρὸς την του B ουτως και η του B πρos την του $Γ$. Aristotle, op. cit., Book V, 1131 b.
2. Aristotle, op. cit., Book V, 1133a, p. 113.
3. Aristotle, op. cit., Book V, 1133b, pp. 113–14. The italicising is mine.
4. A. Grant in *The Ethics of Aristotle* (1866) vol. II, p. 118, n.8.
5. 'ποιει δε την αντιδοοιν την κατ' αναλογιαν η κατὰ διάμετρον συξευξις.' Aristotle, *Ethics*, Book V, 1133a.

6. Aristotle, op. cit., translated by D. P. Chase (1949) p. 112. Most translators and annotators of *Ethics* agree with the above translation and illustrate it similarly. Vide Aristotle, op. cit., trans. by A. Grant, vol. II, (1866) p. 118 and Aristotle, op. cit., trans. by H. Rackham (1926) p. 282 who in a note says: 'The relative value of the units of two products must be ascertained, say one house must be taken as worth *n* shoes. Then the four terms are $\begin{matrix} A & & B \\ & \times & \\ C & & nD \end{matrix}$.' But Henry Jackson in *Ethics* (1879), p. 95 thinks 'συξευξις' is $\dfrac{A + D}{B + C} = \dfrac{A}{B}$.

   See also W. Jaffé, 'Edgeworth's Contract Curve, part 2: Two Figures in its Protohistory: Aristotle and Gossen' in *History of Political Economy* (1974) pp. 384–91.

7. The Latin text of Ceva's essay is given in full in Eugenio Masé-Dari, *Un precursore della Econometria* (Modena 1935) pp. 37–59. There is also a review of Ceva's work in an article by F. Nicolini, 'Un antico Economista matematico', in *Giornale degli Economisti* (1878) pp. 11–23. References to Ceva's text are to the Masé-Dari edition.

   On Ceva, see also G.H. Bousquet et J. Roussier, introduction to the translation of 'De Re Numaria etc.', in *Revue d' histoire économique et sociale* (1958) pp. 129–39.

8. It must be pointed out that the term 'geometry' was used at that time and later to denote the whole branch of pure mathematics. Vide Jacques Moret, *L'emploi des mathématiques en Economic Politique* (Paris 1915) p. 5, n 2.

9. Ceva, op. cit., pp. 38–9.

10. Ceva, op. cit., p. 39, Petitio I and Petitio II. In the Scholium following Petitio II, Ceva says that the external value of money, i.e. its purchasing power, increases when money is exported or there are persons accumulating a great quantity of money or spending on luxuries or when arts and commerce are slack because of a diminution of population. It must be noted that such situations, as accumulation of money and spending on luxuries on the one hand, or exportation of money and slackening of trade on the other, are contradictory, but Ceva is not aware of it. Nor is he aware of any relation between money and the terms of borrowing it or any relation between increase of population and velocity of circulation. Cf. Masé-Dari, op. cit., pp. 27–8.

    G.L.S. Shackle argues that, if we think in terms of the quantity theory, Ceva's view would show to be consistent; because accumulation of money could be thought of as hoarding leading to a reduction of MV of the equation of the Quantity Theory and thus a reduction in P; and spending on luxuries would suggest that the rich 'have for the time being a high propensity to consume, so that T will be high and with MV constant, P accordingly low'. See G.L.S. Shackle, Review of the first edition of the present book, in *Economica* (1964) pp. 195–6.

11. Ceva, op. cit., p. 40.

12. Ceva, op. cit., pp. 41–2.

13. A. Martinelli, quoted by Masé-Dari, op. cit., pp. 12–13, and Masé-Dari

himself (ibid., p. 29) think that this is a serious contradiction on the part of Ceva, because, in his Petitio III he had put copper and silver on the same plane, while now that he examines the effects of changes of their quantities on the value of gold he asserts that the increase in copper coins leads to an increase in the value of gold coins, contrary to what happens when silver coins are increased.

14. This follows from Ceva's argument since:

$$\frac{\text{value of gold coins at } G}{\text{value of gold coins at } I} = \frac{a}{d}$$

and

$$\frac{\text{value of gold coins at } I}{\text{value of gold coins at } H} = \frac{e}{b}$$

15. 'De Numorum duplici valore', Ceva, op. cit., p. 43 *et seq.*

16. The ratio expressing the content of pure metal in the coin, or the 'fineness' of the metal.

17. Propositio I, p. 45, Ceva, op. cit.

18. '... quod nos algebricis utamur notis: etenim subinde praxes trademus, qurbus unus quisque, quandocunque voluerit, poterit traditas rationes per vulgares numeros expedire', Ceva, op. cit., p. 46.

19. F. Nicolini, op. cit., p. 19 wrote, 'We encounter in Ceva a sane conception of science, a clear doctrine of method and above all a bold novelty.'

20. Appendix I of W. S. Jevons, *The Theory of Political Economy*, 2nd edn (1879), does not include Mariotte. The list of works on Mathematical Economics in the English translation of Cournot's *Recherches*, prepared by Fisher, gives the author as 'Esme Mariotte'. Mariotte, however is included in later editions of the *Theory* of Jevons, e.g. see Appendix V of the edition of 1924.

21. In *Oeuvres de Mr Mariotte* vol. I (Leide 1717) pp. 609–701.

22. Mariotte, op. cit., pp. 611–12.

23. Mariotte, op. cit., pp. 629. This is Principe XCI.

24. Principe XCV, p. 629.

25. Principe XCIV, p. 629.

26. Mariotte, op. cit., Principe XCVII, p. 629.

27. Mariotte, Principe XCVIII. The affinity of this idea and certain theories of interest is obvious.

28. Mariotte, Partie II, Article III, op. cit., p. 667. Mariotte appears to imply that the chances of this man gaining or losing are the same, i.e. equal to ½ each.

29. Mariotte, op. cit., p. 667, who adds that of course our man should play 20 écus against 100.

30. F. Hutcheson, *An Essay on the Nature and Conduct of the Passions and Affections with Illustrations on the Moral Sense.* Our references are to the 3rd edn of 1769.

31. Hutcheson, op. cit., pp. 32 *et seq.*

32. Hutcheson, op. cit., pp. 35 *et seq.*, axioms, 3, 5, 8 and 10.

33. Hutcheson also published in 1720, *An Inquiry into the Original of our Ideas of Beauty and Virtue* (London, 5th edn. 1753), where he attempts to

assess the morality of human actions by using mathematical expressions and axioms; see esp. pp. 184, 190 *et seq.* of 5th edn. and W. S. Jevons, Appendix V to the *Theory of Political Economy* (4th edn 1924) and the Preface to the 2nd edn, ibid., pp. xxv–xxvi.

34. The book was published in Naples and bears no date. The British Museum Catalogue gives as its date 1750. The *Enciclopedia Italiana* contains no mention of Spinelli but the Spanish *Enciclopedia Universal* (1927) gives as date of publication 1748. Nicolini, op. cit., p. 20, n 3, estimates that the book was written between 1743 and 1746.
35. Spinelli, op. cit., pp. 5–9.
36. Spinelli, op. cit., p. 8.
37. Spinelli does not use the sign of inequality but simply says 'Se *B* a *C* è in maggior ragione che *E* ad *F*', etc., ibid., p. 8.
38. Ibid., pp. 10–12.
39. Spinelli, op. cit., pp. 35–6. The illustration is contained on p. 35 of Spinelli's book. Symbols *C* and *H* are used to illustrate the arbitrage operations.
40. 'Proposizioni geometricamente dimostrate intorno al valore ed al peso della materia: che servono alla chiara intelligenza dell' opera intrapesa'. op. cit., pp. 63–5.
41. Proposition I, op. cit., p. 63.
42. Op. cit., p. 65. The remaining propositions pp. 66–8 are of a similar nature.

3 The Probabilists

3.1 DANIEL BERNOULLI AND UTILITY THEORY

Bernoulli's contribution to mathematical economics was not intended as such; it was intended as a contribution to the theory of probability and was delivered before the St Petersburg Academy of Sciences in 1738.[1] It was published in the same year under the title 'Specimen theoriae novae de mensura sortis'.[2] In this Bernoulli is concerned with the problem of the value of a game to the individual and arrives essentially to the same conclusions as Mariotte. Contrary, however, to Mariotte, he is not satisfied simply with the logical argument but applies this to the theory of probability by making use, for the first time in a writing of economic character, of both analytic geometry and the differential calculus.

Bernoulli points out that in calculating the mathematical expectation of profit[3] the personal circumstances of the individual are not taken into consideration. But take the case of the holder of a lottery ticket who can, with equal probability, win nothing or 20,000 ducats. The probability to win is therefore 1 : 2 and the expectation of profit is $\frac{1}{2} \times 20{,}000 = 10{,}000$ ducats. If the holder of the ticket is 'a poor devil', Bernoulli asks, will he be silly if he chooses to sell it for a safe sum of 9000 ducats? The answer is negative and Bernoulli suggests that the value of the expected profit must not be taken objectively and independently of the individual but must be determined by the *advantage* derived by each individual.[4] This is really an aspect of what has been called the 'St. Petersburg Paradox' from the city in which Bernoulli's Paper was delivered. The paradox consists in the fact that people do not accept that the value to them of a certain sum they win is equal to the value of the same sum which they lose.

The advantage derived by the individual from the addition to the stock of things, which are useful for the satisfaction of his wants, is related to the height of the wealth already in his possession. Each infinitely small addition to wealth produces an advantage which, most probably, is inversely proportional to the already existing wealth.[5] Thus Bernoulli is not simply satisfied to state the principle of diminishing utility of income but, with noticeable boldness and no justifying arguments in support, goes further and defines an inversely proportional relation between utility of additional income and wealth.

He illustrates[6] his argument in Figure 3.1 to which I have added the 45° line.

AB is the amount of wealth before the chance event, and BC, BD, etc are additions to this wealth. The curve SBS shows the relation between additions to wealth and utility derived. This is given by Bernoulli as concave from below, which would mean that an addition in wealth of say $CD = Gr$ produces a less than proportional increase in utility Hr.

If now, out of a total number of $m + n + p + \ldots = s$ occasions, profit BC, with a consequent advantage CG, occurs m times, i.e. with probability $\frac{m}{s}$, profit BD, with a consequent advantage DH, occurs n times i.e. with probability $\frac{n}{s}$, and so on, the 'mean (average)[7] advantage' will be

$$PO = \frac{m}{s} CG + \frac{n}{s} DH + \frac{p}{s} EL + \ldots = \frac{mCG + nDH + pEL + \ldots}{s}$$

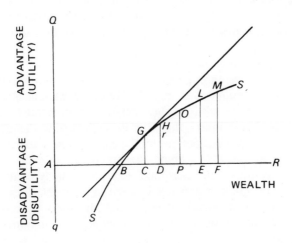

FIG. 3.1.

By referring now to Figure 3.1 we can find that this advantage *PO* corresponds to an addition of wealth *BP*; this is the value of the chance event for the individual and therefore 'the stake which no individual who gives proper care to his wealth circumstances must exceed'.[8]

If now we assume that the increase in wealth is made through infinitely small changes, and *AC* = *x* with its corresponding advantage *CG* = *y*, to an increase *CD* = *Gr* = *dx* there will correspond a utility *Hr* = d*y*. Since, by assumption, the increase in advantage d*y* caused by the increase in wealth d*x* is inversely proportional to the wealth already existing, Bernoulli derives the formula $\frac{dy}{dx} = \frac{1}{x}b$ where *b* is a proportionality factor. Integrating $\int dy = \int b \frac{dx}{x}$ he gets

(1) $$y = b \log x + C$$

If *AB* = *a*, the above equation, when *y* = 0, gives

(2) $$C = -b \log a$$

which substituted into (1) gives

(3) $$y = b \log \left(\frac{x}{a}\right)$$

as the equation of curve *SBS*. This is therefore a logarithmic curve.

This is the contribution of Bernoulli. As Fick remarks,[9] he did not seek to write a treatise in economics but simply felt that he had a good idea which should, for the benefit of science, be put down in writing.

Bernoulli's idea was not noticed by economists but was bound to have reverberations through another channel. It was taken up by Laplace who reproduced it in his '*Théorie analytique des probabilités*',[10] where he distinguishes between mathematical expectation and moral expectation, the latter being defined as the product of the 'value of the good expected' by the expectation where this 'value of the good expected' is nothing else but Bernoulli's 'advantage of profit'. He assumes, after Bernoulli, that an infinitely small increase in wealth is inversely proportional to the total wealth already in the possession of the individual. 'Il est naturel', he writes, de supposer la valeur relative d'une somme infiniment petite, en raison directe de sa valeur absolue, en raison inverse du bien total de la personne intéressée. En effet, il est clair qu'un franc a très-peu de prix pour celui qui en possède un grand nombre, et que la manière la plus naturelle d'estimer sa valeur relative, est de la supposer en raison inverse de ce nombre.'[11]

In Chapter x,[12] Laplace following Bernoulli,[13] puts the argument in mathematical terms. If x is the physical wealth of an individual, and dx the increase in this wealth, the increase in utility ('bien moral' or 'fortune morale'), can be expressed by

$$K \frac{dx}{x} \text{ where K is a constant.}$$

Total utility (fortune morale) y corresponding to total wealth x is therefore

$$y = K \log x + \log h \text{ where h is constant.}$$

Laplace observes that we can never suppose in the natural course of things that x or y will be negative or equal to zero because the man who possesses nothing regards his existence as a good (bien moral) which can be compared with the advantage which could be procured to him by physical wealth, the value of which is very difficult to be determined but which cannot be below what would be absolutely necessary for him to survive'.[14]

Siméon-Denis Poisson also accepted the distinction between mathematical expectation and moral expectation which is the result of the fact that 'the advantage which a gain procures to someone depends on the state of his wealth'.[15, 16]

Others who will deal with the same problem in similar terms include J.L. D'Alembert, A.A. Cournot, J. Bertrand and C. Menger.

3.2 JAMES WALDEGRAVE AND THE THEORY OF GAMES

Another instance of an early application of Probability Theory to a game is contained in a letter sent by James Waldegrave in 1713 to P.R. de Montmort and known from a communication by him to Nicholas Bernoulli[17], a cousin of Daniel Bernoulli, whose contribution we have just seen. Actually the correspondence of Nicholas Bernoulli with 'Cramer and Daniel Bernoulli, had an important role in the pre–1738 history of the Petersburg problem'.[18]

The analysis shows that in the two-person game of '*le Her*' out of the various strategies, which would be adopted by the players, there are two dominating strategies for each player; and each player has a safe strategy by which he can ensure that he will get a minimum and stop his opponent from getting more than a maximum. A combination of these strategies for both players leads to the 'minimax concept' of modern games theory.

As Kuhn points out[19], Waldegrave introduces the concept of mixed strategies and the logic of the 'minimax', and also explicitly solves a matrix game.

NOTES

1. Daniel was the son of Jean Bernoulli, a noted mathematician, and nephew of the famous Jacques Bernoulli, author of the *Ars Conjectandi* (1713).
2. In *Commentarii academiae scientarum imperialis Petropolitanae* (1738) vol. v, pp. 175–92. The work was translated into German by A. Pringsheim under the title *Die Grundlage der modernen Wertlehre: Versuch einer neuen Theorie der Wertbestimmung von Glücksfällen* with an introduction by Ludwig Fick (Leipzig, 1896). It is to this work that we refer. Fick, op. cit., p. 7 mentions that the work had been written in 1730 or more probably 1731.

   See also P.A. Samuelson, 'St. Petersburg Paradoxes: Defanged, Dissected and Historically Described' in *Journal of Economic Literature* (1977) pp. 24–55. Samuelson mentions as precursors of Daniel Bernoulli, his cousin Nicholas Bernoulli, P.R. de Montmort and Gabriel Cramer. Ibid., pp. 24, 53–5.
3. If out of s possible cases such that $s = a_1 + a_2 + \ldots a_n$, the profit g_1, occurs a_1 times, the profit g_2 occurs a_2 times, etc., the expectation of profit is

$$\epsilon = \frac{a_1}{s} g_1 + \frac{a_2}{s} g_2 + \ldots \frac{a_n}{s} g_n$$

$$= \frac{a_1 g_1 + a_2 g_2 \ldots + a_n g_n}{s}$$

   See Bernoulli, op. cit., p. 23.
4. Bernoulli, op. cit., p. 26.
5. 'Jeder beliebig kleine Gewinn einen Vorteil erzeuge, welcher dem schon vorhandenen Vermögen umgekehrt proportional ist', Bernoulli, op. cit., pp. 27–8.
6. Bernoulli, op. cit., p. 32.
7. Bernoulli, op. cit., pp. 26–7 and 31.
8. Bernoulli, op. cit., p. 32. The author points out that if individual circumstances are not taken into consideration and each profit is considered as bringing a steadily directly proportional advantage, line *SBS* would be a straight line. Ibid., p. 33.
9. Ibid., p. 9.
10. Simon de Laplace, *Théorie analytique des probabilités* (1812) p. 187 and

in *Œeuvres*, vol. VII (1847) p. 204. Laplace also distinguishes between 'fortune physique', the sum of goods in a man's possession and 'fortune morale', the value of these goods for the owner. Cf. Laplace, op. cit., vol. VII, pp. 474 *et seq*. Cf. also his *Éssai philosophique sur les probabilités* (1814) p. 21, where the idea is specifically referred to Bernoulli.

11. Simon de Laplace, *Théorie analytique des probabilities* (1812) p. 187 and in *Œeuvres*, vol. VII (1847), p. 204.

12. Laplace, *Théorie analytique des probabilités* (1812), p. 432, *Œeuvres*, pp. 474 *et seq*. But J. Bertrand, *Calcul des Probabilités* (Paris 1888), thought that Bernoulli's idea was absurd.

13. It is not without interest to note that Cournot was a student of Laplace and a friend of Poisson. The work of Bernoulli must therefore have been known to him, although he does not mention it. The first economic writer who, by his own admission, knew of Bernoulli was Friedrich Hermann, *Staatswirtschaftliche Untersuchungen* (München, 1832), who in a note on p. 73 refers to the 5th edn of Laplace, *Éssai philosophique sur les probabilités* (1825), p. 28, 'wo eine ähnliche Schätzung aus Bernoulli angedeutet ist'.

14. Laplace, *Théorie analytique des probabilités* (1812) pp. 432–3. On p. 439 Laplace expressly mentions that the principle was proposed by Daniel Bernoulli.

15. S-D. Poisson, *Recherches sur la probabilité des jugements* (Paris, 1837), p. 72.

16. Before Laplace, Georges-Louis Leclerc, Count of Buffon, in his *Éssai d' Arithmétique Morale*, published in 1777, in discussing the value of money, refers expressly to Bernoulli's contribution and accepts his views. 'Un homme qui a vingt mille livres de bien, ne doit pas l'estimer comme le double du bien d'un autre qui a dix mille livres, car il n'a réellement que dix-huit mille livres d'argent de cette même monnoie, dont la valeur se compte par les avantages qui en résultent.' Buffon, *Œuvres Philosophiques* (Paris 1954) p. 469.

17. Waldegrave James, excerpts from a letter in P.R. de Montmort, *Essay d' Analyse sur les Jeux de Hasard* (Paris 1713) pp. 409–12. Reproduced in W.J. Baumol and S.M. Goldfeld, op. cit., pp. 7 – 9.

18. Samuelson, op. cit., p. 37.

19. H. Kuhn, preface to Waldegrave's letter in W.J. Baumol and S.M. Goldfeld, op. cit., p.6.

4 The Milanese School

We have already explained in our introduction, the reason for the name we have given to the Italian contribution to mathematical economics. We may distinguish two currents of thought in this contribution and a lonely, but most important, contribution by Giambattista Vasco.

The first current starts with Beccaria's inquiry of tariff fixing and its relation with smuggling and ends with Silio thirty years later.

The second is much more lively and varied; it started with Pietro Verri and Paolo Frisi and created a controversy in Italian economic literature which lasted for over half a century. The controversy raged around various simple formulae which, according to their authors, showed how price was determined; it is more of interest because it shows the vigour with which these questions were pursued in Italy in those days, rather than because it marked any great progress towards the solution of the question with which they were interested.

4.1 CESARE BECCARIA AND GUGLIELMO SILIO

Beccaria has made two contributions to mathematical economics.

The first appeared in his work 'Del disordine e dei rimedi delle Monete' in 1762[1]. There he says that the value of goods is in inverse proportion to their quantity and the number of sellers and in direct proportion of competing buyers, of the corresponding tax, of the labour force and of the importance of transport. By utilising the initials of the above factors he gives the formula:

$$v.V : : \frac{mtci}{sp} \cdot \frac{MTCI}{SP}$$

If the mass of gold and silver is divided proportionally to $\frac{mtci}{sp}$, then, if the proportion of gold to silver is de and O the gold, while A is the silver, we shall have

20

$$\frac{mtci}{sp} \; O \cdot \frac{mtci}{sp} \; A :: de$$

Beccaria's second contribution to mathematical economics deals with a specific problem of the connection between tariffs and smuggling. It has the title 'Tentativo analitico sui contrabbandi' and was published in 1764[2] in the periodical *Il Caffé*[3]. This was a literary and scientific periodical of considerable distinction and was the organ of a Society of Friends, which included among its members Paolo Frisi, Pietro Verri and Beccaria.[4]

At the beginning of his essay, Beccaria says that algebra, being a precise and quick method of reasoning about quantities, can be applied to everything which can increase or decrease and consequently it can be applied to political sciences but only up to a point, for political principles depend on a variety of factors which cannot be precisely determined.[5] His attempt is simply intended to give 'a slight idea about how economic science can be analytically considered'.[6]

When the government fixes a customs duty, it legislates that goods smuggled will be confiscated. The merchant therefore who considers importing goods in this illegal way has an inducement and a deterrent; the inducement is that, if he is successful, he will make a profit equal to the tax he has not paid; the deterrent is that if he is caught, he will lose the value of his wares. The problem which Beccaria sets is this: Let us assume that a portion of the goods which a merchant attempts to smuggle is seized while the rest passes through. How large should this latter portion be, so that the merchant should cover exactly his losses from the first portion?[7]

If u is the total value of the goods and x that of the goods smuggled successfully, $u - x$ is the value of the goods, confiscated. If t is the duty for the total value of goods, the portion of duty saved on the quantity x, and therefore appropriated by the smuggler is:

(1) $$\frac{x}{u} t$$

The smuggler is indifferent when his losses $u - x$, equal $\frac{x}{u}t$, his gain. It follows therefore from[8]

(2) $$u - x = \frac{xt}{u}$$

that the value of the goods smuggled must be,

(3) $$x = \frac{u^2}{u + t}$$

if the smuggler is to break even.

Beccarria then experiments with various levels of duty. If the duty is equal to the value of the good, i.e. $t = u$, then

$$x = \frac{u}{2}$$

i.e. the smuggler will be happy if he manages to import illegally at least half his goods.

If the tax is greater than the value of goods, i.e. if $t = u + d$ then

$$x = \frac{u^2}{2u + d} < \frac{u}{2}$$

and smuggling becomes easier as less than half the quantity is needed for the smuggler to break even[9].

If $\quad t = u - d$ then $x = \frac{u^2}{2u - d} > \frac{u}{2}$

The higher the duty, the more profitable therefore becomes smuggling and Beccaria observes that such calculations might prove useful in tariff construction as well as show how much smuggling one may fear.

Beccaria also pointed out that by taking u as constant and x and t as variables, the basic equation $ux + tx = u^2$, if plotted, would give a hyperbola. He did not plot it himself but suggested that 'its inspection by anyone who wants to construct it will show all the different cases' which he had discussed.[10] Beccaria's suggestion was taken up by *Guglielmo Silio*, who not only plotted the curve on the lines suggested but also further extended Beccaria's treatment in his 'Saggio su l'influenza dell' analisi nelle Scienze Politiche ed Economiche applicata ai contrabbandi', which was published in 1792.[11] This was intended, in the author's words, to follow in the tracks of Beccaria and attempt to complete Beccaria's treatment of smuggling[12] and the level of customs duties, a subject full of interest for it is the duty which renders smuggling profitable.[13] Like Beccaria, whom he quoted, he supports the application of analysis to the Social Sciences and his essay is intended to make apparent 'the beneficial and inalterable influence of mathematical achievements and of the calculus'[14] on economic analysis.

The first problem which he discusses deals with the determination of the punishment to be imposed in the case of smuggling.[15] If the smuggler's chance[16] to succeed is n, his profit will be the tax T which he avoids; the mathematical expectation of profit is therefore

$$nT$$

If his chances to be caught are N, he will have to pay a fine p; the mathematical expectation of loss is therefore

$$Np$$

If p is to be a just punishment – and in this he uses the concept of a 'just' game from the theory of probabilities – the two expectations must be equal, or as he puts it $p : T = n : N$, the ratio, that is, of his loss to his gain must be equal to the ratio of his chances of being successful or not. It follows that

$$Np = nT$$

and

$$p = \frac{nT}{N}$$

If the smuggler is asked to pay the amount of duty and the above fine, i.e.

$$S = T + \frac{nT}{N}$$

the punishment is just.

If, however, he is asked to pay a fine less than $\frac{nT}{N}$, the punishment is less than just and by implication smuggling is encouraged. The opposite holds when the fine is larger than $\frac{nT}{N}$.

The second problem[17] is an exact reproduction of Beccaria's problem and solution, to which he returns in connection with his third problem. He then plots[18] Beccaria's equation $ux + tx = u^2$, in the form reproduced on the left (Figure 4.1(a)); to the right (Figure 4.1(b)) we have plotted the same figure in a more conventional form. The curve is the hyperbola *PHG; BC, BF* express the various levels of duty T and *CD, FG* the various quantities of smuggling X, which leave smugglers in their original position. *AB* is the constant V. Since *PHG* is a hyperbola, Silio remarks that we shall have $(AB + BC)CD = (AB)^2$, from which it follows that, since $AB = V$, $BC = T$ and $CD =$

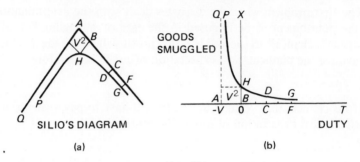

FIG. 4.1

X, $(V + T)X = V^2$ or $VX + TX = V^2$. It can be seen that since V is given, the higher T is, the smaller X is, and in the case where T is infinitely large, X becomes infinitesimal and tends to zero. On the contrary[19] when $T = 0$, X becomes equal to V.

In the third problem itself, Silio seeks to find a quantity of goods to be smuggled, such that the merchant will be able to break even, after he has been able to sell the goods smuggled at a profit additional to the duty he has evaded and which he appropriates. The basic equation then becomes:[20]

$$X + \frac{TX}{V} + \frac{GX}{100} - C = V$$

where, in addition to the symbols used above, G is the percentage of profit at which the goods are sold and C the amount of his expenses. The amount X which he requires to smuggle in order to break even, diminishes as the profit he can secure on the goods smuggled increases, and increases as his expenses increase. This is evident from the solution of the above equation.[21]

$$X = \frac{V^2 + CV}{V + T + (GV/100)}$$

The remaining problems with which Silio deals are couched in much the same terms and discuss such questions as how to reduce customs duty without reducing total revenue which is conceivable because of the reduction in smuggling and in bribing of officials by the smuggler, or how to determine an average duty given all the above data.[22]

4.2 THE MATHEMATICS OF PRICE DETERMINATION AND THE MILANESE SCHOOL

(i) Pietro Verri and Paolo Frisi

Verri cannot be considered as a mathematical economist but certain of his ideas were the seeds from which some of the major contributions of the Milanese School of mathematical economics developed; his ideas therefore, have a place in such a review as ours.

Verri published his *Meditazioni Sulla Economia Politica* in Livorno in 1771 for the first time.[23] It proved to be a great success and made four more editions in the same year. In the sixth edition of the *Meditazioni* which was made in Livorno in 1772 the editor, who was the famous mathematician Paolo Frisi,[24] added various mathematical notes at the end of several chapters of the book by way of illustration of Verri's arguments. At the same time he inserted at the end of the book a review of H. Lloyd's book, *An Essay on the Theory of Money*, and compared the latter's ideas with Verri's. The notes and the review were suppressed in later editions of the *Meditazioni*. Custodi, in his *Scrittori Classici Italiani di Economia Politica*, included the review of Lloyd's book by Frisi but not Frisi's notes; he did however include the less interesting annotation of the *Meditazioni* by Carli which had originally been added to the fifth edition of the book, made in Venice in 1771.[25] It was Frisi's treatment of Verri's argument about the determination of price which created the greatest interest. In the fourth chapter of his book, Verri says that the price depends on two factors, the 'apparent abundance' of the good and the need for it.

The apparent abundance increases with the number of offers, which Verri identifies with the number of sellers. The measure of 'apparent abundance' is for him the number of sellers. But whereas in the editions of the *Meditazioni* in 1771 and 1772, Verri had maintained that the supply corresponds to the numbers of sellers[26] in the edition of 1781 he simply says that the quantity offered corresponds *approximately* to the number of sellers.[27] In general, however, his argument is unchanged. Thus if there is only one seller, he argues, 'the apparent abundance, as we have already seen, will be a minimum; but if there is but only one buyer of this same commodity, the need will be also a minimum, since the price will depend on the equal conflict of two sole opinions. If, however, instead of one buyer, the monopolist has two, then he will be able to increase his demands'.[28] From this it follows that 'if the number of sellers increases, supply increases, other things being equal, and price will continue to fall. If the number of buyers increases, demand increases, ceteris paribus, and price will rise proportionately'.[29] And since he has to deal with quantities, Verri uses 'the language of the science which measures them', in order to be able to express himself with exactitude and puts the argument as follows: 'When the number of sellers is constant, price is proportional to the number of buyers; when the number of buyers is constant, prices increase in the same proportion that the number of sellers decreases.'[30]

This is the argument which Frisi takes up[31]. If we call P the price of a good at a time when the number of sellers is V and the number of buyers C, and p the price at another time when the number of sellers is v and that of buyers c, the relation between the two prices will be[32]

$$P : p :: \frac{C}{V} : \frac{c}{v}$$

He then examines whether the function relating the price to the numbers of sellers and buyers could be of the form

$$P = \frac{M(C + A)^m}{(V + B)^n}$$

where A, B, M, m and n are constant. He rejects this because of two reasons:

If the number of buyers is zero the price must be zero. If, therefore, in the above function $C = 0$, for P to be equal to zero, A must be zero. At the same time, given the number of buyers, if there are no sellers the price must rise outside any limits. Where, therefore, $V = 0$, an infinite P requires that B must be also equal to zero.[33] This argument, valid mathematically, reduces the above formula to

$$P = \frac{C^m}{V^n}$$

and the relation of the prices of a good at two different times would be:

$$P : p = \frac{C^m}{V^n} : \frac{c^m}{v^n}$$

But Frisi rejects even this form for another reason, of questionable mathematical validity. His reasoning is that, given the number of sellers, if the number of buyers becomes infinite, price must become infinite of the same order. But if we have $m = 2$, in the case where C is infinite, price would become infinite of the second order;[34] or if $m = \frac{1}{2}$ or $\frac{1}{3}$, etc, price would be expressed by a radical infinite; 'le quali supposizioni', he concludes, 'non sembrano verosimili'.[35] The same argument he uses for the case where, given C, the number of sellers is infinite and then he argues that P must be an infinitesimal of the first order. In both cases therefore, m and n 'must not differ much from unity'.

And so one must have always $P = C/V$ or, for two prices,[36]

$$P : p = \frac{C}{V} : \frac{c}{v}$$

At the end of the book[37] Frisi took up again the same question and examined whether the function linking prices and numbers of sellers and buyers could be expressed by

$$P = \frac{MC + aC^{1/2} + bC^{1/2} + \ldots}{MV + aV^{1/2} + bV^{1/2} + \ldots}$$

where a, b, M are constant. Given C, an infinite V would make P infinitesimal, and given V, an infinite C means an infinite P. The additional terms, would mean an infinitesimal or infinite price of radical order, a result 'which is not likely'.[38] His conclusion from all this discussion is that the formula for the price should be $P = C/V$ where $P =$ price, $C =$ number of buyers and $V =$ number of sellers.

Frisi's next task is to enquire when the price will be a maximum or a minimum.

When dP, dC, dV are the 'successive and simultaneous'[39] variations in price and the numbers of buyers and sellers, he finds that the price will be a maximum or minimum when

$$dP = \frac{VdC - CdV}{V^2} = 0, \text{ from which he gets } \frac{dC}{dV} = \frac{C}{V}$$

This result he interprets in the following way:

When the number of buyers increases or diminishes in a proportion greater or smaller than that of the number of sellers, the price will be a maximum or a minimum when the simultaneous variations are proportional to the changing quantities themselves.[40]

But of course the condition that

$$dP = \frac{VdC - CdV}{V^2} = 0$$

is not a sufficient but only a necessary condition for a maximum or a minimum; all it says is that price at this point is stationary and what Frisi's rule shows is simply under what conditions price would remain unchanged.[41]

In Figure 4.2 any point on line OP indicates one and the same price. Since $P = \frac{C}{V} = \frac{2C}{2V}$, etc., Frisi's $\frac{dC}{dV} = \frac{C}{V}$ means that, as the tangent is the same, price will be the same for $\frac{C + dC}{V + dV}$ and $\frac{C}{V}$.

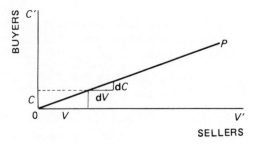

FIG. 4.2

The other mathematical demonstrations of Frisi are:

(a) If P is the price of the commodities[42] in general and at that time the value of money is U and if at another time, when price is p, the value of money is u, we shall have, as price and value of money are inversely related

$$P : p = u : U$$

and since $P = \frac{C}{V}$ and $p = \frac{c}{v}$

$$u : U = \frac{C}{V} : \frac{c}{v}$$

the value of money, that is, is inversely related to the number of buyers and directly related to the number of sellers.

(b) If the demand for money is R and its supply O, the rate of interest I is

$$I = \frac{R}{O}$$

The price of money is therefore no longer linked with numbers of suppliers or those demanding it but is linked with supply and demand[43]. By applying the same condition for a maximum or minimum rate of interest, which he imposed in the case of price, he finds

$$\frac{dR}{dO} = \frac{R}{O}$$

i.e. the maximum or minimum rate of interest is found not only when demand (or supply) increases infinitely or supply (demand) diminishes to zero but also in intermediate stages, 'when supply or demand is proportional to their simultaneous changes'.[44]

(c) In Chapter xxi of the *Meditazioni* Verri asserts that the problem of political economy is to increase as much as possible the annual production with the least effort possible. This would mean that given the amount of the annual production, one must expend the minimum effort to achieve this production; and given the amount of labour, one must achieve the maximum production.

Frisi gives as the form of the function which would satisfy both the above conditions:

$$R + AT = B \text{ or } R = B - AT$$

where R is the amount of production, T the amount of labour and A and B constants. When $dR = 0$ and R is a maximum, $dT = 0$ and T is a minimum.[45]

(d) Finally there is a curious contribution by Frisi, which we only mention because it is the second suggestion made by a member of the Milanese School for the application of analytic geometry to economic problems.[46]

In Chapter XXVI of the *Meditazioni* Verri had suggested that the more distance among men is diminished, the greater and more active becomes industry. This Frisi takes up and suggests that the curve showing the relation between distance and industry will be a hyperbola, whose equation is $XY = A^2$ where X is the distance, Y is the industry and A is constant. This curve would therefore be something like Figure 4.3 shown here.

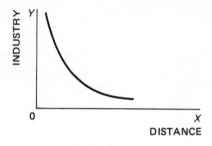

FIG. 4.3

The relation however will be represented by only a section of the curve because there is a limit to the expansion of inustry and one could not imagine *Y* becoming infinite.

(ii) Henry Lloyd

Lloyd published his book *An Essay on the Theory of Money* anonymously in London in 1771. We include him, however, among the authors of the Milanese School because it was to these authors that his work was known and these authors that he influenced. Lloyd remained entirely unknown as a mathematical economist in his own country.[47]

Lloyd had been very friendly with Verri:[48] they had many discussions and there is so much similarity in their views that it is very difficult to decide which of them was influenced more by the other. They both called money 'the universal merchandise'. Regarding this definition Verri admits that 'I have discussed much on this and on other arguments of political economy with the English General Lloyd'.[49]

Because of the similarity of their views, Frisi inserted a review of Lloyd's book in the sixth edition of Verri's *Meditazioni* (1772). It is through this review that Lloyd's influence on Italian economic thinking was perpetuated.

Lloyd believed that the price of a commodity is a function of the quantity of money circulating and the quantity of the good itself.[50] If therefore we call *P* the price, *Q* the quantity of money in circulation and *M* the quantity of the good, we have the equation[51]

$$P = \frac{Q}{M}$$

He further assumes that *y* indicates the variation of the quantity of the good. If instead of a quantity M we have a quantity yM, price will become P/y; this would mean that a doubling of the quantity of the good, when the quantity of money remains unchanged, would cut its price by a half.[52] We thus have:

$$\frac{P}{y} = \frac{Q}{yM} \text{ or } yP = \frac{Q}{M/y}$$

Frisi suggests that the formulae expressing Verri's and Lloyd's ideas $P = C/V$ and $P = Q/M$ may be combined in a more general formula

$$P = \frac{C \cdot Q}{M \cdot V}$$

which would mean that prices are generally in compound ratio, consisting of the direct ratio of the number of buyers and the quantity of money and inverse ratio of the number of sellers and the quantity of the good.[53]

Lloyd also dealt with the subject with which Ceva and Spinelli had occupied themselves, namely the relation between gold and silver. If S is the quantity of silver, G the quantity of gold, p their ratio, Lloyd gives the relation $p = S/G$. If the quantity of gold increases by y, the ratio becomes $p/y = S/yG$ and if it decreases by y, it becomes[54]

$$yp = \frac{S}{G/y}.$$

For the rate of interest he gives the solution:[55]

$$I = \frac{B}{O}$$

where I is the rate of interest, B the number of those demanding loans, O the number of those who make loans. A change in quantity of money y affects I inversely. Thus:

$$\frac{I}{y} = \frac{B}{yO} \text{ and } yI = \frac{B}{O/y}$$

(iii) The controversy following the Verri–Frisi demonstration

The Verri–Frisi contribution was bound to arouse discussion concerning both the economic argument of Verri and its mathematical treatment by Frisi. It is not our aim, however, to describe the controversy but only to trace the contributions to mathematical economics connected with it.

(a) In an article in the *Nuovo Giornale de' Letterati d' Italia* in 1773[56] an anonymous author identified as G. B. Venturi,[57] Professor of Mathematics and Philosophy in the University of Modena, takes Frisi to task for attempting to show that the price must increase exactly in proportion to the number of buyers and in inverse proportion to the number of sellers. 'All his calculations', Venturi says, 'finally show nothing else but what we already knew, that is, that price increases the more buyers increase or sellers decrease and vice versa.'[58]

Frisi had argued that $P = C/V$ where P = price, C = number of buyers and V = number of sellers; and that such formulae as $P = C^m/V^n$ could not have the indices m and n different from unity because if, say, C became infinite or infinitesimal and $m = 2$, P would become infinite or infinitesimal of the second order.

The anonymous author has two remarks to offer: first, that it is absurd to speak of the number of sellers or buyers becoming infinitely small since no man can be smaller than unity and, secondly, that if one applied Frisi's argument one could reduce Newton's Law of attraction to absurdity.[59]

He is on a much less secure ground when he criticises Frisi's use of the differential calculus. He makes three criticisms, two of which are not in my opinion warranted.

(a) That infinite variations in the numbers of sellers or buyers are very difficult to conceive. But when we have very large numbers of buyers or sellers, small variations in C or V may be approximately considered as infinitesimal.[60]

(b) He objects that C and V are independent of one another and Frisi had treated them as if they were related. But Frisi was applying Verri's argument and Verri had expressly stated that an increase in the number of buyers increases the number of sellers and producers.[61]

(c) Frisi had found as the condition for a maximum or minimum price $C/V = dC/dV$. If we assume that dV retains the same value and take for dC a quantity larger than that which would make $dC/dV = C/V$ (i.e. if $dC/dV > C/V$) we should by Frisi's first formula $P = C/V$ have an increased price. But then how can $dC/dV = C/V$ indicate a maximum condition? The author does not go further to explain the reason of the contradiction but this is evident from what we said above that the point, that is, where $dC/dV = C/V$ is not a maximum or minimum point but a point where price is stationary.[62]

The anonymous author of the *Nuovo Giornale* will, however, remain known in the history of the development of mathematical economics for another reason. He was the first who suggested the use of geometry for the study of a three-variable function, without actually drawing the curves he suggested.[63] Given $P = C/V$ we could have

(a) C variable and V constant. The locus of the equation will be a straight line.[64] There will be a maximum price only when C is infinite and a minimum price when $C = 0$. (See Figure 4.4.)

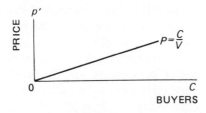

FIG. 4.4

(b) V variable and C constant; the locus of equation $P = C/V$ will be a hyperbola (Figure 4.5). The maximum price occurs only when $V = 0$, and the minimum when V is infinitely large.[65]

(c) Where both V and C are variable the locus of the equation $P = C/V$ is the surface of a solid so that if it is cut by a plane perpendicular to the axis of V and parallel to that of C the section of the surface will always give a straight line; but if it is cut by a plane perpendicular to the first plane and therefore perpendicular to the axis of C, we shall always get a hyperbola as a section.[66]

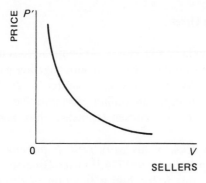

FIG. 4.5

But though he himself used mathematics extensively in his arguments, the anonymous author is doubtful of the value of the mathematical method in economics.

We hope that these reflections, he says,[67] 'will serve as a shining example to everyone of the danger one runs when one wants to make use of mathematics in fields outside the realm of Nature and when one attempts to express with lines and analytical symbols moral quantities, which depend on a thousand factors and which are not at all susceptible of any exact measurement'.

Pietro Ferroni in an essay entitled 'Esame di Alcuni Passi Delle Meditazioni sulla Economia Politica del conte Pietro Verri'[68] criticises both Verri's argument and the use of the mathematical method in economics. He thinks that Verri did not distinguish between the idea of price, in which the number of sellers, that is, the competition of sellers, enters as one of its elements, and the idea of quantity of the commodity. He proposed therefore the following rule: 'The apparent abundance of a commodity ... is measured solely by its quantity which is offered for sale; while, the price of the same commodity increases or decreases in proportion to the smaller or greater number of sellers, when the above mentioned quantity is supposed to remain unchanged.'[69]

On the use of the mathematical method, he denies that ideas of maximum and minimum in their strict mathematical sense could be applied, for it would be absurd to assume that the number of sellers increases infinitely while the number of buyers remains finite, or that there are no sellers when the number of buyers remains finite. 'Lontano adunque', he exclaims, 'da fraseggiare in materia di scienze pratiche col linguaggio dell' algebra o della geometria delle curve.'[70]

(iv) Giammaria Ortes

Ortes was a Venetian and some of his contributions might warrant his inclusion in the School of Geometricians together with Ceva, Spinelli and Mariotte. As he, however, indirectly contributed to the controversy which raged in Italian economic literature after Frisi's demonstration, we have chosen to include him under the Milanese School.

In the fourth book of his work *Dell' Economia Nazionale* which was published in Bologna in 1774,[71] Ortes discusses the value of consumable goods; this is for him a function of the demand and the

supply or quantity of the good ('massa') and may be represented by
the formula

$$v = \frac{r}{m}$$

where v is the value, r the demand and m the quantity of the good.[72]

Goods like land, fire and water, although extremely useful, have no
value because 'they are incomparably greater in quantity than any
other kind of good' and the formula of their value becomes[73]

$$v = \frac{r}{\infty} = 0$$

On the contrary, if the quantity of a particular kind is very small or
zero, its value, when demand is finite, rises to infinity. This can be
expressed by[74]

$$v = \frac{r}{0} = \infty$$

But though the value of individual goods may vary from zero to
infinity, Ortes maintains that the value of consumable goods in
general will remain constant, because, he says, in this case, with an unchanging population and unchanging preferences (needs)[75] demand is
measured by what he calls 'the common need of the nation which itself
is invariable'.[76] To this he adds the assumption that the mass of
consumable goods in general does not change.

This believed constancy in value Ortes represents by the formula[77]

$$v = \frac{r}{m} = \frac{1}{1} = 1$$

The formulae which Ortes uses in the theory of money are of a
similar form. The value of money rises with a rise in its demand r and
falls with a rise in its quantity d, so that it can be expressed by[78]

$$v = \frac{r}{d}$$

Ortes adds however that, in general, both the demand for and the
quantity of money, and therefore its value, will remain unchanged[79]
and

$$v = \frac{r}{d} = \frac{x}{x} = 1$$

Ortes did not simply and in passing employ mathematical formulae in his economic arguments; he was consciously a fervent supporter of the use of the mathematical method in economics. In the preface of his book *Errori popolari intorno all' Economia Nazionale*, published anonymously in 1771,[80] he makes a strong plea for the application of the mathematical method to economic analysis; such application does not simply mean counting, weighing and measuring but it implies that, before calculating, one must discover and understand 'the reasons, the aims, the motives and the relations according to which those goods consumed by all can increase or diminish in the nations'.[81] He is more emphatic in his *Annotazioni dell' Autore del libro degli Errori popolari sull' Economia Nazionale* which he published later in the same year to answer various criticisms.[82] Answering a reviewer of his earlier book, who had remarked that geometric spirit can contribute much to the advancement of economic science and that with this all economists agree, Ortes points out that he believes that the use of Mathematics cannot simply contribute but is the indispensable means through which 'one can reconnoitre and regulate the Science of Economics'.[83]

The *Errori popolari* itself is an attempt to treat certain economic questions by following the procedure of a geometric treatise.

He sets down certain axioms or what he believes are 'general truths, derived from immutable and necessary principles from which there is no deviation',[84] and to these he opposes some of what he thinks are popular errors. From these axioms he proceeds to particular cases which he investigates.[85]

(v) Luigi Valeriani Molinari and Melchiorre Gioja

Economic thinking had advanced much by 1806, when Valeriani published his *Del prezzo delle cose tutte mercatabili*, from the time when Verri and Frisi had expressed their view that the price is simply in compound proportion to the numbers of sellers and buyers. Verri had already in the 1781 edition of the *Meditazioni* suppressed Frisi's notes and introduced the word 'approximately' in his argument. Supply is no longer 'measured by the number of sellers' but 'approximately measured' by this number;[86] and Ferroni had delivered his essay before the Società de' Georgofili. It was evident that Frisi's formula was not adequate; if it were not to be discarded it should be revised and Valeriani attempted to 'put sense'[87] into it by substituting for the numbers of sellers and buyers, the supply and the demand of the good.[88]

Valeriani distinguishes between 'value in genere or in the abstract' of a good and its 'specific value'. The 'value in genere' is nothing else but the 'total utility' of a good. 'Il pregio del pane', he writes,[89] 'se si considera cosi in astratto ed in genere come proveniente dal bisogno di alimentarsi è non meno grande, che importante, e molto più del pregio di tutto ciò che non serve che all' abbigliamento, alla voluttà ed al lusso.'

But while 'value in the abstract' is always equal to the need, the *specific* value of a good depends not only on the 'value in genere' of the good but also on its quantity. Valeriani is thus grappling with the problem of utility and its relation to the quantity of the good, though for Valeriani the value of a good is not determined by marginal utility but by the average utility: it is in other words the quotient of total utility 'in the abstract' divided by the quantity of the good. But as value in the abstract is directly proportional to the need for the good and this need may be expressed by the demand for the good, the specific value, argues Valeriani,[90] may be expressed by the quotient of the demand for the good by its supply or by

$$p = \frac{i}{o}$$

where p is the specific value, i the demand and o the supply.[91]

Exchange of two goods will, Valeriani continues, take place in accordance with their specific values. Thus, if for a certain good its specific value is $P = I/O$, while for another the specific value is $p = i/o$, the exchange value or price of the first in respect of the second will be[92]

$$P : p = \frac{I}{O} : \frac{i}{o}$$

Regarding the Frisi formula, Valeriani felt that the number of sellers or buyers did influence the outcome but that on the other hand one should not identify quantities supplied or demanded with the numbers of sellers or buyers; 'one buyer demanding one unit has not the same power to increase the value of the good as the buyer who demands ten units'[93] and the same holds for the seller. But this does not mean that demand and supply do not partly depend on the number of buyers and sellers.[94]

Valeriani repeated his formula in many of his subsequent works[95] and in the two answers he published against Gioja's remarks made in the latter's book *Nuovo Prospetto delle Scienze Economiche*.[96]

Melchiorre Gioja in his discussion of the formation of prices examines both the Verri–Frisi and the Molinari version.[97]

Verri, as mentioned, had argued and Frisi had expressed algebraically the argument, that $P = C/V$ where P = price, C = number of buyers and V = number of sellers. But they, Gioja remarks,[98] stretched a truth so much as to make it false. For it would be absurd to assume that, if in a city there are 64 makers of hats and the hats sell at 10 lire, in another city with 32 hatmakers the hats must sell for 20 lire; or that whenever there is the same ratio of buyers to sellers prices will be the same.[99]

Frisi had made it clear that he assumed unchanged conditions of supply and demand, of population, of the circulation of money and all other circumstances[100] and that he was only interested in the study of the variations of the numbers of sellers and buyers but Gioja can point out that even in such a case the relation between price and numbers cannot be simply proportional because:

(a) Prices cannot increase indefinitely as sellers decrease or buyers increase, because the seller himself will not be eager to put up his price if the lower price is more profitable, and because beyond a certain point the limited financial circumstances of the purchasers will not permit them to buy.[101]

(b) Prices cannot fall without limit in response to a fall in the number of buyers or an increase in the number of sellers because (i) sellers cannot sell for long below their cost; (ii) buyers consume more at a lower cost; (iii) an increase in the number of sellers may mean an increase in their expenses; the more difficult collusion becomes, the more buyers will be affected adversely, because either quality will suffer or price will rise; (iv) the quantity demanded by a single buyer may be more than that demanded by twenty. The number of buyers is therefore not enough; what is needed is the quantity demanded or offered.[102]

Turning now to Valeriani's formula, Gioja remarks that this has in part put sense into the Frisi formula but he denies its general validity, because he observes that beyond a certain point the increase in the number of sellers will, by reducing their collusion to zero, reverse the process of decreasing prices; any further increase in the number of sellers will, owing to their increasing costs, increase prices.[103]

It was against this criticism that the two answers of Molinari, which we mentioned above, were aimed.[104]

Melchiorre Gioja did not use mathematics only in connection with his controversy with Frisi and Molinari.[105] Thus in the sixth volume of his *Nuovo Prospetto delle Scienze Economiche* published in 1817 he applies economic theory to the estimation of the value of a forest, which, he says is the value of its product *ad infinitum* discounted to find its present value.[106]

He calculates the present value of a product A which will be produced after n years; this value for a rate of interest r per annum will be:

$$\mathbf{a} = \frac{A}{(1 + r)^n}$$

which is nothing else but an aspect of the compound interest formula.[107]

The value of the product A, however, must be the net value; if, therefore, for n years a sum of expenses and taxes equal to E is paid every year, we must deduct the total sum of E's adjusted for interest, from the gross return A. The total deduction is nothing else but the final value of an annuity and this is equal to[108]

$$D = \frac{E[(1 + r)^n - 1](1 + r)}{r}$$

Adeodato Ressi in his book *Dell' Economia della Specie Umana*,[109] speaking of the theory of value, sides with Valeriani 'who contributed to this argument the most profound thought and has solved it under all its possible relations by reducing the values of all marketable things to a very simple formula'.[110] This formula Ressi attempted to correct into $p = A\dfrac{d}{o}$ where p = value, d = demand, o = supply and A the price of the market on the day when the transaction took place. Ressi has completely misunderstood Valeriani and it is with justice that A. Loria remarks:[111] 'As if A is not precisely the term which is wanted and which must result from the division of d by o.'

Another author who, though not connected directly with the controversy described above, could be mentioned is Cagnazzi who in 1813 published in Naples a book with the title *Elementi di Economia Politica*. There[112] he gives a formula which he claims shows the equilibrium which must always exist between the circulation of money and the circulation of goods. If M is the quantity of money and c its velocity of circulation, while D is the quantity of goods and C their velocity of circulation

$$Mc = DC \text{ and therefore } M = \frac{D \cdot C}{c}$$

It is very difficult to see what Cagnazzi really means, for he equates money with the quantity of goods and not their value expressed in money; had he done this he would have given a version of the quantity theory.

4.3   GIAMBATTISTA VASCO AND DYNAMIC ECONOMICS

Vasco is the earliest writer on dynamic process analysis but his work remains entirely unknown to this day even among his own compatriots.[113]

His contribution occupies some pages in his book *Saggio Politico della Moneta* which was published in 1772[114] and is reproduced in Custodi's *Scrittori Classici Italiani di Economia Politica*[115].

A country, says Vasco, may fix the relation between gold and silver independently and in accordance with its particular conditions; but on the other hand, it may take into consideration the ratios between gold and silver existing in the other countries and take as its ratio the arithmetic mean of the ratios of all other nations; if all nations adopt the latter procedure, we shall see that individual differences of the ratios will tend to diminish and they will tend towards an equilibrium value.[116]

Let us assume, he says, that the Spanish ratio is 1 : 15 and the Portuguese 1 : 10. If France decides to fix its ratio at a point which is the arithmetic mean of the Spanish and the Portuguese ratios, she will fix it at 1 : 12 because

$$(\frac{1}{15} + \frac{1}{16})\frac{1}{2} = \frac{1}{12}$$

Now Spain and Portugal decide to adjust their ratios. Spain takes the mean of the Portuguese ratio reigning till then and the French ratio,

i.e. $$(\tfrac{1}{10} + \tfrac{1}{12})\tfrac{1}{2} = \frac{1}{10\frac{10}{11}}$$

and Portugal the mean of the Spanish ratio reigning before and the French ratio,

i.e.
$$(\tfrac{1}{15} + \tfrac{1}{12})\tfrac{1}{2} = \frac{1}{13\frac{1}{3}}$$

But then the ratio of France will again be 1 : 12 because

$$(\frac{1}{10\frac{10}{11}} + \frac{1}{13\frac{1}{3}})\tfrac{1}{2} = \tfrac{1}{12}$$

and it will always remain the same while 'Spain and Portugal will always tend to approach more and more the ratio of France'.[117]

His argument will perhaps become clearer if we put it in *modern dynamic* equation form. Thus if f is the ratio of France, s the ratio of Spain and p the ratio of Portugal we shall have:

(1) $f_t = \dfrac{s_{t-1} + p_{t-1}}{2}$

(2) $s_t = \dfrac{f_t + p_{t-1}}{2}$ and using (1)

$\quad s_t = \tfrac{1}{4}s_{t-1} + \tfrac{3}{4}p_{t-1}$ (4)

(3) $p_t = \dfrac{f_t + s_{t-1}}{2}$ and using (1)

$\quad p_t = \tfrac{1}{4}p_{t-1} + \tfrac{3}{4}s_{t-1}$ (5)[118]

We shall then have Table 4.1:[119]

TABLE 4.1

Time	France $f_t = \dfrac{s_{t-1} + p_{t-1}}{2}$	Spain $s_t = \tfrac{1}{4}s_{t-1} + \tfrac{3}{4}p_{t-1}$	Portugal $p_t = \tfrac{1}{4}p_{t-1} + \tfrac{3}{4}s_{t-1}$
0	—	$\tfrac{1}{15}$	$\tfrac{1}{10}$
1	$\tfrac{1}{2}(\tfrac{1}{15} + \tfrac{1}{10}) = \tfrac{1}{12}$	$\tfrac{1}{60} + \tfrac{3}{40} = \dfrac{1}{10\frac{10}{11}}$	$\tfrac{1}{40} + \tfrac{3}{60} = \dfrac{1}{13\frac{1}{3}}$
2	$\tfrac{1}{2}(\tfrac{11}{120} + \tfrac{9}{120}) = \tfrac{1}{12}$	$\tfrac{11}{480} + \tfrac{27}{480} = \dfrac{1}{12\frac{12}{19}}$	$\tfrac{9}{480} + \tfrac{33}{480} = \dfrac{1}{11\frac{3}{7}}$
$\downarrow$	$\downarrow$	$\downarrow$	$\downarrow$
∞	$\tfrac{1}{12}$	$\tfrac{1}{12}$	$\tfrac{1}{12}$

Thus while the ratio of France, having reached the equilibrium, remains on it, the ratios of Spain and Portugal approach with oscillations the same equilibrium. Vasco gave a similar table to the above (Table 4.2), which we reproduce[120], and where the original ratio of Spain is $\frac{1}{b}$ and that of Portugal $\frac{1}{c}$.

TABLE   4.2

Time	Spagna	Francia	Portogallo
I	$\dfrac{1}{b} = \dfrac{2c}{2bc}$	$\dfrac{b + c}{2bc}$	$\dfrac{2b}{2bc} = \dfrac{1}{c}$
II	$\dfrac{3b + c}{4bc}$	$\dfrac{b + c}{2bc}$	$\dfrac{3c + b}{4bc}$
III	$\dfrac{3b + 5c}{8bc}$	$\dfrac{b + c}{2bc}$	$\dfrac{3c + 5b}{8bc}$
IV	$\dfrac{9b + 7c}{16bc}$	$\dfrac{b + c}{2bc}$	$\dfrac{9c + 7b}{16bc}$
V	$\dfrac{15b + 17c}{32bc}$	$\dfrac{b + c}{2bc}$	$\dfrac{15c + 17b}{32bc}$
VI	$\dfrac{33b + 31c}{64bc}$	$\dfrac{b + c}{2bc}$	$\dfrac{33c + 31b}{64bc}$
VII[a]	$\dfrac{63b + 65c}{128bc}$	$\dfrac{b + c}{2bc}$	$\dfrac{63c + 65b}{128bc}$

NOTE

[a]   The equilibrium value is $\dfrac{b + c}{2bc} = \dfrac{1}{2c} + \dfrac{1}{2b}$. If we split each term of Spain into its two component parts we shall see that the first part is 0, $\dfrac{3b}{4bc}$, $\dfrac{3b}{8bc}$, $\dfrac{9b}{16bc}$, $\dfrac{15b}{32bc}$, $\dfrac{33b}{64bc}$, $\dfrac{63b}{128bc} \rightarrow \dfrac{1}{2c}$ (oscillating), and the second part is $\dfrac{1}{b}$, $\dfrac{1}{4b}$, $\dfrac{5}{8b}$, $\dfrac{7}{16b}$, $\dfrac{17}{32b}$, $\dfrac{31}{64b}$, $\dfrac{65}{128b} \rightarrow \dfrac{1}{2b}$ (oscillating). We can analyse the series for Portugal in the same way. It must be noted that Vasco considered it as self-evident from his table that there would be a tendency towards the equilibrium value $\dfrac{b + c}{2bc}$.

But Vasco goes further; he gives the general formula of the series[121] as

$$\frac{(2^{n-1} \pm 1)b + (2^{n-1} \pm 1)c}{2^n bc}$$

where n is the number of terms or periods, b and c the denominators of the two ratios when the numerators are equal to 1; in the series which has as denominator of the first term b, + or − must alternate in such a way that when n is even we have $(2^{n-1} + 1)b$ and $(2^{n-1} - 1)c$;[122] in the series which has a denominator of the first term c, + or − must alternate in such a way that, when n is even, we have[123] $(2^{n-1} - 1)b$ and $(2^{n-1} + 1)c$.

It is easy to see, Vasco observes, that though the terms in the two series are parallel they can never be equal except when n becomes infinite, but they always tend towards one another, and *their difference becomes smaller and smaller*. The equilibrium is thus, we might say in modern terms, stable.[124]

Vasco now experiments with another model which has different lags. If, he says, instead of supposing that Spain and Portugal *simultaneously* calculate their ratios from the latest ratio of each other and that of France, we assume that each of the three nations calculates its ratio *in turn* from the latest ratios of the other two countries, we shall find not only that the paths for the values of Spain and Portugal are different from what we got from the first model but also that the ratio of France no longer remains unchanged. If we start with proportion for Spain 1 : 15 and Portugal 1 : 10, the proportion of France being the mean of these two will be 1 : 12; Spain now calculates its ratio by taking the mean of the ratio of France 1 : 12 and Portugal 1 : 10 and finds it to be 1 : $10\frac{10}{11}$; but now comes the change: Portugal calculates its ratio from that of France 1 : 12 and the new ratio of Spain 1 : $10\frac{10}{11}$ instead of the old ratio 1 : 15. Portugal's new ratio is therefore 1 : $11\frac{3}{7}$ and the new ratio of France[125] is 1 : $11\frac{7}{43}$.

We may put this model, too, in conventional dynamic equations. Thus using the same symbols as before we have[126]

$$(6) \qquad f_t = \frac{s_{t-2} + p_{t-1}}{2} \qquad \text{where } f_t = f_{t+1} = f_{t+2}$$

$$f_{t+3} = \frac{s_{t+1} + p_{t+2}}{2}$$

$$(7) \qquad s_{t+1} = \frac{f_t + p_{t-1}}{2} \qquad \text{where } s_{t+1} = s_{t+2} = s_{t+3}$$

$$s_{t+4} = \frac{f_{t+3} + p_{t+2}}{2}$$

(8) $\qquad p_{t+2} = \frac{f_t + s_{t+1}}{2} \qquad$ where $p_{t+2} = p_{t+3} = p_{t+4}$

$$p_{t+5} = \frac{f_{t+3} + s_{t+4}}{2}$$

From these equation we have the Table 4.3, when the initial values for $s_t = 1 : 15$ and $p_t = 1 : 10$.

TABLE 4.3

Time	France $f_t = \dfrac{s_{t-2} + p_{t-1}}{2}$		Spain $s_t = \dfrac{f_{t-1} + p_{t-2}}{2}$		Portugal $p_t = \dfrac{f_{t-2} + s_{t-1}}{2}$
-1	—		$\frac{1}{15}$		—
0	—		$\frac{1}{16}$		$\frac{1}{10}$
1	$\frac{1}{2}(\frac{1}{10} + \frac{1}{15}) = \frac{1}{12}$		$\frac{1}{15}$		$\frac{1}{10}$
2	$\frac{1}{12}$	$\frac{1}{2}(\frac{1}{12} + \frac{1}{10}) = \dfrac{1}{10\frac{10}{11}}$			$\frac{1}{10}$
3	$\frac{1}{12}$		$\dfrac{1}{10\frac{10}{11}}$	$\frac{1}{2}(\frac{1}{12} + \dfrac{1}{10\frac{10}{11}}) = \dfrac{1}{11\frac{3}{7}}$	$\dfrac{1}{11\frac{3}{7}}$
4	$\frac{1}{2}(\dfrac{1}{10\frac{10}{11}} + \dfrac{1}{11\frac{3}{7}}) = \dfrac{1}{11\frac{7}{43}}$		$\dfrac{1}{10\frac{10}{11}}$		$\dfrac{1}{11\frac{3}{7}}$
5	$\dfrac{1}{11\frac{7}{43}}$		$\dfrac{1}{11\frac{5}{17}}$		$\dfrac{1}{11\frac{3}{7}}$
↓	↓		↓		↓
∞	$\dfrac{1}{11\frac{1}{4}}$		$\dfrac{1}{11\frac{1}{4}}$		$\dfrac{1}{11\frac{1}{4}}$

Vasco himself gives the table of the values of ratios in the following form (Table 4.4),[127] where $\frac{1}{b}$ is the initial ratio of Spain and $\frac{1}{c}$ the initial ratio of Portugal.

TABLE 4.4

Time		
-1	Spain	$\dfrac{c}{bc} = \dfrac{1}{b}$
0	Portugal	$\dfrac{b}{bc} = \dfrac{1}{c}$
I	France	$\dfrac{b + c}{2bc}$
II	Spain	$\dfrac{3b + c}{4bc}$
III	Portugal	$\dfrac{5b + 3c}{8bc}$
IV	France	$\dfrac{11b + 5c}{16bc}$
V	Spain	$\dfrac{21b + 11c}{32bc}$
VI	Portugal[a]	$\dfrac{43b + 21c}{64bc}$

NOTE

[a] Portugal's $\dfrac{43b + 21c}{64bc} = \dfrac{43}{64c} + \dfrac{21}{64b}$ can be seen to tend to $\dfrac{2}{3c} + \dfrac{1}{3b}$ which is the equilibrium value as we mention below.

Vasco gives also the general formula of this series.[128] This is:

$$\frac{Ab + (2^n - A)c}{2^n bc}$$

where $A = 2^n - \dfrac{(2^n - 4)}{3} - 1$ when n is an even number, and

$A = 2^n - \dfrac{(2^n - 2)}{3} - 1$ when n is an odd number.

Though Vasco was satisfied simply to demonstrate that the ratios approach their equilibrium values in his table, we could easily see from his formula that this is so. For if we carry out the substitution of

A in the formula,[129] we would have:

$$\frac{1}{c} - \frac{1}{3c} + \frac{4}{3 \times 2^n c} - \frac{1}{2^n c} + \frac{1}{3b} - \frac{4}{3 \times 2^n b} + \frac{1}{2^n b}$$

but as n tends to ∞ the above expression becomes

$$\frac{1}{c} - \frac{1}{3c} + \frac{1}{3b} = \frac{2}{3c} + \frac{1}{3b}$$

which is the equilibrium value and the equilibrium is stable.[130]

This is Vasco's contribution; the fact that it was restricted to a few pages of his work left it entirely unknown;[131] older authors were not able to appreciate its significance and modern dynamic authors do not engage very often in the study of these older text-books. Vasco's example, and that of Du Pont, of whom we shall presently speak, were left without imitation for over fifty years until T. Perronet Thompson made another formal contribution to dynamic economics.[132] He was of course, preceded by Canard who has had most interesting ideas about the dynamic equilibrium and the path towards it but who, however, did not put these particular ideas of his into a mathematical dynamic form.[133]

NOTES

1.   In P. Custodi, *Scrittori Classici Italiani di Economia Politica*, parte moderna, vol. XII. See also G.H. Bousquet, 'Histoire de l'Economie mathématique ...', op. cit., p. 124.

2.   *Il Caffé*, vol. I (Brescia, 1765) p. 118. Cf. Augusto Montanari, *La matematica applicata all' economia politica da Cesare Beccaria, Guglielmo Silio, Luigi Molinari Valeriani e Antonio Scialoja* (Reggio Emilia, 1892) p. 10.

3.   The article is reproduced in P. Custodi, *Scrittori Classici Italiani di Economia Politica*, parte moderna, vol. XII, pp. 235–41. It is to this edition that we refer. It may also be found on pp. 122–3 of *Il Caffé: ossia brevi e varii discorsi distribuiti in fogli periodici dal Giugno 1764 a tutto Maggio 1765* (Milano, 1804), first semester.

4.   Other members were Alessandro Verri, Baillon and Sebastiano Franci. The periodical lasted for only two years. See *Il Caffé*, pp. 3–4.

5.   Beccaria, op. cit., p. 237.

6.   Ibid., p. 238.

7.   Ibid., p. 239. The symbols used are Beccaria's.

8.   Beccaria gives the equation (2) as $x + \dfrac{tx}{u} = u$, which is the same as

(2) above. Equation (3) is given in the form $x = \dfrac{uu}{u + t}$. Ibid., p. 239.

9. Ibid., p. 240. The signs of inequality are actually used by Beccaria.
10. Ibid., p. 240.
11. Silio in the *Nuova Raccolta di Opuscoli di Autori Siciliani,* vol. V (Palermo, 1792) pp. 91–173.
12. Ibid., p. 122.
13. Ibid., p. 104.
14. Ibid., p. 122.
15. Ibid., pp. 127 *et seq.*
16. These probabilities, Silio observes, can be calculated by taking into account the numbers of successful and unsuccessful attempts at smuggling. Ibid., p. 137.
17. Silio, op. cit., pp. 138 *et seq.*
18. Ibid., p. 151. The symbols he uses are slightly different from Beccaria's. Thus he writes $VX + TX = V^2$, where $V = u$, $t = T$ and $x = X$.
19. Ibid., p. 152, where Silio's argument is as follows: 'Crescendo $BC = T$ diminuira $CD = X$ in guisa, che per divenire $X = 0$, cioè infinitesimo, fa di mestieri che infinito sia il tributo.' He also adds that 'quando sia il tributo $T = 0$, sarà $X = V$'. Ibid., p. 152.
20. Ibid., pp. 147–9, the terms are reproduced as given by Silio.
21. Ibid., pp. 147–9.
22. Ibid., pp. 172–3 conclude by making another plea in favour of the application of mathematics to political economy.
23. Three are the most important editions of the *Meditazioni* the first of 1771, the sixth of 1772, which includes Frisi's notes, and the edition of 1781 in Milan where Verri revised certain of his arguments and supressed Frisi's notes. There are French translation, one made in 1773 and another by F. Neale in 1823. The latter appears to have been made from the sixth edition of 1772 but leaves out the notes by Frisi. The first five editions were made in 1771. When we refer to an edition of 1771, we refer to the third edition made in Genoa.
24. Frisi, Verri and Beccaria were friends and members of the Society *Il Caffé.* For the identification of Frisi as the editor of the notes, we have Custodi's evidence that the review of Lloyd's book was written by Frisi (vide, Custodi, op. cit., vol. XV, p. lxiii and vol. XVII, p. 369) in conjunction with the evidence in Venturi's review of the 6th edn of *Meditazioni,* in *Nuovo Giornale de' Letterati d'Italia,* vol. III, May and June 1773, p. 237, that the notes and the review of Lloyd's book were written by the same person. Cf. also A. Montanari, *La teoria matematica del valore e uno scrittore emiliano del secolo scorso* (Reggio Emilia, 1891) pp. 12 *et seq.*
25. In addition to the sixth edition which can be found at the British Museum, Frisi's notes are reproduced in full in F. Fuoco, *Applicazione dell' algebra all' Economia Politica,* edited by Mauro Fasiani, Appendix F, pp. 259–67.
26. Verri, op. cit. (1771) p. 22; (1772) p. 32. Of Verri's contribution to monopolistic theory, which was significant as indicated by the above passage, nothing has been written so far.

27. Verri, *Opere filosophiche* (Paris, 1784) p. 201, which reproduces the Milan edition of 1781.

28. See note 26.

29. Verri, op. cit. (1772) p. 33. These passages occur on p. 23 of the edition of 1771.

30. See note 29.

31. Verri had already preceded Frisi in commenting on an aspect of Frisi's work. See Verri's comments pp. 210–11 of *Il Caffé*, op. cit., second semester, to an article by P. Frisi on 'Human Influences', ibid., pp. 206–10. Verri wrote also an encomium of Frisi but it is interesting to note that in the bibliography of Frisi's printed and unprinted works given there by Verri, the notes to the 6th edn of the *Meditazioni* are not included. Vide Pietro Verri, *Memorie appartenenti alla vita ed agli studii del signor Paolo Frisi* (Milan 1787) pp. 90–6.

32. P. Frisi, 'Note dell' Editore' in Verri's *Meditazioni*, 6th edn (1772) p. 37.

33. Ibid., p. 38. 'Poichè dato il numero de' compratori, e non essendovi alcun venditore, il prezzo contrattabile deve crescere oltre qualunque limite, è inoltre manifesto che sarà ... B = 0.'

34. That is while *C* would simply become infinite, *P* should become infinite of a higher order. See also Frisi in Verri, op. cit., p. 245.

35. Ibid., p. 38.

36. Ibid., p. 38.

37. Verri, op. cit., p. 232, where he notes that this should be read in conjunction with the note on pp. 37–8.

38. This would of course contradict Frisi's initial hypothesis that *P* must be of the same order as *C* or *V* when they become infinite; *a, b, c*, etc. must therefore be equal to zero.

39. Frisi, op. cit., p. 43. The proof, not provided by Frisi, is:

   (1) $dP = \dfrac{\partial P}{\partial C}\, dC + \dfrac{\partial P}{\partial V}\, dV = 0$ when (2) $P = \dfrac{C}{V}$, (3) $\dfrac{\partial P}{\partial C} = \dfrac{1}{V}$ and

   (4) $\dfrac{\partial P}{\partial V} = -\dfrac{C}{V^2}$ Substituting (3) and (4) into (1) we get Frisi's formula.

40. Ibid., p. 43. Frisi points out that in addition to the above, price will be a maximum when *C* becomes infinitely large, or *V* infinitely small; price will be a minimum when the opposite happens.

41. Helmut Reichardt, in *A. A. Cournot*, pp. 75–6 criticising Frisi misses in my opinion entirely Frisi's point by examining variations in price in respect only of changes in the number of buyers and playing on the ideas of relative and absolute maximum: Frisi considered *simultaneous* variations in both *C* and *V*.

42. Ibid., p. 84, Verri had contrasted the 'merce particolare' (commodities) to the 'merce universale' (money).

43. Ibid., pp. 92, 97.

44. Ibid., p. 97. The objections made against $dC/dV = C/V$ hold also here.

45. Verri, op. cit., p. 134. This problem, as Frisi points out, is an isoperimetric problem. The same problem is discussed in the note on p. 155, where a maximum of production in each branch of agriculture is required for a minimum of workers. Calling *R* the production in the

particular branch and N the number of workers employed there, we have the formula $AN + R = B$ where A and B are constant.

46. Ibid., p. 152. The first suggestion came from Beccaria in his treatment of smuggling. Like Beccaria, Frisi did not plot his curve.
47. See Jevons, Preface to the second edition of *The Theory of Political Economy* (p. xlv–xlvi of 2nd edn) where he mentions that it was an Italian, Prof. L. Cossa, who identified for him Lloyd as the author of his copy of the *Essay on the Theory of Money*.
48. Cf. A. Valeri, *Pietro Verri* (1937) p. 158; Frisi, in 'Estratto del libro intitolato: An Essay on the Theory of Money, London 1771' in Verri, *Meditazioni Sulla Economia Politica*, 6th edn (1772) p. 237.
49. Letter from Verri to his brother dated 11 April 1781 from the Archive Andreani–Sormani–Verri, quoted by Valeri, op. cit., p. 159.
50. Lloyd, op. cit., ch. IX; Frisi, op. cit., p. 243.
51. Or $PM = Q$, i.e. price by the quantity of good = quantity of money. The velocity of circulation is left out.
52. To this Frisi, op. cit., p. 244, opposes Verri's $P = C/V$ which, he says, assumes as given the quantity of money, the supply and demand of the good and all other circumstances and seeks only variations arising from numbers of sellers and buyers.
53. Verri, op. cit., p. 247.
54. Lloyd, op. cit., chs X and XI.
55. Lloyd, op. cit., ch. XII; Frisi, op. cit., p. 248. Frisi mentions, op. cit., p. 241, that Verri's thesis that the state of industry is in inverse proportion to the distance among men, which led to the formula $XY = A^2$ is equivalent to Lloyd's thesis that the state of arts, manufacture and commerce is in inverse proportion of the space occupied by a number of people. Lloyd, op. cit., ch. IV.
56. 'Meditazioni Sulla Economia Politica: Edizione sesta accresciuta dall' Autore, Livorno 1772, nella Stamperia dell' Enciclopedia in ottavo', in *Nuovo Giornale de' Letterati d' Italia*, vol. III (Modena 1773) pp. 228–83. It is to this edition that we refer.
57. By A. Montanari, in *La teoria matematica del valore e uno scrittore emiliano del secolo scorso* (Reggio Emilia, 1891), pp. 12 *et seq.* There are, however, some doubts about the author's identity.
58. Venturi, *Nuovo Giornale*, p. 237.
59. Ibid., pp. 240–1. Newton's law is $v = 1/d^2$ where v the attraction is the inverse quadratic of distance d. If distance is infinitely small or large, attraction becomes infinitely large or small of the second degree, and, if one followed Frisi, one would have to exclude all functions of distance. This would mean making attraction simply inversely proportional to distance 'il quale sembrerebbe forse geometricamente dimostrato, purchè tutti i fenomeni della Natura contro di esso non reclamassero', the author ironically observes, ibid., pp. 241–2.
60. See also Montanari, op. cit., pp. 14 *et seq.*
61. Verri, 'Meditazioni sulla Economia Politica' (1772) p. 30.
62. Venturi, *Nuovo Giornale*, p. 243. On p. 281 the author refers to Frisi's other formulae $XY = A^2$ and $R + AN = B$ which do not advance, at

all, he thinks the solution of the problems discussed.

63.   The figures in the text have been drawn according to Venturi's instructions.

64.   Ibid., p. 244. 'Se si riguardi come variabile la sola *C*, e la *V* si prenda per costante, il luogo dell' equazione *P* = *C*/*V* sarà una linea retta, e non vi sarà altro massimo valore di *P* se non quello che corrisponde a *C* = ∞, nè altro minimo se non quello che corrisponde a *C* = 0.'

65.   Venturi, *Nuovo Giornale*, p. 244.

66.   Ibid., p. 244.

67.   Ibid., p. 245.

68.   This was delivered before the Società de' Georgofili di Firenze on 2 March 1796 and is reproduced in Custodi, *Scrittori Classici Italiani*, parte moderna, vol. XVII (1804) pp. 384–99, to which we refer.

69.   Ferroni, op. cit., p. 390. Condorcet also discussed Verri's ideas on price. 'Je sais bien que le prix augmente quand le nombre des acheteurs augmente, et qu'il diminue quand celui des vendeurs s'accroît, mais est-ce dans le même rapport?' Condorcet, *Œuvres complètes*, vol. I (Paris, 1847–9) pp. 281 *et seq.*

70.   Ferroni, op. cit., p. 392.

71.   *Ortes' work is reproduced in Custodi, Scrittori Classici Italiani di Economia Politica, parte moderna, vols XXI–XXV.*

72.   Ortes, op. cit., in Custodi, vol. XXII, p. 45.

73.   Ibid., p. 48.

74.   Ibid., p. 49; Ortes, a poet at the same time, adds, 'Tale sarebbe il valore della gioventù perduta, della fedeltà in amore e simili altri beni chimerici e immaginarii.'

75.   Ortes, op. cit., in Custodi, op. cit., vol. XXII, pp. 45 and 365.

76.   Ortes, op. cit., in Custodi, vol. XXI, p. 211. Cf. also André Jean-Faure, *Giammaria Ortes: Un Vénitien du Settecento* (1934) p. 328.

77.   Ortes, op. cit., in Custodi, op. cit., vol. XXII, pp. 45 and 365 A. Loria, in 'Teoria del Valore', *Archivio Giuridico* (Bologna, 1882) p. 25, in reviewing Ortes observed that his assumptions are erroneous but his result will be valid, if in $v = r/m$ we interpret Ortes to mean not that the quantity of goods remains unchanged but rather that an increase in national wealth brings about an equal increase to the supply and demand of the product.

78.   Ortes, op. cit., in Custodi, op. cit., vol. XXII, pp. 365–6.

79.   Ibid., pp. 365–6.

80.   Reproduced in Custodi, op. cit., vol. XXV.

81.   Ibid., p. 11.

82.   The book is reproduced in Custodi, op. cit., vol. XXV, pp. 235 *et seq.*

83.   Ibid., p. 237.

84.   Ortes, *Errori popolari*, in Custodi, op. cit., vol. XXV, pp. 14–15.

85.   The quality of his results is not at all comparable to his method, as may be instantly seen by referring to his axiomatic truths, which are '(a) Rendite nazionali dipendono dalle occupazione; (b) Rendite nazionali sono di chi le consuma; (c) Rendite nazionali non possono nè mancare nè abbondare; (d) Rendite ecclesiastiche non possono eccedere; (e) Rendite ecclesiastiche accrescono le communi; (f) Ecclesiastici decaduti per la loro povertà; (g) Economia ecclesiastica dee conformarsi alla

comune presente.' Vide, Ortes, op. cit., p. 17. Another instance where Ortes uses mathematics is on p. 270 of his *Calcolo sopra il valore delle opinioni umane* in Custodi, op. cit., vol. XXIV.

86. See Verri, op. cit., edn of 1784, p. 201; A. Valeri, op. cit., p. 160.

87. M. Gioja, *Nuovo Prospetto delle Scienze Economiche*, vol. III (Milan 1815) p. 9 n. 1.

88. Valeriani had a distinguished public career in Milan and was Professor of Economics at the University of Bologna. See A. Montanari, *La matematica applicata all' economia politica* (1892) p. 22. It is interesting to note that G. Pecchio, *Histoire de l'Économie Politique en Italie* (Paris, 1830 translated from the Italian edition of 1829) p. 376, mentions that it was in 1798 that Valeriani published 'a dissertation on the word value which is not without metaphysical merit'.

89. Valeriani, *Del prezzo* (1806) p. 28.

90. Ibid., p. 29.

91. Ibid., p. 30. This formula Valeriani though was similar to the formula for *specific* gravity, which is equal to $\frac{m}{v}$, or to the mass of a body divided by its volume. See Molinari Valeriani 'Contro la sentenza del celebre Inglese Giuspubblicista-Economico Adam Smith', (Bologna 1821) p. 7 in *Ricerche Critiche ed Economiche 1819–1822*.

92. Valeriani, op. cit., pp. 32 and 46–7. If for example the specific value of good *A* is 8 while that of *B* is 4, the price of *A* in respect of *B* is 2.

93. Valeriani, op. cit., p. 31.

94. The specific value, he says, 'è in ragione composta della diretta de' bisogni espressi dall' inchiesta *tanto più pienamente quanto è maggiore il numero de' richieditori*, e dell' inversa della quantità della cosa espressa dall' offerta *tanto più pienamente quanto è maggiore il numero degli offeritori*' [my italicising]; Valeriani, *Del prezzo*, p. 30.

95. *Operette concernenti quella parte del gius delle genti e pubblico che dicesi pubblica economia* (Bologna, 1815) pp. 24–7; *Saggi di Erotemi su quella parte del gius delle genti e pubblico che dicesi pubblica economia*, (1825) pp. 115–36 and 160 *et seq.*

96. Valeriani not only gave a formula for the price but studied the effect of the changes in value on prices. He distinguishes between an *absolute*

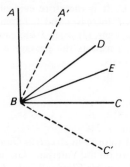

FIG. 4.1n

change in price following a change in the specific value of one good only and a *relative change* where both specific values of goods exchanged change but in a different proportion. He illustrates the effect of changes in prices on the whole price system by a geometrical illustration (Figure 4.1n). The lines *AB, DB, BE, BC* represent goods and the angle between any two of them represents the price (or exchange value) of the one in respect of the other. If *AB* rotates to a position *A'B* the relative prices of all other goods to this one have changed but the relative prices of all other goods between them have remained unchanged. If at the same time that *AB* rotates to *A'B*, *BC* rotates to *BC'* the relative prices of all other goods to these two change but their own prices between them remain unchanged. Whether the relative price of *A'B* to *BC'* remains unchanged or not depends on whether the angle *ABA'* is equal or not to angle *CBC'*.

97. Melchiorre Gioja, *Nuovo Prospetto delle Scienze Economiche* (Milano, 1815–17).

98. Gioja, op. cit., vol. IV (1815) p. 7.

99. Ibid., p. 12.

100. Frisi, op. cit., p. 244.

101. Gioja, op. cit., vol. III, p. 7.

102. Ibid., pp. 8–9.

103. Ibid., p. 9n.

104. Valeriani Molinari, *Apologia della formola p = i/o* (Bologna 1816); *Discorso apologetico in cui si sostiene recarsi invano pel celebre Autore del 'Nuovo prospetto delle scienze economiche' contro l'Apologia della formola p = i/o* (Bologna, 1817). I have not been able to consult these books but according to Montanari, *La matematica applicata*, p. 25 Valeriani mentions that his formula was approved by mathematicians and economists like Fontana, Mascheroni and Longo and maintains that contrary to what Gioja supports, the increase in the numbers of sellers can never harm the purchasers, given free competition between buyers and sellers and among the sellers themselves.

105. In vol. I, p. 43 of *Nuovo Prospetto* there occurs a passage which is not strictly mathematical but could be very easily put into mathematical terms. 'Capital is formed and increases in the measure that production exceeds consumption; in other words capital *A* is equal to production *P* minus consumption *C*. It is therefore evident that *A* can increase in three ways: (1) when *P* increases and *C* remains constant, (2) when *C* decreases and *P* is constant, (3) when *P* increases and *C* decreases at the same time.' In certain aspects the passage is a precursor of modern macro–economic analysis.

106. Gioja, op. cit., vol. VI, p. 316.

107. Ibid., vol. VI, p. 316.

108. Ibid., vol. VI, p. 318.

109. 1807, Pavia, 4 vols, 1817–20.

110. Ressi, op. cit., vol. III, p. 248.

111. A. Loria, 'Teoria del valore', in *Archivio Giuridico* (Bologna, 1882) p. 51, note I. A final word on the Valeriani–Gioja controversy was written by Domenico Vaccolini in his *Elogio di Luigi Valeriani Molinari* (1829),

who after mentioning that the controversy remained unresolved adds, 'Ma il tempo, che giudica degli scrittori e pone ciascuno al posto che gli appartiene darà la palma all' Economista filosofo (quali mostrossi veramente il Valeriani) sopra l'Economista compilatore (qual parve più spesso quel suo illustre avvessario).' Ibid., p. 12. Others who mentioned the controversy were Carlo Bosellini, *Progressi delle scienze economiche in Giornale Arcadico di Scienze, Lettere ed Arti*, vol. XXIX (Roma, 1826) p. 72, who mentions the controversy without comments and A. Marescotti, *Discorsi sulla Economia Sociale*, vol. II (1856) pp. 39–41, who says that Valeriani's formula is inadequate to render a precise idea of all the elements of value.

112. Cagnazzi, op. cit., p. 217 in note.
113. One finds sporadic references in Italian books about Vasco having produced some 'formulette' but no mention of the essence of his contribution to mathematical economics is made. See, for example, G. Rossi, *La Matematica applicata alla teoria della ricchezza sociale* (Reggio Emilia, 1889), pp. vii–viii; M. Fasiani, op. cit., p. 91; A. Montanari, *La matematica applicata*, p. 9, n. 2, does not consider Vasco as having written mathematical economics because 'l'uso della matematica, fatto dal Vasco, non è per certo esposizione di un metodo destinato alle ricerche di economia, nè una speciale di tali ricerche fatta per mezzo dell' analisi, ma sibbene il puro e semplice impiego di un calcolo in una questione di calcolo'.
114. Pecchio, op. cit., p. 226.
115. Custodi, op. cit., vol. XXXIII, parte moderna, pp. 109–15, note, to which we refer.
116. Vasco, op. cit., p. 109.
117. Ibid., p. 110.
118. It is immediately obvious that if we add (4) and (5)

$$s_t + p_t = s_{t-1} + p_{t-1}$$

and so $f_t = f_{t+1}$ and f_t is in equilibrium. Equations 1–5 and the table are *not* Vasco's; they are our interpretation of his argument.
119. Thus (see Figure 4.2n) if the arrow means 'influences the' we shall have for:

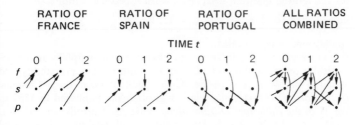

| RATIO OF FRANCE | RATIO OF SPAIN | RATIO OF PORTUGAL | ALL RATIOS COMBINED |

TIME *t*

FIG. 4.2n

120. Vasco, op. cit., p. 111.
121. Vasco, op. cit., p. 112.

122. This we may represent by $\dfrac{[2^{n-1} + (-1)^n]b + [2^{n-1} + (-1)^{n+1}]c}{2^n bc}$

   This is the general formula for Spain.

123. This we may represent by $\dfrac{[2^{n-1} + (-1)^{n+1}]b + [2^{n-1} + (-1)^n]c}{2^n bc}$

   This is the general formula for Portugal.

124. Although Vasco does not prove it, it is easy, by using his formula, to prove formally the stability of the system. He simply says, ibid., p. 112, 'È facilissimo ad osservare in questa formola, che sebbene i termini paralleli delle due serie non possano mai essere uguali essendo disuguali b e c, se non quando n *diventi infinito*, si vanno però sempre più indefinitamente accostando a non avere in breve progressione che *piccolissime e trascurabili differenze*' [my italicising].

125. Vasco, op. cit., p. 113.

126. These reactions may be illustrated by Figure 4.3n (which, of course, like equations (6)–(8) are our own).

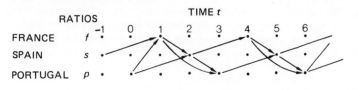

FIG. 4.3n

   There are, in addition, two similar currents of reactions; one emanating from s_0 and p_1 and another from s_1 and p_2. Thus the Spanish ratio influences the Portuguese ratio after one lag and the French after two lags; f influences s after one lag and p after two lags; and p influences f after one lag and s after two lags; there is thus a period of three lags before the value of each ratio changes.

127. Vasco, op. cit., p. 114.

128. Ibid., p. 115.

129. It does not matter whether we take the value of A as if n is even or odd for the term in question disappears when n becomes infinite.

130. Substituting for $b = 10$ and $c = 15$, we get $\frac{2}{30} + \frac{1}{45} = \dfrac{1}{11\frac{1}{4}}$ as the equilibrium value of ratios.

131. It is not even included in Jevons's or Fisher's bibliographies on mathematical economics. Vasco has dealt also with various probability and actuarial problems in a review of the book of Gian–Luigi Chianale *Institutions d'Arithmétique* which was originally published in 1787 in vol. IV of the *Biblioteca Oltramontana*. Vide also Custodi, op. cit., vol. XXXV, pp. 110–36, 264–5, 456–7 and 271, all dealing with actuarial problems.

132. T. Perronet Thompson, 'The instrument of Exchange' *Westminster Review*, vol. I (1824) pp. 171–205 and *An Exposition of fallacies on*

rent, tithes, etc. (1826) pp. 39–40. We deal with Thompson's contribution further below.

133. Canard, *Principes d'Économie Politique*, p. 51. The argument therefore advanced by W.J. Baumol in his *Economic Dynamics* 1951, pp. 11 *et seq.* that the history of dynamics starts with the English classical economists and that these early attempts did not include dynamic process analysis is not correct.

5 The French Contribution

5.1 FRANÇOIS VÉRON DE FORBONNAIS

Forbonnais has the distinction of being the first author to use expressly mathematical reasoning and symbols in French, a language which was later to become the channel of some of the most important developments in mathematical economics. The second volume of his *Élémens du Commerce* published anonymously in 1754 contains two such instances.

In Chapter VIII, Forbonnais, dealing with the rate of exchange, observes[1] that if there is parity of the rate of exchange of two countries and parity of the rate of exchange of the second country with a third country, as well as parity between the first and the third country, a position of equilibrium will be established which he calls 'pair politique'. If the rates of exchange are

$$a = b$$
$$b = c$$
$$c = a$$

it is clear that there will be no benefit in exchanging the various currencies.

But if
$$a = b$$
$$b = c$$
$$c = a + d$$

the parity will be broken. One, by exchanging a for b, and then exchanging b for c and c for $a + d$, makes a profit of d. The parity will be re-established when

$$a + d = b + d$$
$$b + d = c + d$$
$$c + d = a + d$$

If now, through any reason, $c + d$ is exchanged in the third country for $a + d + f$, the same chain of reactions will be repeated.

An elementary conception of some form of equilibrium and its disturbance was thus formulated and put into mathematical form.[2]

The second instance of the use of mathematics by Forbonnais is a treatment, similar to that of Spinelli, of the problem of bimetallism.[3]

If in Europe $a = 15b$ where a is a pound of gold and b a pound of silver and a country raises this proportion so that $a = 16b$, neighbouring nationals could bring a and get for it $16b$. Exchanging $15b$ in their own country they would make a profit of a pound of silver.

Equation $a = 15b$ is a first condition of equilibrium. Given this, there is a second condition, namely that a pound of gold must be exchanged for 15 pounds of silver of the same title. Thus if we indicate absolute purity of gold by $16c$ and absolute purity of silver by $6d$, the second condition requiring equality of titles would give

$$16c = 6d \quad \text{or} \quad 8c = 3d, \text{ etc.}$$

If we had in addition to $a = 15b$, $8c = 4d$, it would pay foreigners to bring in gold and exchange it for silver of a higher title.

Adding the two conditions of equilibrium together, we have a general condition

$$a + 16c = 15b + 6d$$

or

$$a + 8c = 15b + 3d$$

If one of these proportions is broken it must be established by the other: thus $a + 16c = 30b + 3d$, i.e. a pound of pure gold is exchanged for 30 pounds of half-pure silver.[4]

5.2 PIERRE SAMUEL DU PONT DE NEMOURS

Du Pont de Nemours is the earliest French contributor of importance to mathematical economics. He has the distinction of being the first professional economist to have actually used a diagram in illustrating an economic argument set out in essentially dynamic terms, two years after Vasco had for the first time used the dynamic form of process analysis in economics.

Du Pont's contribution was originally made in a memoir delivered in 1774 before a gathering of physiocrats at the house of the Marquis de Mirabeau. After it was revised it was sent, as part of a letter, to the son of Carl Friedrich von Baden, and was published together with other letters in 1892.[5] It appears that the memoir was sent with the

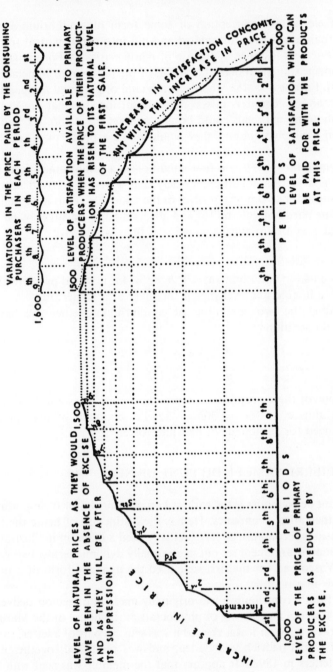

FIG. 5.1   Dupont's diagram

intention of interesting Daniel Bernoulli, whose unique contribution we have already seen, in the problems dealt with in the memoir, a plan of which he had already seen. No evidence of Bernoulli's reactions can, however, be found.

Du Pont appears to be preoccupied with the need of correctly evaluating the effects of various measures as a guide to the formulation of a sound policy, and believes that mathematics could help much towards this end.[6] The infinite relations among the members of a society are interdependent but have regularity 'for nothing in nature occurs without rule'.[7] It is true that the effects of a particular measure of policy cannot yet be precisely known but simply surmised at. But in the same way as mathematicians were able to determine the effects of opening a hole in a water reservoir, they could, if they applied themselves to the task, provide answers to questions of policy. One way to achieve this, he thinks, is by finding curves which will represent the effects of various measures of policy, the 'curves of policy' – 'courbes politiques'. 'There are many kinds of these, others rising, others falling,'[8] he writes, and expresses the hope that Daniel Bernoulli 'may be able to calculate them and other mathematicians will follow his example and shed light on these matters which are so important for mankind.'[9]

By way of illustration he attempts to construct such a curve (Figure 5.1), not basing himself on any empiric data but, as he says, with the help of his intuition.[10] This curve attempts to show the effects on price through time of the suppression of an excise tax. A convinced physiocrat, Du Pont *a priori* believes that the benefits from the suppression of the tax will ultimately accrue to the owners of the land – the primary producers as he calls them. But the diffusion of the tax back to the primary producers will take place gradually through time. The immediate result of a removal of a tax on commerce or manufacture would be that the merchants or manufacturers will find that they are in a position either to cut the prices of their products or increase the price paid for their materials; Du Pont thinks that they will pass some of the profit to either side 'with the view of securing from the ones an increase in sales and from the others supplies of good quality'.[11] But 'by degrees, while the means of payment increase among buyers and a more vigorous competition makes itself felt among them, the prices rise for them to the same point at which they were before the suppression of the excise, in such a way that the reform of the excise turns out in the end to be entirely to the advantage of the primary producers'.[12]

Thus the price of primary producers tends through time towards a new equilibrium which is the old price increased by the amount of the excise; while the price of buyers, after being initially displaced, tends to return to its old equilibrium level.

To draw his curve, Du Pont has to make more explicit assumptions about the form of his relations. This he does by assuming[13] that 'the increase in the price obtained by the primary sellers is assumed for each period to amount to three-fourths of the increase of the preceding period'.[14] The result is the curve on the left-hand side of the diagram, where time is measured on the abscissa and the increase in the price of primary producers on the ordinate. Our author shows that at the end of the ninth period the curve reaches the equilibrium level of 1500; he has failed, however, to show that this equilibrium level is approached asymptotically through time.

Du Pont makes clear that his hypothesis is arbitrary and may not be realistic. 'A greater or smaller proportion', he writes,[15] 'is possible. And there are good reasons to believe that their proportion is diminishing, so that while the proportion in the second period is three fourths that of the first, that of the third may very well be equal to two thirds of the second, that of the fourth one half of that of the third and that of the fifth only one third of that of the fourth, and so on.' But while he makes explicit that there may be changes in the value of the parameter, his diagram shows properties which need other assumptions, which are not made explicitly and which must be made if certain of its features are to be justified. The first is that the various points of price through time are not joined by straight lines but by curves which are convex to the abscissa. This would mean that while at the end of each period the increase in price turns out to be three fourths of the increase in the previous period, the speed of adjustment inside the period is not uniform, the rate of increase being slower at the beginning than at the end of each period. The second assumption concerns the curve on the right of the diagram which measures time on the abscissa and the increase in satisfaction to be derived by primary producers, as a result of the increase in price on the ordinate. It can be seen immediately that Du Pont assumes a constant marginal utility of income since the increase in the price – and the concomitant increase in income of the primary producers – are shown to be exactly proportional to the increase in satisfaction.[16]

Du Pont shows in his diagram a third curve illustrating the path through time of the price paid by the consuming buyers. The equilibrium price in this case is higher than the equilibrium price received by the primary producers, the difference between them 'reflecting the costs of processing, transporting, or storing'.[17] The deviation from equilibrium is in each period measured by the perpendicular dropped from the trough of each arc of the curve to the chord of the same arc.[18]

Du Pont also visualises conditions under which his curves would shift. 'If', he writes,[19] 'new waterways were constructed, if inventions of ingenious machinery which simplifies labour and reduces expenses were forthcoming, then the prices of the sellers would be higher.'

Du Pont's contribution to mathematical economics remained unnoticed until Spiegel published his translation. But though this author mentions, in his introduction to the translation, the importance of Du Pont's diagram in the history of the development of mathematical economics he has failed to appreciate the other part of his contribution, the ideas, that is, expressed in both the text and by his diagram of a dynamic path through time towards equilibrium.

Before concluding this section on a leading Physiocrat, it should be added that the 'tableau économique' of François Quesnay is mathematical in character.

This is especially true of the first version of the 'tableau' which appeared in 1758 and referred to the circulation of the net product.[20] This version, which had come to be known as the 'zig-zag' version, as well as the later versions used by other Physiocrats and especially Mirabeau[21] are essentially dynamic in character because they try to trace the distribution of the net product among the three classes through time; and they further attempt to show how this distribution is affected through time, if there is a change in the basic parameters such as an increase in capital or the imposition of additional indirect taxes.

5.3 ACHYLLE-NICOLAS ISNARD AND GENERAL EQUILIBRIUM

In 1777 Le Trosne, in an interesting passage of his book *De l'ordre social*, writes about the applicability of mathematical methods to economics:

Le calcul est une formule par laquelle on opère sur des quantités mesurables et comparables, entre lesquelles on cherche à découvrir un rapport quelconque. Le résultat présente l'inconnue qu'on cherchoit, et que l'auroit eu beaucoup de peine à découvrir sans cette formule. La science économique s'exerçant sur des objects mesurables est susceptible d'être une science exacte et d'être soumise au calcul.[22]

Also, Condillac's book *Le Commerce et le Gouvernement* published in 1776 shows a markedly mathematical undercurrent beneath his arguments but as it contains no mathematics and no reference to the mathematical method it cannot fall within the scope of this review.[23]

The next important contribution in French after Du Pont and in fact one of the most important contributions in the history of the development of mathematical economics was that of A. N. Isnard, who in 1781 published anonymously a *Traité des richesses*,[24] in two volumes.

In the first volume, he examines the relations of goods among themselves. He assumes that there is no money as a first step; if then a units of a certain commodity are exchanged for b units of a second commodity, the exchange value of a unit of the first commodity in terms of units of the second is b/a or $b:a$.[25] If we call M the first commodity and M' the second commodity we have

$$aM = bM'$$
$$\frac{M}{M'} = \frac{b}{a}$$

This may be written as $M : M' :: \frac{1}{a} : \frac{1}{b}$. The greater is, therefore, the number of units received for a given quantity of good M, the greater is its value; on the contrary, the greater is the number of units of the good M given in exchange for a certain quantity of good M', the smaller is the value of M.

If in fact, Isnard says, we assume that in a market there are only these two goods, and the quantity intended for exchange[26] of good M is a while that of the second good M' is b, their value is determined by the above equation.

If there are three commodities, the quantity of each will be exchanged in a certain proportion for a quantity of each of the other two; thus if a of M is divided between M' and M'' in a proportion am to an where $m + n = 1$ and if b of M' is divided between M and M'' in a proportion of bp to bq where $p + q = 1$, while c of M'' is divided into cr which goes to M and cs which goes to M', we may find the relative value of any good in respect of another. These results we may summarise in the Table 5.1.[27]

TABLE 5.1

Units given in exchange by	Units received in exchange by			
	M	M'	M''	Total payments in kind
M	—	am	$an = a(1-m)$	a units of M
M'	bp	—	$bq = b(1-p)$	b units of M'
M''	cr	$cs = c(1-r)$	—	c units of M''
Total Receipts in kind	$bpM' + crM''$	$amM + csM''$	$anM + bqM'$	$aM + bM' + cM''$

Thus a units of M are exchanged against bp units of M' and cr units of M'' or in Isnard's notation

(1) $$aM = bpM' + crM''$$

and consequently the unit of M is exchanged for

$$\frac{bpM'}{a} + \frac{crM''}{a}$$

The unit therefore of a commodity has a value 'which is in direct proportion to the sum of offers and in inverse proportion to its quantity. But as the offers are composed of many commodities which are heterogeneous, it is not possible to deduce from the equality, or the equation of which we have just spoken, the relation of two particular commodities; to find the relation of commodities taken two by two, one would have to form *as many equations as there are commodities*'.[28] Thus Isnard has conceived the idea of a general equilibrium and its determination and he proceeds to give the three equations which may be directly deduced from our table. These, in addition to (1) above which we reproduce again, are:

(1) $$aM = bpM' + crM''$$
(2) $$bM' = amM + csM''$$
(3) $$cM'' = anM + bqM'$$

But of these three equations only two are independent;[29] and though we have equal equations to commodities, we could not find the absolute values of M, M' and M''; but to find the relative values any two equations are sufficient and this Isnard has done:[30]

$$(4) \quad M : M' : M'' :: \frac{r + p - pr}{a} : \frac{s + m - sm}{b} : \frac{n + q - nq}{c}$$

Isnard emphasises that his expressions are quite general. We may, he says, assume on the one extreme that the quantity of each commodity is divided equally in exchange between the other two and thus have $m = n$, $p = q$, $r = s$, or we may assume that each commodity goes to only one owner of each of the other commodities so that $n = q = s = 0$. We may even progressively change the amount of each offer and see how the change influences all values.[31]

Now has come the moment to introduce money.[32] If we have several commodities M, M', M'', M''', etc., whose values a, b, c, d are known, we may compare all commodities to one of them, money M. Thus

$$M : M' = a : b, \, M : M'' = a : c, \, M : M''' = a : d.$$

Our author applies a similar analysis to the examination of the costs of production.[33] If we suppose that to produce a quantity of 40 units of M we must consume 10 units of M and 10 units of M', while to produce a quantity of 60 units of M' we need $5M + 10M'$, we shall need for the production of $60M' + 40M$ a sum of $15M + 20M'$.

If we assume that $M = M''$ and $M' = 2M''$ or $M' = 3M''$ we shall have (Table 5.2):

TABLE   5.2

Producers of	Expenses in kind		Product		Surplus value of product minus expenses	
					in M'' when $M'' = M = \dfrac{M'}{2}$	in M'' when $M'' = M = \dfrac{M'}{3}$
	M	M'	M	M'		
M	10	10	40		$40 - (10 + 20) = 10$	$40 - (10 + 30) = 0$
M'	5	10		60	$120 - (5 + 20) = 95$	$180 - (5 + 30) = 145$

Thus a change in the price of a commodity affects the net revenue of both producers.[34]

Volume II of the *Traité des richesses*, dealing mainly with taxation, contains no mathematics except for a section where Isnard attempts to set up an economic system composed of

$$100M, \ 120M', \ 150S, \ 180S', \ 200T, \ 240A, \ 300I, \ 360F$$

where M, M' are primary materials, S, S' subsistence wages, T jobs, A money, I industrial units and F land and where the total value of the system in 1980A, as he assumes that $M = A, \ M' = \frac{3}{2}A, \ S = A,$ $S' = \frac{1}{2}A, \ T = \frac{1}{2}A, \ I = \frac{3}{4}A$ and $F = 2A$ (Vol. II, pp. 4–5.)

5.4 CONDORCET

Marie-Jean Caritat, Marquis de Condorcet, though a professional mathematician, used mathematics in his economic writings only once in his *Vie de Monsieur Turgot*, which was published anonymously in London in 1786.

There, discussing in a note[35] the various ways in which indirect taxation could be replaced by direct taxation and the effects of such a change, he used some simple mathematics, the only innovation of which is that he used the sign $\int$ as a sign of summation of finite quantities.

A change may be effected according to Condorcet in three ways, of which the first one is when an indirect tax is converted in total into direct tax by a single operation. If a' was the net product of a piece of land when a direct tax b' and its share of indirect tax i' had been deducted, and we assume now that both taxes are removed, the value of the net product of this particular piece will become

$$a' + b' + i'$$

Consequently the total sum of the values of the net products of the whole land will be

$$\int \overline{a + b + i} \qquad \text{when}$$

$a', a'', a''', \ldots, a^n$ are the various values of the net product for different lands after taxation has been deducted

$i', i'', i''', \ldots, i^n$ the various indirect taxes imposed on each piece of land respectively and

$b', b'', b''', \ldots, b^n$ the direct tax.

But the total tax I is now to be imposed as a direct tax; this will be distributed in proportion to the net product of each piece; thus the share of property a' will be.[36]

$$I \times \frac{(a' + b' + i')}{\int a + b + i}$$

Since the tenant of the land used to pay the indirect tax i', he will have to go on paying it and the landlord will pay the remainder

$$I \times \frac{(a' + b' + i')}{\int a + b + i} - i'$$

As he himself formerly paid the tax b', the excess he is now asked to pay is

$$I \times \frac{(a' + b' + i')}{\int a + b + i} - i' - b'$$

Condorcet gives a treatment on similar lines, when he examines the other two ways in which indirect taxation changes into indirect. These are (*a*) when only a part of indirect tax is changed into direct and this is distributed according to the net product of the properties,[37] and (*b*) when the proprietors of the land have to pay a certain amount of direct tax instead of the amounts of direct and indirect taxes of which they are relieved.[38]

5.5   NICOLAS-FRANÇOIS CANARD AND THE THEORY OF THE 'LATITUDE OF PRICE'

(i) His work

If Vasco's contribution has remained entirely unknown, Canard has acquired a certain notoriety, which he does not deserve at all. Although not an economist by profession, he wrote an essay on whether in an agricultural country, all taxes fall ultimately on land, a subject proposed by the French *Institut National des Sciences et Arts*. To answer the question and oppose the physiocratic ideas, Canard had to analyse the sources of wealth and go into the principles of political economy. He did this with a refreshing novelty and an ingenuity of approach which made Canard one of the most important mathematical economists of this period. The crowning of the work by the Institute[39] had an immense influence on its future for it was no longer an ordinary book but a book which had received the approbation of the most illustrious body in France, an honour which was not bestowed on the works of better known economists.[40] It was perhaps natural that professional economists would judge with more than average severity the views of this 'outsider', whose approach was outside conventional lines; in their critique they concentrated on the defects of the book, while its merits were either ignored or not appreciated because of their novelty. J. B. Say, L. Say, Cournot and Walras repeating one another in their disapproval of the Institute's decision, to whom Jevons, Bertrand and even Schumpeter are added, speak of the work in very derogatory terms. Canard's book, writes Schumpeter,[41] 'is sometimes listed among early contributions to mathematical economics (on *the strength of a few algebraic formulae that mean nothing*) but would otherwise partake of the blessings of *deserved oblivion*, had not a misfortune befallen it. This misfortune consisted in its being "crowned" by the same French Academy that later on failed to extend any recognition to Cournot and Walras. And those Olympians, who felt their neglect the more bitterly on account of the honour done to Canard, visited him with a scathing contempt that bestowed upon him an unenviable immortality: in the history of scientific bodies, Canard is forever sure of a place'.

It is perhaps significant, as we shall see further on, that Canard did not receive elsewhere the same treatment which he received at the hands of his compatriots.[42] He had considerable influence in Italy and it was an Italian author, F. Fuoco, who made a vigorous attempt to defend his method if not his results. But in the end it was Say's, Cournot's and Jevons' works which survived together with what they said about Canard.

Canard's work may be broadly divided into his theory of value and its application, especially to the theory of taxation.

He believes that everything, which has exchangeable value, derives its value from the quantity of labour employed upon it. As there are different qualities of labour, however, Canard does not think that the quantity of labour, which could ideally serve as a measure of the exchangeable value, could in fact serve to determine the price. For this reason, he argues, one must fall back to the market to discover the determinants of price. In the market, where buyers and sellers are gathered, the buyers try to secure the lowest price possible and the sellers the highest price possible. When buyers consider what price to pay they have in mind a maximum price which they cannot exceed; in the same way sellers have a minimum price, below which they will not fall. The actual price will therefore settle somewhere between these two limits. The distance between these two limits, the difference, that is, between the maximum and the minimum price is called by Canard *Latitude*.[43]

The lower limit is the price of the 'necessary labour' which has been applied to the object; the price of this labour is equal to the subsistence wages.[44]

The upper limit, depending on what buyers are willing to pay, varies according to the use for which the object is intended:

(a) If the good is not a necessity, there is a diminishing demand as price rises: the seller, therefore, even if he could, would not force the price beyond that point, where what he gains from the increase in price, he loses by the diminution in sales. 'There is', says Canard,[45] 'a point of increase such that he gains on the one side as much as he loses on the other. This point is the limit of the latitude for the seller, because, if he wanted to increase his price beyond this, his profit would decrease rather than increase.' This is the very kernel of monopoly theory which Cournot was later to develop.[46]

(b) If the good is a necessity, the price would be limited by the 'natural wages' of the buyer; 'if the merchant wanted to exceed this, either the wages would increase in proportion or the workers would revolt so as not to die of hunger'.[47]

(c) If the purchaser intends to transform the good and resell it, the price cannot be higher than that which would leave to the purchaser only his natural wages out of the price he would receive by reselling the object.[48]

The actual price will, we have said, be somewhere on the 'latitude'. The question, however, is at what point. Canard sees the solution in terms of force.[49] If the sellers are more powerful, they will be able to secure for themselves a greater part of the latitude and set a higher price; the opposite happens, if buyers are the more powerful. If they are equally powerful they will share the latitude and price will be settled half-way between the two limits.

Thus Canard presents this interesting and quite 'modern' result: The actual level of price will be determined by the relation of the force of the sellers to that of the buyers.

The force of either side is determined by two factors:

(a) Their need to buy or to sell; the smaller the need to buy or to sell, the higher is the force of the side.

(b) Their competition among themselves; the smaller this competition, the higher is the force of the group against its opposites.[50]

If, therefore, L is the latitude and x the part which is added by the sellers to the minimum price, $L - x$ is the part which buyers have been able to deduct from the maximum price (Figure 5.2).

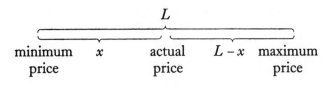

$$L$$

| minimum price | x | actual price | $L - x$ | maximum price |

FIG. 5.2

The actual values of x and $L - x$ and therefore the level of actual price are determined in proportion to the forces of sellers and buyers. Thus

(1) $x : (L - x) =$ force of sellers : force of buyers.

But the force of the buyers is $\dfrac{1}{BN}$ where B is their need and N their competition; and the force of sellers is $\dfrac{1}{bn}$ where b is their need and n their competition.[51] The above equation therefore becomes $x : (L - x) = \dfrac{1}{bn} : \dfrac{1}{BN}$ or

(2) $x : (L - x) = BN : bn$ or

(3) $bnx = BN (L - x)$

This is Canard's basic equation. He has called it 'équation des déterminations'[52] and it 'expresses the equality of moments of the two opposing forces which are in equilibrium. It is to the principle of equilibrium of these two forces that the whole theory of political economy refers, in the same way that the whole theory of statics refers to the principle of equilibrium of the lever'.[53]

Solving (3) for x we get:

(4) $x = \dfrac{BN}{BN + bn} L$

and if S is the natural wage for producing the good and therefore its minimum price, the actual price p of the good will be:[54]

$$(5) \qquad\qquad p = S + \frac{BN}{BN + bn} L$$

Equation (4) shows the amount by which the sellers are able to increase price above its minimum. Thus, says Canard, if $bn = 0$, i.e. if either the need of sellers is zero, or there is a monopoly (and consequently $n = 0$) while BN is finite, $x = L$. The sellers will impose the *maximum* price and this, as we mentioned before, is, in the case of goods which are not absolutely necessary for *survival, at the point where profits are a maximum.*[55]

If on the contrary we have a monopsony[56] with $N = 0$ or the need of buyers to buy is zero, $x = 0$. The price thus becomes a *minimum* and this is determined by the *barest cost, whose covering is absolutely essential for the survival of the producer.*

Canard did not examine the case of bilateral monopoly, that is, where $n = N = 0$ but it can be immediately seen that his formula gives x as *indeterminate*. In such a situation therefore *anything may happen* and x may settle at any point of the latitude. Canard was thus able to produce a formula which not only gave realistic results in monopolistic situations but also in other situations of conflict. Thus if the conflict among sellers becomes extremely acute (and n, therefore, tends to infinity) $x = 0$ and price becomes a minimum; if it is among buyers that the conflict is acute (and $N \rightarrow \infty$ while n is finite) $x = L$ and price is at a maximum. If there is acute conflict among the ranks of both buyers and sellers (and both n and N tend to ∞) the result becomes indeterminate.

The sum $x = \dfrac{BN}{BN + bn} L$, which the seller secures above his natural wage forms his rent and Canard distinguishes three kinds of rent, the rent of land, the rent of capital and industrial rent.[57]

Absolute equilibrium is said to exist when the force of the sellers is equal to that of the buyers[58] and since $BN = bn$

$$(6) \qquad\qquad x = \tfrac{1}{2} L$$

'Mais cet équilibre', says Canard,[59] 'est un point fixe vers lequel tendent toujours les valeurs des choses, et où elles ne s'arrêtent jamais. La vicissitude des évènements, l'instabilité des goûts, des besoins factices, l'opposition des intérêts et mille causes diverses, les tiennent dans une fluctuation continuelle qui les élève et les abaisse alternativement, relativement à ce niveau.'

Thus Canard, not only has conceived the idea of a dynamic equilibrium, but also may be considered as a precursor of the theory of external shocks as a generating force of fluctuations. These same ideas, that a deviation from equilibrium will take time to die out and will generate damped oscillations through time around the equilibrium value, he repeated in his examination of the imposition of a new tax which disturbs the equilibrium position.[60]

Canard's formula (5)

$$p = \frac{BN}{BN + bn} L + S$$

had presupposed, apart from the uniformity of sellers or buyers in their groups, that each seller was the producer of the product, who had transformed it from its raw condition to its final stage, and then sold it to the final consumer.

Now he proceeds to remove this assumption. If, he says, the product passes through various hands during its various stages, the same process of bargaining will take place at every instance when the semi-finished product changes hands. At every such instance there will be a maximum price which the seller hopes to secure as opposed to the minimum one and the difference between the two will form the *partial latitude* at this stage.

These partial latitudes make up the total latitude 'which is not different from that which would exist if all branches of the different sellers were merged into one which sold immediately to the consumers',[61] and which he had already defined as the difference between the maximum price secured under monopoly and the minimum price secured under 'the monopoly of the consumer'[62] (monopsony).

If therefore, there is a series of producers *A, B, C*, etc. each selling to his immediately next, and

$\Lambda = L + L'' + L''' + \dots$

where Λ is the total latitude, while L, L', L'', etc. are the partial latitudes when *A* sells to *B*, *B* sells to *C*, etc., and if further

$b, b', b'', \dots$

are the needs of *A, B, C*, etc. respectively as sellers and

$n, n', n'', \dots$

their competition as sellers;

$B, B', B'', \dots$

are the needs of *B, C, D*, etc. respectively as buyers and

$N, N', N'', \dots$

their competition and

$S, S', S'', \ldots$

is the natural wage of the work on the product done by A, B, C, etc.

we shall have as price of the product when the good passes from A to
B.

$$p = S + \frac{BN}{BN + bn} L$$

The price of the product when the good passes from B to C will be
the cost of the product to B, that is what he paid for it plus the natural
wage of the labour which he applied to it plus the share of the partial
latitude which will, as in the first case, be apportioned in proportion
to the forces of B and C. Thus:

$$p' = p + \frac{B'N'}{B'N' + b'n'} L' + S'$$

$$= S + \frac{BN}{BN + bn} L + S' + \frac{B'N'}{B'N' + b'n'} L'$$

and in general the price of the good at any stage will be[63]

$$(7)\quad P = S + \frac{BN}{BN + bn} L + S' + \frac{B'N'}{B'N' + b'n'} L' + \ldots$$

If $N = N' = N'' = \ldots = 0$, i.e. if there is a monopsony at all stages,
then

$$(8)\qquad P = S + S' + S'' + \ldots$$

Each seller will not receive more than the natural wage for the work he
did. 'This is the limit of the diminution of prices.'[64]

If on the contrary $n = n' = \ldots = 0$, i.e. there is a monopoly
throughout

$$(9)\qquad P = S + S' + S'' + \ldots + L + L' + \ldots$$
$$= S + S' + S'' + \ldots + \Lambda$$

This is the upper limit of prices and it may be seen that the difference
between the two limits is the total latitude.[65]

If at each stage the forces of sellers and buyers are equal and so BN
$= bn$, $B'N' = b'n'$, etc., formula (7) becomes[66]

$$(10)\quad P = S + S' + \ldots + \tfrac{1}{2}(L + L' + \ldots) = \tfrac{1}{2}\Lambda + S + S' + \ldots$$

And since equality of forces is for Canard the condition for absolute
equilibrium in the case where there is a single class of sellers-

producers, this is also a condition for equilibrium in the case where there is more than one selling branch. But there is an additional condition. The partial latitude, which is divided between seller and buyer, is for Canard the rent of labour, over and above the natural wage. If there is to be equilibrium there must be equilibrium among the rents of the various branches, that is among the partial latitudes, so that the application of labour in all branches is equally advantageous. This is the second condition for the existence of absolute equilibrium. 'When the equilibrium is established', says Canard, 'each branch must have for its share of the entire latitude Λ a part proportional to its *capacity*, which means that, other things being equal, the branch which does work double to that done by another, must absorb a portion of the latitude equal to double the latitude of the latter.'[67]

If therefore, c, c', c'', etc. are the capacities of each branch and Σ the sum of the partial capacities of all branches, we must have:

$$(11) \qquad L = \frac{c}{\Sigma} \Lambda, L' = \frac{c'}{\Sigma} \Lambda$$

and formula (10) showing the conditions of equilibrium becomes

$$(12) \qquad P = S + S' + \ldots + (c + c' + c'' \ldots) \frac{\Lambda}{2\Sigma}$$

and as $c + c' + \ldots = \Sigma$

$$(13) \qquad P = S + S' + \ldots + \tfrac{1}{2}\Lambda.$$

The second assumption, which Canard had made, was that at each stage the sellers (or buyers) in a group were uniform, which meant that their forces were the same.[68] He was therefore able to treat the group as if it were an individual. Now he removes this assumption too. In a group of sellers the force of each individual is directly proportional to the capacity of his work and inversely proportional to his need and his competition.[69]

If therefore f, f', f'', etc. are the forces of sellers in a group, so that

$$(14) \qquad f = \frac{c}{bn}, f' = \frac{c'}{b'n'}$$

where c is the capacity, b the need and n the competition,[70] and F is the force of the consumers collectively, the total latitude Λ will be divided in proportion to their forces.

If x is the share of sellers and $\Lambda - x$ that of the purchasers, we shall have $(f + f' + f'' + \ldots): F :: x : (\Lambda - x)$ or

(15) $$x = \frac{(f + f' + f'' + \ldots)}{(f + f' + f'' + \ldots) + F} \Lambda$$

Canard's contribution is remarkable in another respect also. He described the idea of general equilibrium and introduced analysis at the margin.[71]

Apart from absolute equilibrium, which exists when the forces of buyers and sellers are equal and to which we have already referred, Canard examined another kind of equilibrium, that which determines the employment of labour in such a way as to produce the most advantageous combination of his three kinds of rent. This equilibrium he considers as the basis of political economy,[72] and is achieved through free competition by adjustments of the quantities or units at the margin which he calls *'extrémités'* – 'extreme quantities'.

Free competition allocates labour in such a way that the equilibrium among the three kinds of revenue or 'rent' (the rent of land, the rent of capital and the industrial rent) is maintained.[73]

Canard describes figuratively the sources of rent as forming with their ramifications, a system of canals which communicate with one another; and he adds: 'The three sources of rent form a system of ramifications and the entire mass of consumption forms another analogous system. When the quantities at the margin ("les extrémités") of some branches of consumption diminish, the branches of the sources of rent must equally and reciprocally diminish. Thus the marginal quantities of the branches of these two systems coincide with one another so that they increase or decrease simultaneously.'[74]

In other words what Canard is saying is that:

(a) there exists an equality between quantities demanded and quantities produced. If there is a fall in demand, production will be accordingly adjusted so that the equality is reestablished. This is really a version of Say's Equality.
(b) The adjustments of both quantities demanded and quantities produced are effected through marginal changes.

Marginal analysis, in the Ricardian sense, and in anticipation of Ricardo, is used by Canard in his discussion of land rent.

He points out that the discussion of rent and land utilisation should be carried out in terms of marginal lands, of those lands, i.e. of inferior quality which are brought last into cultivation or taken out first. 'The marginal units of all branches of production which belong to the rent of land (i.e. all marginal lands) consist of all estates of inferior quality whose repairs or taxes increase or decrease'[75] and whose cultivation increases or decreases in accordance with their return to the landlord.

Canard uses his ideas of the margin to show how general equilibrium is established, so that benefits are equalised.

> When the benefits decrease in a branch, those who constitute the margin abandon it, as we have seen, and seek to attach themselves to other branches which offer them greater advantages. The number of workers in the less-fortunate branch diminishes until the benefit *is re-established at the same level with that of the other branches.*[76]

The opposite process is followed in the case of the increase in the benefits of a branch.

And Canard concludes[77]: 'Human Labour forms a unique system of ramifications which *all communicate with one another and which constantly tend to bring back all benefits* to level and to the extent that a thousand separate causes raise them or lower them relatively to that level.'[78]

This is the highly ingenious and original analysis of Canard. His application to the theory of taxation, which earned him his unfortunate immortality is an application of his 'balance of forces' analysis.

Canard points out that in the case of the imposition of a new tax, it will take time for its effects to be diffused throughout the economy and a new equilibrium to be reached. Canard called this difficulty of re-establishing the equilibrium the 'Frottement' ('Rubbing in') of the tax and pointed out that during this adjustment period there are marginal adjustments in production due to the new tax. The process of the diffusion of the new tax is described by Canard as follows.

When a new tax is imposed the natural desire of the person who pays it is to 'pass it on' to the purchaser of the good, who is not at all eager to accept this; a conflict follows and the extent of the tax shifted is proportional to the 'forces' of the two conflicting sides. This is generally known as Canard's 'principle of the equal diffusion of taxation' and is based on an erroneous conception of Canard's views. 'The tax will be *proportionately* diffused, not equally.'[79]

If therefore T is the tax, x the part paid by the purchaser, BN his need and competition, $T - x$ the part of the tax borne by the seller whose need and competition are b and n we shall have

$$x : (T - x) = BN : bn \quad \text{or}$$

(16)
$$x = \frac{BN}{BN + bn} T$$

and since price before tax is $p = S + \dfrac{BN}{BN + bn} L$

the new price will be

(17)
$$P = S + \frac{BN}{BN + bn} (L + T)$$

According to his ideas about equilibrium, a new tax is a disturbing cause; before it can be diffused it causes conflicts and fluctuations which take time to die out. It is this which made Canard remark, 'Donc on peut avancer cette grande vérité, que tout vieil impôt est bon et tout nouvel impôt est mauvais',[80] a remark on which his critics concentrated in order to throw as much scorn on him as they could.

(ii) The controversy round Canard and later French authors

One of the first authors who commented on Canard's work was Francis Horner in a review of the book in the *Edinburgh Review*.[81]

He outlines in great detail the arguments of the book which he says 'has added nothing to our knowledge of Political Economy'[82] and criticises in length Canard's contention that labour is the source of all value. He finds him inconsistent because, after having established the labour theory of value as a general principle, Canard does not apply this in the determination of prices but develops a theory in terms of mutual competition.[83] He is particularly critical of Canard's use of Algebra, who, he says, 'has only translated into a language less readily understood, truths of which the ordinary enunciation is intelligible and familiar to all. We will not deny that some branches of political economy, especially those which relate to circulation, money and the analysis of price, admit of being treated with a precision which almost approaches to mathematical exactness. But a subject may possess this precision without requiring or even admitting the symbolic representation of algebra'.[84] He does not exclude the use of analogies from mathematics 'but the frugal and classic taste, with which Beccaria has interspersed allusions of this nature, forms a contrast to the pedantry and profusion with which M. Canard has overloaded his composition'.[85]

Jean-Baptiste Say had a two-way attack against Canard. He indirectly spoke against the use of mathematics and formulae in economics because they are 'most evidently inapplicable to political economy' and form 'the most dangerous of abstractions';[86] and made a direct attack against Canard's ideas on taxation[87]. 'Que penser en conséquence d'une doctrine qui a obtenu l'approbation d'une société illustre et où l'on établit qu'il importe peu que l'impôt pèse sur une branche de revenu ou sur une autre, pourvu qu'il soit anciennement établi.'

The same line was followed by J. B. Say's brother, Louis Say, who in his *Considérations sur l'industrie et la législation*[88] criticises Canard's method of using mathematics in a way which shows his complete ignorance of mathematics. 'Algebra', he says,[89] 'does not facilitate the research for the truth except when the quantities expressed by letters are real and possible. Most of the ideas which M. Canard expresses by letters in his calculations being incorrect, they can be considered, in terms of mathematics, as impossible quantities.' Moreover, algebraic calculation is impossible in economics where quantities change in a complicated and uncertain way and where we have to take into consideration such factors as the weather, human desires, human power and so on.[90]

He refers to Canard's argument that every new tax is bad while every old tax is good and ends by saying that he treated Canard's work at such length because it was crowned by the Institute.[91]

Cournot, also referring to Canard's work, says that it was the only application of mathematics to economics he knew. In his *Recherches* he denied any value to the book. 'These pretended principles are so radically at fault and the application of them is so erroneous, that the approval of a distinguished body of men was unable to preserve the work from oblivion.'[92] Years later Cournot admitted that Canard's work had provided him with his starting point. 'C'était là mon point de départ, et certes il n'avait rien d'encourageant', he remarks,[93] and yet as we have already seen some of Cournot's principal ideas on monopoly had their origin in Canard.

J. Bertrand criticises Canard's mathematics. 'Citizen Canard, although professor of mathematics, ignores or forgets the elements of the calculus of functions,' he writes;[94] 'as he knows that the price of a commodity increases with the number of buyers, with their needs and the revenue at their disposal, and decreases with the number and eagerness of sellers, the translation (of these) into algebraic language is for him immediate; $B + Ax$ is in effect, following Canard, the type of every increasing function of variable x and $B' - A'x$ that of decreasing functions; this is the point of departure and the basis of his theory.' And Bertrand wonders: 'How did he become the laureate of the Institute?'[95]

I fail to understand what relation Bertrand's criticism can have with Canard. He, in essence, accuses Canard for having used linear functions instead of functions of a higher order. But Canard was using economic arguments, of the value of which Bertrand has nothing to say, and even today, when mathematical economic analysis is so much advanced compared to its state at the time of Canard, it is considered legitimate to use linearity as an approximation.

Canard's work did not have the same reception in Italy. There, authors with a considerable standing in their time were prepared to take the work seriously, discuss it and even adopt some of its ideas. Canard, writes Fasiani,[96] 'was then read and commented upon by many Italian authors' and his 'theory of the latitude had various reflections in the doctrines of our country'.[97]

Cagnazzi, in his *Elementi di Economia Politica* (1813), refers extensively to Canard's work.[98] M. Gioja, whom we also mentioned before, gives, over a series of pages, quotations from Canard's theory of the determination of price[99] but thinks that 'the algebraic formula by which Canard has represented the elements of price is more ingenious than useful'.[100] It is, however, evident that Gioja was influenced by Canard's theory of the latitude because in his own theory he determines the limits of price, between a maximum and a minimum.[101] Another author who referred to Canard's views, considering them as worthy of attention, was A. Scialoja, in his *I principii della Economia Sociale esposti in ordine ideologico*.[102]

But it was Fuoco who commented most extensively on Canard's work. As however his comments on Canard and his critics form an integral part of his contribution to mathematical economics, we have chosen to examine his views on Canard simultaneously with the examination of his whole work.[103]

The only French author of his time who was considerably influenced was Simonde de Sismondi, who in the Introduction to his *De la Richesse Commerciale*,[104] admitted that many times in the earlier chapters of his book he had nothing better to do than repeat Canard's ideas. He does not, however, imitate Canard in the use of mathematics except once, 'car appliquer ce langage à une science qui n'est point exacte c'est s'exposer à des erreurs continuelles'.[105] His main attempt at mathematical economics is when he tries to show that in both a closed economy and with foreign trade a country, ceteris paribus, will be progressing, declining or stationary according to the level of wages.

The argument is in agreement with Sismondi's general ideas on value. A nation is progressing, stationary or declining in accordance with whether the national revenue exceeds, is equal to, or is below the nation's expenses. The national revenue is equal to the national product less the 'necessary' salary for the labour which produced the national product. Thus, if D are the expenses, P the national product and N the 'necessary' salary, the nation will be

$$\text{progressing if } P - N > D$$
$$\text{stationary if } P - N = D$$
$$\text{declining if } P - N < D$$

However, the salary for necessary work N, which produced this year's production is, according to Sismondi, last year's necessary salary; this year's necessary salary is paid in advance of next year's production; if this salary is $N + x$ and x is positive it will mean that next year's production will be increasing. It is this years salary which determines this year's consumption. In an economy which has no foreign trade, Sismondi assumes that consumption is equal to production.

(1) $$D + (N + x) = P$$

therefore $$P - N > D \text{ if } x > 0$$

If a country is permanent debtor, then

(2) $$D + (N + x) = P + C$$

where C is the amount of the debt and therefore the country will be progressing if $x > C$ and stationary if $x = C$
If a country is a permanent creditor then

(3) $$D + (N + x) = P - C$$

and therefore $$P - N > D \text{ if } x + C > 0$$

'From which it results', Sismondi concludes,[106] 'that the progressive or declining state of a country depends always on the value of x or of the difference between the necessary salary of a year and that of the following year.'

Sismondi indicates that irrespective whether the country has a positive or negative balance of trade it will be progressing, declining or remaining stationary depending on the relative values of C and x.

Thus an economy with a negative balance, will be progressing if $x > C$ where C is the negative balance, and it will be declining if $x < C$.

Alternatively an economy with a positive balance of trade C, will be progressing if

$$x + C > 0$$

In the case therefore that x is negative, there will still be progress if $C > -x$

From the above according to Sismondi it is evident that even a country with a negative trade balance may continue progressing, even if its balance worsens every year, as long as $x > C$.

The next French author to use mathematics in an economic argument was Du Bois-Aymé in his book *Examen de quelques questions d'Économie Politique et notamment de l'ouvrage de M. Ferrier intitulé Du Gouvernement*.[107] There are two cases.

The first is where he compares the power due to the riches of two countries.[108] This power he maintains is in proportion to the goods available to each country over and above its indispensable requirements for consumption and reproduction.

Thus if N, n are the numbers of inhabitants in the two countries
C, c the value of goods absolutely necessary to each inhabitant
V, v the total value of goods in the two countries respectively

$V - NC$ is the value of goods available over the minimum requirements of the first country, while $v - nc$ is the value of goods available over the minimum requirements of the second country. The relation of the power of the two countries $\frac{R}{r}$ is then[109]

(1) $$\frac{R}{r} = \frac{V - NC}{v - nc}$$

The second case is the discussion of the relation between the salary of the unskilled worker and that of the skilled worker, who needs to undergo a period of apprenticeship at a certain expense. The condition is that the salary of the skilled worker should be such as to give him over his shorter working life total earnings equal to his earnings as a general labourer plus his costs of apprenticeship. Thus

$$(k - t)j = k'j' + tj'$$

where $k - t$ is the working life of the skilled worker and k' that of the unskilled, j and j' their respective salaries and t the period of apprenticeship. From this he gets

$$(2) \qquad \frac{j}{j'} = \frac{k' + t}{k - t}$$

If the first worker has also such a talent that the relation of the value of his work J to the value of the work of an ordinary skilled worker j is n then[110]

$$(3) \qquad \frac{J}{j'} = \frac{n(k' + t)}{k - t}$$

and if j' is taken as the unit of measurement of the value of a day's work.

$$(4) \qquad J = \frac{n(k' + t)}{k - t}$$

and the author calculates[111] the value of an object which takes T days to be manufactured from a value of raw materials c as

$$(5) \qquad V = T \times J + c = T \times \frac{n(k' + t)}{k - t} + c$$

Jevons in his bibliography refers also to Barnabé Brisson as having contributed to mathematical economics in his *Éssai sur le système général de navigation intérieure de la France* (1829). All the pages to which he, however, refers have been written by Brisson's editor, Duleau, and they contain very little mathematics apart from the calculation of the sum to be set aside annually to pay for the amortisation of the cost of excavating the proposed canals.[112]

5.6 L.F.G. DE CAZAUX

Cazaux in the *Élémens d'Économie Privée et Publique* which appeared in 1825, uses some simple mathematics in the belief that 'contrary to J. B. Say's opinion ... mathematical analysis is very suitable for application to Political Economy'.[113] His formulae are simple applications of proportion and aim at clarifying Cazaux's peculiar ideas about value.

Value for Cazaux is not simply the price of a thing; it is this price as affected by the 'value' of money; but the value of money is measured, according to Cazaux, by the rate of interest. Failing to see that trade in commodities will mean flow of money in the opposite direction, he maintains that only when the rate of interest of money is different between two areas, will money flow from one to the other; thus since there is no flow except as a result of the rate of interest, he argues, this rate must be the measure of the value of money.[114]

Thus if v and V are the respective values of one thing at two different periods or places, p, P its respective prices at the respective periods or places and i, I the respective rates of interest then, 'as the values increase in direct compound proportion of the price of the thing and of the value of interest of money',[115] we shall have this proportion:

$$v : V :: ip : IP$$

or
$$v = V\frac{ip}{IP}$$

from which he derives various results by assuming $i = I$ or $p = P$. Cazaux also has a formula purporting to show how rich one really is.[116] Thus, if S represents the annual net income of an individual, S' the money worth of things one annually desires to purchase and R his wealth, then

$$R = \frac{S}{S'}$$

As S' is always higher than S 'nobody ever believes himself really rich'.[117]

5.7   GERMAIN GARNIER AND JEAN-BAPTISTE SAY

The Comte Germain Garnier, the translator of the Wealth of Nations into French, used in his '*Abrégé élémentaire des principes de l'économie politique*'[118] which appeared in 1796, a diagram to illustrate the relation between demand, income and price.

This diagram which is a pyramid is given in Figure 5.3. The price is measured on the vertical line by the side of the pyramid.

Garnier gives two interpretations of his pyramid:

(a) it represents the number of people who are willing to buy a certain product at a certain price or

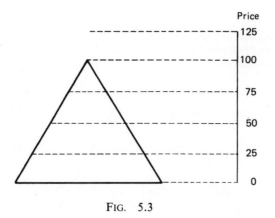

Fig. 5.3

(b) it represents the share of his wealth that each individual is willing to use for the purchase of a good at a certain price.

Under (a), the higher the price, the fewer people are willing to purchase the good. At zero price all people, represented by the base of the pyramid, will want the good; at a price of, say, 100, very few people, represented by the apex of the pyramid, will be able to afford it. And the price of, say, 125 is prohibitive for all.

Under (b), at zero price, an individual does not care what share of his wealth he will spend on purchasing the good. But as the price rises he is willing to spend a progressively smaller share of his wealth on the good.

Garnier's ideas have obviously influenced J.B. Say, who in the second volume of his *Cours Complet d'Économie Politique Pratique* published in 1828 included a diagram[119] to illustrate the relation between demand, income and price, which is reproduced below.

Say starts from two propositions. The first is that wealth is so distributed that individual fortunes 'are the more numerous the smaller they are and become rarer the larger they become'.[120] The second proposition is that the higher the fortune of a person, the higher price he is willing to pay for a given commodity.

His diagram (Figure 5.4) is a pyramid, on the vertical axis of which the price of the commodity is measured. The horizontal axis measures the numbers of individuals who possess a certain fortune. Thus line *AA*, being the locus of a number of vertical lines, represents the numbers of individuals having a certain fortune, while line *BB*, which is smaller than *AA*, represents the number of individuals having a greater fortune.

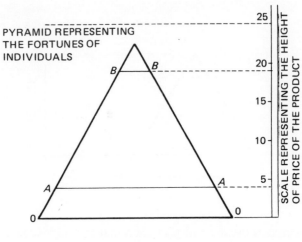

FIG. 5.4

It becomes immediately evident that the higher the price, the shorter the horizontal line will be. 'The higher is the section, the rarer will be the fortunes capable to reach this level of cost.'

Thus in the diagram 'a number of fortunes represented by the vertical lines which do not exceed the line *AA* could afford the price represented by the fourth degree in the scale; a number of fortunes represented by the vertical lines which do not exceed line *BB* could afford the price represented by the 19th degree in the scale; and the 24th degree would represent a price which no fortune could afford'.[121]

Free goods would be demanded by all in the country and this is 'represented by the lowest horizontal line at the base of the pyramid'.[122]

But Say was not, in general, in favour of the application of mathematics to economic analysis. In his *Traité d'Économie Politique* he had this to say of such applications. 'Political economy like mathematics is based on an abstraction; in mathematics one deals in magnitudes, in political economy one deals in values. As values are susceptible of increase or decrease they belong to the domain of mathematics but as they are subject to the action of the faculties, needs and the will of man, they return to the domain of morals. And this, by the way, shows how it is superfluous to apply the formulae of algebra to the demonstrations of Political Economy. No quantity, there, is susceptible of a rigorous evaluation.'[123]

Another early French author who used mathematical analysis, including the differential calculus, is J.H.T. Du Villard de Durand.[124] He attempts to measure the desirability of an investment by using the expected rate of return. He also shows how one may find the period for which a given investment may give the maximum rate of return.[125]

NOTE

1. Forbonnais, *Élémens du commerce*, 2nd edn., vol. II (1766) pp. 113–14.
2. Forbonnais, op. cit., p. 114.
3. Ibid., pp. 128–9.
4. Ibid., p. 130.
5. Du Pont, 'Des courbes politiques' in *Carl Friedrichs von Baden brieflicher Verkehr mit Mirabeau und Du Pont*, ed. C. Knies, vol. II (Heidelberg, 1892) pp. 289–300 to which we refer. This edition does not contain Du Pont's diagram but this and the text in translation are reproduced in Pierre Samuel Du Pont de Nemours *On Economic Curves*, translated with an introduction by H. W. Spiegel, The Johns Hopkins Press, 1955.
6. I believe that Spiegel wrongly translates the word 'politique' as political economy; Du Pont is advising a future Prince and it would seem that the literal translation of 'politique' as 'policy' is nearer the meaning of the author. Thus Du Pont, op. cit., p. 290, writes 'La conquête des géomètres ajouterait beaucoup à la réputation *des principes de saine politique* qui doivent faire le bonheur des humains'; Spiegel, op. cit., p. 1 translates the words in italics as 'the correct principles of political economy'. I believe that 'the principles of a sound policy' would be more correct.
7. Du Pont, op. cit., p. 290.
8. Ibid., p. 299.
9. Ibid., p. 299.
10. Ibid., p. 299.
11. Ibid., p. 296.
12. Ibid., p. 297.
13. Ibid., p. 297.
14. Ibid., p. 297. Du Pont's model may be put into a conventional dynamic form:

$$P_t = p_{t-1} + \tfrac{3}{4}(P_{t-1} - P_{t-2})$$

which has as its general solution

$$P_t = A + B(\tfrac{3}{4})^t.$$

Solving for Du Pont's figures we get $P_t = 1500 - 500(\tfrac{3}{4})^t$ and it is immediately clear that $t \rightarrow \infty$, $P_t \rightarrow 1500$. A table of values derived from our equation shows that:

Period	P_t
0	1000
1	1125
2	1218.8
↓	↓
∞	1500

which exactly correspond with Du Pont's drawing.

15. Ibid., p. 297.
16. It is therefore evident that Du Pont, most probably, ignored Daniel Bernoulli's own contribution to mathematical economics.
17. Du Pont, op. cit., p. 298.
18. Ibid., p. 298.
19. Ibid., pp. 298-9.
20. See R.L. Meek 'The 1758-9 Editions of the Tableau Économique' in M. Kuczynski and R.L. Meek (eds), Quesnay's *Tableau Économique* (1972).
21. Victor Riquetti, Marquis de Mirabeau, 'Tableau économique avec ses explications' in VI partie, *L' Ami des hommes* (1760). Extracts are published in R.L. Meek, *Precursors of Adam Smith, 1750-1775* (Dent, 1973) pp. 120-46.
22. Guillaume François Le Trosne, *De l'ordre social* (Paris, 1777) Discours VIII, p. 320, n.2.
23. Condillac's work is included in Jevons' bibliography appended to the second edition of the *Theory of Political Economy*, who also, however, in the preface to the same edition mentions that Condillac made no explicit attempt at mathematical treatment. Jevons, op. cit., 2nd edn (1879) p. xxx.
24. A. N. Isnard, *Traité des richesses*, 2 vols (London and Lausanne, 1781).
25. Isnard, op. cit., vol. I, p. 17.
26. Isnard uses the word 'le superflu', ibid., p. 18.
27. This table is not given by Isnard; only the argument and the equations are his. Isnard, op. cit., pp. 19-20. Nevertheless he and Lang, with whose work we deal further below, may be considered as precursors of 'linear programming'.
28. Isnard, op. cit., p. 19.
29. If we know what the first and the second exchanged with the third, we automatically know what the third exchanged with the first two.
30. By solving equations (1) and (2) we find for

$$\frac{M}{M'} = \frac{b(ps + r)}{r} : \frac{a(s + rm)}{r} \text{ and for } \frac{M'}{M''} = c(s + rm) : b(1 - mp)$$

Adjusting therefore and dividing throughout by abc we have

$$M : M' : M'' = \frac{bc(ps + r)}{abc} : \frac{ac(s + rm)}{abc} : \frac{ab(1 - mp)}{abc}$$

and substituting $s = 1 - r$ in the first part, $r = 1 - s$ in the second, and $p = 1 - q$, $m = 1 - n$ in the third we get Isnard's result

$$M : M' : M'' = \frac{r + p - pr}{a} : \frac{s + m - sm}{b} : \frac{n + q - nq}{c}$$

31. Isnard, op. cit., p. 21.

32. Ibid., pp. 21 *et seq.*

33. Ibid., pp. 34 *et seq.*

34. Ibid., p. 36. On pp. 40 *et seq.* Isnard, in order to demonstrate that distribution of the surplus among workers, producers and landowners depends on the respective values of their services, gives an example where he assigns particular values to the cost of subsistence of workers, the costs of producers, and the cost of maintaining and renewing fixed wealth. On p. 31, Isnard gives the formula $x = \dfrac{R}{B - E}$ where R is the value of fixed wealth, $(B - E)$ its net revenue per annum and x their relation. On p. 48 he gives the ratio $F : F' :: B : B'$ where F is the value of capital employed in agriculture and F' the capital employed in industry and B, B' the respective net returns of their products. There is also on p. 43 another formula for the net receipts from the sale of a product where $p = B - aF$ and p is the net revenue, B the total revenue, a the quantity and F the costs per unit. On p. 293, finally, the problem of the rates of exchange of two countries with bimetallistic systems is treated mathematically.

    On Isnard, see also: W. Jaffé, 'A.N. Isnard: Progenitor of the Walrasian General Equilibrium Model', *History of Political Economy* (1969) pp. 19–43.

35. Condorcet, op. cit., pp. 158–66.

36. Ibid., p. 159.

37. Ibid., p. 161.

38. Ibid., p. 163. On p. 164 Condorcet mentions that real quantities may be substituted in his formulae; 'on n'en connaîtra que des valeurs approchées, mais l'on pourra connaître les limites des erreurs de cette détermination. ... On verra donc si cette erreur est assez considérable pour faire un tort sensible'.

39. On 5 January 1801 (15 Nivôse an IX). See Institut National, 'Prix proposés dans la séance du 15 Nivôse an IX'. It was published as a book under the title *Principes d'économie politique* (Paris an X) 1801.

40. The title of the memoir submitted to the Institute was *Éssai sur la circulation de l'impôt* and according to the anonymous reviewer L.B. in the *Décade philosophique, littéraire et politique*, vol. II (an X) p. 386, was half the size of the book but similar in its essentials.

41. Schumpeter, *History of Economic Analysis* (1954) p. 499. The italicising is mine.

42. It must however be mentioned that in 1920 Edgar Allix published a sympathetic review of Canard's work under the title 'Un précurseur de l'école mathématique: Nicolas–François Canard' in the *Revue d'Histoire Économique et Sociale* (Paris, 1920) pp. 38–67. Enthusiastic was also the immediate reaction of the reviewer in *La décade philosophique, littéraire et politique*, vol. II (an X) pp. 385–99 who wrote: 'Il y a peu d'hommes auxquels il soit donné de saisir les grandes questions avec autant de puissance que l'a fait dans cette occasion le C. Canard. C'est le sujet et non les livres d'économie politique qu'il a

fouillés. Il a résolu la question proposée par l'Institut et répandu des lumières nouvelles sur la science.' Ibid., p. 398. He is also seriously taken by M. Desrenaudes in his review of Garnier's translation of Smith's *Wealth of Nations* in the same periodical, vol. IV (an X) pp. 528–9.

43. Canard, op. cit., p. 28.
44. Ibid., p. 32.
45. Ibid., p. 34.
46. A. Cournot, *Recherches sur les principes mathématiques de la théorie des richesses* (1838) ch. V.
47. Canard, op. cit., p. 35.
48. Ibid., p. 35.
49. There occurs a passage in Isnard, op. cit., vol. I, p. 4, from which Canard possibly drew his inspiration. 'Supposons que l'état social commence entre deux membres; s'ils sont *égaux en force* et s'ils ont les mêmes désirs ils chercheront ce qui leur sera utile à chacun; le propre de l'un sera égal au propre de l'autre: si on *suppose les forces inégales, ce que chacun trouvera sera proportionné à ses forces*.' [My italicising.]
50. Canard, op. cit., p. 29.
51. We may also assume that the force of sellers is the need and competition of their opponents, i.e. BN and that of buyers is bn. The results are the same as in equation (2). Vide Canard, op. cit., p. 29.
52. Canard, op. cit., p. 30.
53. Ibid., pp. 30–1.
54. Ibid., pp. 35–6.
55. Ibid., p. 36.
56. Or 'acheteur-monopoleur' as Canard calls him, ibid., p. 46.
57. Ibid., p. 11.
58. Ibid., p. 49.
59. Ibid., p. 51.
60. See also Allix, op. cit., p. 58.
61. Canard, op. cit., p. 48.
62. Ibid., p. 48.
63. Ibid., p. 49.
64. Ibid., p. 46.
65. Ibid., pp. 47–8.
66. Ibid., p. 49.
67. Ibid., p. 50.
68. BN was different from $B'N'$ but this was a comparison of a group of sellers at different points in time not of the members of the group at the same point of time.
69. Canard, op. cit., p. 53.
70. Ibid., p. 53.
71. On these aspects see also G.H. Bousquet, 'N.F. Canard, Précurseur du marginalisme', *Revue d' Économie Politique* (1957) pp. 232–5. Also G.H. Bousquet, 'Le Système mathématique, etc.', op. cit., p. 968–9
72. Canard, op. cit., p. 20
73. Ibid., pp. 13–15.
74. Ibid., p. 20.

75. Ibid., p. 18.
76. Ibid., p. 60; my underlining.
77. Ibid., p. 61.
78. Ibid., p. 61; my underlining.
79. Ibid., p. 158–64; Allix, op. cit., p. 54.
80. Cauard, op. cit., p. 192.
81. The article was published anonymously under the title 'Canard: Principes d'économie politique' in no. II (Jan. 1803) pp. 431–50. This had, of course, been preceded by the reviews in the *Décade*, which we have already mentioned.
82. Canard, op. cit., p. 432.
83. Ibid., p. 439.
84. Ibid., p. 439.
85. Ibid., p. 439.
86. J.B. Say, *Traité d'économie politique*, vol. I (1803) p. xxxix.
87. Say, *Traité*, etc. vol. II (1803) livre 5*me*, p. 492.
88. Paris (1822) ch. IV, pp. 112–19.
89. L. Say, op. cit., p. 114.
90. Ibid., p. 115. F. Fuoco, in *Saggi Economici* (1825), attacked all these ideas of Say. We refer further below to Fuoco's views.
91. 'On dira peut-être que nous avons traité avec trop d'importance l'ouvrage de M. Canard; mais pouvions-nous passer légèrement sur un ouvrage qui a été couronné par l'Institut national dans sa séance du 15 nivôse an IX (5 Janvier 1801) ainsi qu'on le voit dans son titre?' L. Say, op. cit., pp. 118–19. See also *Nouveau dictionnaire d'économie politique*, vol. I (1891) p. 299, edited by L. Say and J. Chailley.
92. Cournot, *Researches into the Mathematical Principles of the Theory of Wealth* (Eng. transl.) p. 2.
93. Cournot, *Revue sommaire des doctrines économiques* (Paris, 1877) p. 10.
94. J. Bertrand in '*Théorie mathématique de la richesse sociale par* Léon Walras (1883) et recherches sur les principes mathématiques de la théorie des richesses par A. Cournot (Paris, 1838)' *Journal des Savants* (Paris, 1883) pp. 499–508.
95. Bertrand, op. cit., pp. 499–500. W. S. Jevons, in his preface to the 2nd edn of the *Theory of Political Economy*, considers Canard's work as nonsense. See p. xxv of the fourth edition.
96. Fasiani, op. cit., p. 79.
97. Ibid., p. 112 n. The same author remarks elsewhere, 'A study of the influence exercised by Canard on Italian authors of the beginnings of last century and the subsequent fading of his fame, would undoubtedly be very interesting and praiseworthy.' Ibid., p. 79 n.
98. Cagnazzi, op. cit., pp. 191 *et seq* and 195.
99. Gioja, *Nuovo Prospetto delle Scienze Economiche*, vol. III (1815—1817) pp. 32–5.
100. Ibid., p. 32.
101. Ibid., vol. III, pp. 2 and 33–4.
102. Scialoja, op. cit., 1846 (1840) p. 313 n.
103. Canard was also mentioned by Karl Heinrich Rau in his *Grundsätze der*

Volkswirthschaftslehre, which was published in 1826. See Rau, op. cit., 4th edn (1841) p. 161 n.

104. J. C. L. Simonde (de Sismondi), *De la richesse commerciale ou principes d'économie politique, appliqués à la législation du commerce* (Genève, 1803) pp. xx–xxi.

105. Sismondi, op. cit., vol. I, p. 105.

106. Ibid., p. 106.

  See also P. Barucci, '*Un tentativo di Trattazione Matematica della* Bilancia Nazionale da parte di Sismondi', *Economia e Storia* (Milano, 1966) pp. 481–91. Barucci mentions that the note was used by M. Gioja, in his *Discussione economica sul Dipartimento d' Olona* (1803).

107. Paris, 1823.

108. Du Bois-Aymé, op. cit., pp. 71–7, where in addition to the formula itself he gives various applications.

109. Aymé maintains also that the prices of the two countries are proportional to the numbers of good available.

  Thus $\dfrac{P}{p} = \dfrac{V - NC}{v - nc} = \dfrac{R}{r}$. Du Bois-Aymé, op. cit., p. 71. This argument is reproduced in Fuoco, *Saggi Economici*, vol. Ц, pp. 104–8.

110. This *n* is 'a function of the number which would express the probability of finding such a skilled worker among a given number of workers'. Du Bois-Aymé, op. cit., p. 103.

111. Ibid., p. 104. This argument is verbatim reproduced in Fuoco, op. cit., vol. II, pp. 102–4.

112. Brisson, op. cit., pp. 160–1 and ii and xiii.

113. Cazaux, op. cit., p. 20 n.

114. Ibid., pp. 19–20.

115. Ibid., p. 21.

116. Ibid., pp. 36–7.

117. Ibid., p. 38. The formula is further adjusted on p. 43 to deduct from *S* the taxes, the interest on debts and 'the foolish annual expenses' the individual has to meet out of his income.

118. G. Garnier (1754–1821), *Abrégé élémentaire des principes de l' économie politique* (Paris, 1796) pp. 195–6 of the 1846 edn.

  See also V.K. Dmitriev, *Economic Essays on Value, Competition and Utility*; (1974) pp. 196–7, where, however, the diagram is ascribed to J. Garnier (1813–1881).

119. J. B. Say, op. cit., vol. II, between pp. 334–5. 'The table was given', he says, ibid., p. 322, 'to make visually apparent how as the price of a product falls, it meets with more consumers'.

120. Ibid., p. 321. Say treats in this section price and cost as identical.

121. J. B. Say, op. cit., pp. 334–5, where he adds: 'The section of the pyramid represents more exactly the number of portions of fortune which each individual can and wishes to devote to the acquisition of a commodity, the price of which rises by a given amount.'

122. Ibid., p. 322.

123. J. B. Say, *Traité d'économie politique*, vol. I (1803), discours préliminaire, p. xxxix.

Of Say's views on Canard's work we have already spoken when discussing the controversy caused by Canard.

124. J.H.T. du Villard de Durand, *Recherches sur les Rentes, les Emprunts, et les Remboursements* (Paris et Généve, 1787). Excerpts are reproduced in W.J. Baumol and S.M. Goldfeld, op. cit., pp. 153–4.

125. See note 124.

6 Two Eclectic Authors — Fuoco and Lopez De Peñalver

6.1 FRANCESCO FUOCO

The examination of Fuoco's work comes naturally after the review of both the Milanese school and the French contribution, for his work is a product of the influence of both currents. He is, in fact, the first author to have gone systematically into the literature of mathematical economics available then and to have presented a systematic defence of the application of mathematical methods in economic analysis. It is for this that he deserves a special place in the history of early developments in mathematical economics rather than for any original mathematical formulations of his own.

There are many passages in his *Saggi Economici*[1] published between 1825 and 1827, where Fuoco uses mathematical methods and analogies in his argument. His important contribution is the fourth essay in the second volume of his work, which has the title *Applicazione dell' Algebra all' Economia Politica.*[2]

His defence of the application of the mathematical approach takes two forms. On the one hand, he attempts to describe the scope and limitations of such a method and on the other he discusses and tries to answer the objections made against such an application by various authors.

Economic quantities like price, value, abundance, scarcity, need, etc. 'are things which can be expressed algebraically and reduced into algorithmic functions once their respective relations have been determined'.[3] The calculus can then be applied and results, like the limits of these functions, and their maximum or minimum values, obtained. Thus the application of algebraic language is not only easy and natural but also most useful as new truths may be discovered.[4]

But Fuoco does not want an indiscriminate use of algebra; he wants the results obtained with its help checked to see whether they correspond, not to unintelligible jargon, but either to established truths or new truths at which one could arrive also by more roundabout ways, through analogous reasoning, though this last route could not shed full light on the problem and solve it rigorously.

'La catena dell' espressioni algebriche però dovrebbe servire di sola e semplice guida, e nulla impedirebbe che sostituito il linguaggio ordinario non si aggiungessero tutti i ragionamenti suppletori, de' quali si avesse bisogno, per arrivare al risultato ottenuto col soccorso dell' Algebra.'[5]

Thus Fuoco is an advocate of a temperate use of mathematics. 'Intemperateness is an evil everywhere; and especially in applied sciences because in these it is easy to take the chimeric for the real and the abstract for the concrete.'[6]

The objections to which Fuoco refers against the use of mathematical methods are especially those L. Say made in connection with Canard's work and P. Ferroni made in connection with the Verri–Frisi formula, to both of which we have referred in the appropriate places.

Canard had had a considerable influence on Fuoco. In the third essay of the second volume of Fuoco's *Saggi*, 'Teoria de' Limiti applicata all' Economia Politica',[7] he has adopted, in discussing the reward of labour, land and capital, Canard's idea of a minimum and a maximum reward, with the reward actually paid being somewhere between these two extremes. Again his idea that there is a limit to the growth of population, which is approached through oscillations, may be partly due to Canard's conception of the approach towards equilibrium when a new tax is imposed.[8] On the other hand, he is no admirer of Canard's idea of the proportionate diffusion of taxation. Having quoted extensively[9] from that section of Canard's *Principes* he says he has done so 'to show how much influence an ingenious work can exercise on minds: that of Canard merited to be crowned by the Institute of France but the Institute showed itself to be ignorant of both the nature of various taxes and the law according to which these are assessed and imposed'.[10] But in Canard's theory of the latitude, Fuoco sees a useful contribution. Canard he says 'did not exceed the limits set for the useful and discreet application of Algebra; he has given algebraic formulae which present no complications, no obscurities and much less impossibility of calculation'.[11]

He has therefore many scornful remarks to make both against L.

Say's critique of Canard and his connected refutation of the usefulness of mathematics to economic analysis. Even supposing that
Canard had used mathematics intemperately, which in fact he did not,
Say's attack should have been directed against the specific use of
mathematics made by Canard and not against the use of mathematics
in general. Answering Say's contention that algebraic calculation is
impossible in economics, where quantities change in a complicated
way and where we have to take account of such factors as the weather,
human desires, human power and so on, Fuoco says that such
exogenous disturbances and causes cannot have a place in economic
analysis. To include all quantities suggested by Say would not only be
useless but would have as a result 'the most extravagant love-story' (il
più stravagante romanzo).[12] On the other hand Say had maintained
that Canard's ideas, being incorrect, had expressed impossible
quantities, which made the solution impossible, as the solution of
problems is only possible where quantities expressed by letters are
both real and possible; to this Fuoco answers that mathematics, using
negative, imaginary, indeterminate, infinite and similar quantities,
can solve various problems; and giving Canard's well known passage,
where the theory of the latitude is expounded,[13] he declares, 'We shall
not refer either to the nature of the doctrine contained in this passage
(being outside our present scope) or to the special deductions which
M. Canard has drawn from this to determine the price of things; but
we shall ask M. Say and all those who think in the same terms, where
are those quantities, which he calls impossible, to be found? Is the
contrast of the forces of competition among sellers and buyers not
calculated and expressed in the most elegant, speediest and clearest
manner?'[14]

Fuoco, also, objects to Ferroni's strict mathematical interpretation
of the ideas of maximum and minimum. Ferroni, he says, would be
right if we had abstract quantities which could become infinite or
infinitesimal. But here we are dealing with concrete quantities and
abstraction cannot and must not be such as to render these quantities
impossible.[15] He thinks that the maximum price would be that point
where general prosperity becomes a maximum, if we were to interpret
truly Verri's ideas.[16]

Of the mathematical formulations we find in Fuoco's work, we can
distinguish those belonging to him from those he has taken from
previous authors and quotes without acknowledgement.[17]

To the first category belong a mathematical exposition of Ricardo's
theory of rent.[18] An interesting adaptation of Valeriani's theory may

also be mentioned. According to this the quantity of offers constitutes the competition of the sellers and the competition of the buyers is represented by the total sum demanded. 'The competition, which makes price vary and finally determines it, is that resulting from the excess of the ones (offers) over the others (supply).'[19] Price would be in constant proportion of this excess and would be 'like the immediate effect of the *resultant* of two opposing forces';[20] and he adds: 'If the two forces are expressed by the two convergent sides of a parallelogram, the resultant will be its diagonal'; it is this diagonal therefore which expresses excess supply or demand and in accordance with which price varies (see Figure 6.1.).[21]

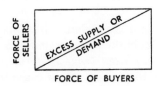

FIG. 6.1

The third instance is where he shows the relation between the quantity of productive force and the time during which the force has been employed.[22] Thus if f is the quantity of productive force, t is the time and q the quantity of the product, we have the following relations

(1) $$q = ft, \quad \text{or} \quad f = \frac{q}{t}, \quad \text{or} \quad t = \frac{q}{f}$$

But time is in inverse proportion to the velocity of the force and therefore a force with greater velocity needs a smaller amount of time to produce the same results as a slower force. Calling the velocity v, we have

(2) $$f = vt$$

Substituting (2) into (1)

(3) $$q = vt^2$$

from which it follows that

(4) $$t = \sqrt{\frac{q}{v}}$$

It must also be mentioned that Fuoco attempted, in analogy to the concepts of dynamics and statics in physics, to define economic statics and dynamics.[23]

In addition to these, Fuoco reproduced under the title 'Examples of some principal applications of algebra to the objects of Political Economy'[24] Valeriani's formulae of price determination,[25] Du Bois-Aymé's treatment of the comparision of the power of two nations and wages differentials[26] and Frisi's comment on Lloyd and Verri.[27] Most of these are reproduced word for word from the original without acknowledgement to their authors.

6.2   LOPEZ DE PEÑALVER

Another eclectic author and keen admirer of Canard is the Spaniard Lopez de Peñalver who published a work under the title '*Reflexiones sobre la Variacion del Precio del Trigo*' (Madrid, 1812)[28].

His aim is to analyse the factors which cause the changes of the price of wheat, the limits within which this price can move as well as its relation to the wage level.

Lopez de Peñalver points out that it is very important to know the limits within which the price of wheat can move; and in order to do this, it is essential to undertake empirical research, which he admits it is difficult to undertake in his days; but he visualises a state in the future where empirical research and what we call today econometric studies would be widely and professionally used.

'It is of the greatest importance,' he writes of the price of grain[29] 'that, in all matters the government should know what is *much* and what is *little*, without holding onto vague and uncertain expressions. The determination of these limits must be the object of the greatest care, in all circumstances, and this will no doubt be the case when the calculus will be something current and when we shall know better to apply its results. But this calculus supposes that the continuous work of six or eight men, and even of a whole office, will be reduced, at the end of a year to two or three numbers.' And he adds: 'There will come a day when the elements of political economy will, to a large extent, become a branch of the calculus; and the verification of the given quantities will be the aim of permanent institutes, which governments will appreciate, for they will have recourse to them: to fix and allocate the taxes, to determine the number and the rate of customs duties on entry and exit, to learn the causes of the prosperity and of the depression, to know what one must hope or fear and to verify the truth of certain theoretical points of the utmost importance.'

Lopez de Peñalver is aware of the limitations of empirical research but also of the advantages of the application of mathematical methods to economic analysis. 'The given quantities, i.e. knowledge acquired through experience in economic matters, cannot and need not have a geometrical rigour; but it is sufficient that they have a certain approximation, when one knows well to employ them and when one examines the extent of one's own mistakes. Sometimes the results deducted are more exact than those which one derives from the reality. With experience and the calculus, one can resolve, with a few words, a great number of questions which in the books occupy numerous pages without at the same time indication of the truth.'[30]

Lopez de Penālver is critical of the fact that while the application of mathematical methods to economic analysis had been neglected, some authors had used incorrectly expressions and comparisons drawn from geometry and arithmetic. He is particularly critical of J.B. Say's use of the pyramid in an analogy.[31]

On the contrary he is full of praise for the work of Canard and considers that he deserves an important position among those who very successfully applied mathematical analysis to economics. He thinks that Canard's success is largely due to the fact that in a new Science he introduced new terms and notions, which he defined.

Lopez de Penālver is aware of the work of Verri from whom he quotes with approval[32]; he also refers among others, to the work of Smith, of Condorcet and of Condillac.

Coming to the main object of his essay, which is to determine the limits within which the price of wheat can vary, Lopez de Penālver gives as his basic formula

(1) $$\text{n.e.} = \frac{A}{B} f \qquad \text{where}$$

n is the proportion of daily wages spent on bread, e the actual level of daily wages and $n.e.$ the daily wages spent on bread; A the price of a measure of 12.5 litres of wheat; B the quantity of bread produced from 12.5 litres of wheat and f the quantity of bread consumption by the worker and his family per day. $\frac{A}{B}$ is the price of bread.

What therefore Lopez de Peñalver is saying is that the daily wage spent on bread is equal to the cost of the daily bread consumption by each worker.[33]

From (1) he gets

(2) $$A = \frac{B \cdot n \cdot e}{f}$$

which shows the price of wheat as in proportion of the daily wages, of its proportion spent on bread and of the bread-producing capacity of wheat and in inverse proportion of loaf consumption.

Lopez de Peñalver estimates that on the average $B = 90$ lb of bread and $f = 3$, therefore (2) takes the form:

(3) $$A = \frac{90}{3} \times n \,.\, e = 30 \, n \,.\, e$$

The price of wheat should be thirty times the daily wages spent on bread. This price may vary within narrow limits; for example if f is smaller, then the price of wheat, given the daily wages spent on bread, may be higher; but if f is too low, it will fall below the minimum level for survival, and population will decline.

Peñalver then proceeds to evaluate the limits within which n, the proportion of wages spent on bread, can move. For this purpose he assumes that the worker distributes his spending of his wages in four proportions (see Table 6.1[34]):

TABLE 6.1

	Proportion of daily wages spent on	*Actual amount spent*
Bread	n	$n \,.\, e$
Oil, salt, wood and other food	n'	$n' \,.\, e$
Lodging and clothes	n''	$n'' \,.\, e$
Wine	n'''	$n''' \,.\, e$

where $n + n' + n'' + n''' = 1$

Peñalver considers that, given the level of wages e, and of course B and f, the price of wheat is at an appropriate level and workers live fairly comfortably when $n = {}^4/_{10}$ i.e. when they spend ${}^4/_{10}$ of their wages on bread.

'The price of wheat begins to worsen when the wage-earner spends only ${}^3/_{10}$ of his salary to buy his bread; in this case, he asks more for his labour, and the return to capital employed in agriculture, is not enough to cover expenses and charges. The minimum price of wheat is thus:

$$A = 9e^{,35}$$

This results from (3) when $n = {}^3/_{10}$.

The maximum proportion out of his salary which the worker can spend on bread is, according to Peñalver, ${}^7/_{10}$. Beyond this 'starts the reign of hunger'[36].

The maximum price of bread is, therefore

$$A = 30 \times 0.7e = 21e$$

'One sees, therefore that the price of wheat has a certain latitude or that it may vary between certain limits without a parallel change in wages.'[37]

Lopez de Peñalver uses a mathematical illustration to show the differential advantage of a location which is nearer the market than another[38] and to indicate how this affects the price secured by each producer at the point of production.

If A and A' are the respective values of a product at two different locations

n and n' their respective distances from the market

p the cost of transport per unit of distance

he points out, that as the *price* at the market, is uniform because of competition

$$A + np = A' + n'p \qquad \text{which leads to}$$
$$A - A' = (n' - n)p$$

Therefore, the price at the point of production is different depending on the relative distance from the market. 'When one takes the price of the nearer product or that of the more distant, there will always be an advantage for the first over the second. ... From this arises the inequality of the value of the product of soils as a function of the distance which separates the places of production and those of consumption and of the difficulty or the impossibility of taking advantage of the cultivation of certain products because of the state of agriculture and of what has been established through the present considerations.'[39]

NOTES

1. F. Fuoco, *Saggi Economici*, vol. I (Pisa, 1825); vol. II (1827). To these editions we refer.
2. Ibid., vol. II, pp. 61–120. A very brief summary of the work is given by Gustavo del Vecchio, 'Francesco Fuoco, opponent of J.B. Say on the use of algebra in Political Economy', in *Econometrica 1933*, p. 220. The work is reproduced in M. Fasiani, op. cit., pp. 135–85.
3. Fuoco, op. cit., vol. II, 116.
4. Ibid., p. 76.
5. Ibid., vol. II, p. 116.
6. Ibid., vol. II, p. 117.
7. Ibid., vol. II, pp. 9 *et seq.*
8. Fuoco knew Malthus's ideas to which he refers in this work. See ibid., pp. 25–6 and 31–2.
9. Fuoco, op. cit., vol. I, pp. 105–6.
10. Ibid., vol. I, p. 106.
11. Ibid., vol. II, p. 79.
12. Ibid., vol. II, p. 82. The same ideas were expressed in his introduction to the *Applicazione*. There criticising Du Bois-Aymé, he says that we have to have a general theory, which could only be applied to particular cases, after allowing for deviations due to the particular case. See op. cit., pp. 63–6.
13. Canard, op. cit., pp. 29 *et seq.*
14. Fuoco; op. cit., vol. II, pp. 83–4.
15. Ibid., vol. II, p. 86.
16. Ibid., vol. II, p. 87. Fuoco also refers to Gioja, op. cit., vol. I, p. 8, who had also said that the use of algebraic formulae is impossible in economics – though he himself had used some, as we have seen – because of the number and indefinite variety of the elements to be calculated; to this Fuoco answers that his general remarks on the application of mathematics, apply also. Fuoco, op. cit., vol. II, p. 91 n.
17. Especially Du Bois-Aymé and P. Frisi.
18. Fuoco, op. cit., vol. I, pp. 22 *et seq.* and 112.
19. Ibid., vol. I, p. 190.
20. Ibid., vol., p. 190.
21. Ibid., vol. I, p. 190 n.
22. Ibid., vol. II, pp. 93–4. Contrary to what he had supported about the determination of price in his *Teoria de' Limiti* (vol. II, pp. 9 *et seq.*) Fuoco supports a cost of production approach in his *Applicazione* (vol. II, pp. 61 *et seq.*). On pp. 96–7 he gives the value of a commodity v as equal to l the quantity of labour employed to produce it, where
$v = l = c + i + s + p + d$ and c = raw materials, i = interest, s = salaries p = profit as reward of management and d = profit from exploitation of workers.
23. Fuoco, *Introduzione allo studio della economia industriale* (Napoli 1829) pp. 136 *et seq.*
24. Fuoco, *Saggi*, vol. II, pp. 100 *et seq.*

25. Ibid., vol. II, pp. 98 and 100–1.
26. Ibid., vol. II, pp. 102–8.
27. Ibid., pp. 108–12.
28. It has been reproduced, with an introduction by F. Estape in *Anales de Economia 1953–55*, pp. 207–52. Extracts from it have been translated and published by G.H. Bousquet in *"Lopez de Peñalver: Réflexions sur les variations du prix du blé* (Une étude économétrique de 1812)", *Revue d' Histoire Économique et Sociale*, 1961, pp. 496–509. Also Bousquet, *Histoire de l' économie Mathématique* etc. op. cit., pp. 128–9.
29. Lopez de Peñalver, in *Anales* etc. pp. 210–21; Bousquet, op. cit., pp. 498–9.
30. Peñalver, *Anales*, p. 243; Bousquet, op. cit., p. 499.
31. Lopez de Peñalver, op. cit., p. 245. Peñalver cites two more instances of the use of the pyramid to illustrate an argument: Don Juan Danvilla y Villarosa who 'built a pyramid with the landlords possessing the large estates at the base and the prince at the top'; and Steuart 'who also formed a pyramid more regular than those of the others and which has the advantage to have, at least, some sense'. Ibid., p. 245.
32. Lopez de Peñalver, op. cit., p. 246.
33. Ibid., p. 212.
34. Ibid. pp. 215–7.
35. Ibid., op. cit., p. 217
36. Ibid., p. 217. The average price is given $A = 15e$. Ibid., p. 223.
37. Ibid., p. 218
38. Ibid., pp. 230–1.
39. Ibid., p. 231.

7 The German Contribution

7.1 CLAUS KRÖNCKE AND THE QUANTITY THEORY

Kröncke, a road engineer by profession, is the first German author known to have used mathematics in his economic writings. In a book published in 1804[1] which, though purporting to be a treatise on taxation, is really a book of economic principles, Kröncke uses ample mathematics, about the value of which he is most explicit, 'I believe that the whole Political Economy allows and even demands such a method of treatment', he writes.[2]

Kröncke's main contribution is in the theory of money. He was the first author to introduce the velocity of circulation into the formula of the equation of exchange. The idea was not his[3] but he was the first, as far as I have been able to ascertain, to use symbolic writing for explaining the role of the velocity of circulation of money. Lloyd, we have already seen, had given the formula $P = \dfrac{Q}{M}$ where P = price, Q = quantity of money and M = the quantity of goods; he thus made no allowance for the velocity of circulation of money.

Kröncke examines the quantity of 'money capital' r, which is necessary for a country;[4] this, he says, depends on ϕ, the money value of all goods sold during a certain time and on m, or the times that on the average money is used for buying and selling during the same time. We have therefore[5]

$$r = \frac{\phi}{m}$$

Since ϕ the money value of goods is made up of their quantity multiplied by their price, we can translate the above equation into the more familiar terms of the Fisher equation

$$M = \frac{PT}{V} \text{ where } r = M, \phi = PT \text{ and } m = V.$$

Given the quantity of things and the velocity of circulation, the quantity of money determines the 'values' of things.[6]

Kröncke, having in mind a metallic currency, thinks that the quantity of money in circulation must be as small as possible.[7] As, however, we do not want to decrease ϕ, the best way to achieve this is by increasing m, i.e. the velocity of circulation.

Kröncke also makes an interesting calculation to show why money is useful as a measure of value.[8] If we had three things, he says, A, B and C, there are three comparisons to be made: A with B, A with C and B with C. For 4 things there are 6 comparisons, for 5 things 10 comparisons and in general for n things there are

$$(n - 1)\frac{n}{2} \text{ comparisons to be made.}$$

If, however, we know the comparision of A to B and of B to C we may calculate the comparison of A to C. Thus

	Things		Comparisons
For	2	we need	1
	3		2
	.		.
	.		.
	.		.
	n		$(n - 1)$

when we use money as a common means of comparison. If $n = 1000$, without money we would have to make 999×500 comparisons while money enables us to have only 999 comparisons.[9]

Kröncke used mathematics extensively to determine the value of factors of production under different conditions of location of production and market. If goods are produced and sold in the same place, the values of two factors are in proportion to the quantity of the product each factor produces during a given time. Thus

value of factor A: value of factor B :: $b : d$

where b is the quantity of the product produced by A and d the quantity produced by B.

If, however, the place of production or marketing differs, the relative values of factors are affected, for there are costs of transportation to be taken into consideration. Kröncke, like Thünen after him, calculates these costs in terms of units of the good transported. Thus if factor A produces p units of a good, and m units are given up as payment for transportation, only $p - m$ units reach the market and these are the measure of the value of A compared to that of a factor B, which also produces p units but owing to its different location pays n units for transportation. Thus if value of factor A is g and that of B is h, we shall have

$$g : h :: p - m : p - n$$

and

$$g = \frac{h(p - m)}{p - n}$$

The value of the product is proportional to the quantity of the factor used to produce it.[10]

7.2   JOSEPH LANG AND MACRO-ECONOMICS

Joseph Lang is the first real macro-economic mathematical economist. Kröncke had, before him, defined national income and wealth[11] and Isnard had presented a model of a closed exchange economy but it was Lang, who, not only followed Isnard's lead, but was able for the first time to create a macro-economic mathematical model where the problems of distribution, production, money and prices are viewed in their interdependence and the analysis is pursued with consistency and clarity to the ultimate limits the model will allow.

His book bears the title *Grundlinien der politischen Arithmetik*[12] but his is an entirely novel conception of Political Arithmetic. It is the mathematical part of the Science of Economics[13] and its aim is to search for the *general* relation of interdependence existing among economic quantities. 'It abstracts from everything particular and given, and uses Algebra in order to find these general laws.'[14]

Lang must have known Isnard's work for his influence is obvious. Like him, he assumes that a portion of the commodity is held by the producer and only the rest is offered for exchange.[15] Like him, he examines what products each producer gets in exchange for his product. But Lang's model is much more sophisticated, for he has introduced two innovations, both necessary for his later treatment.

The first is that, while Isnard examined individual commodities, Lang distinguishes three broad classes of goods and introduces aggregation. These are primary products, manufactured goods and services to include those of land, of capital and of the state.[16] According to the product every individual helps to produce, he is classified in one of these three classes. We thus have the class of primary producers, the 'manufacturing class' and the 'service class'. It must be stressed that the manufacturing class includes not the capitalists but industrial workers, engineers, management, etc.

The second innovation is the introduction of money right from the start as an integral part of the analysis. This introduces a complication. Isnard, by working in real terms, was able to write his equations immediately; thus a quantity a of M is exchanged for a quantity bp of M' and cr of M'' and the equation is[17]

$$aM = bpM' + crM''$$

Any saving that the owner of quantity M wants to make has been taken care of before arriving at a which is the quantity intended for exchange (the 'superflu').

But in Lang's model it is different; a quantity of, say, a of M is 'superfluous' as such but it is exchanged for money and this is in turn used to buy the other commodities. There is no certainty that the money receipts will be equal to the money payments of an individual or of a class. To achieve this, Lang makes the following assumptions:

(a) The quantity of money circulating among the classes is given and does not change.
(b) There is no saving of money (hoarding). No class withdraws any money from circulation ('sondern sie gibt alles Geld dass sie von den beiden andern Klassen empfangen hat, wieder in die Zirkulation, d.h. an die beiden andern Klassen, zurück'.[18])
(c) No class can give more money than that acquired.
(d) There are no debts between classes; if we take a sufficiently long period for our model, debts are cancelled out by repayments.[19]

Having established the equality between money receipts and money payments, Lang proceeds,[20] on much similar lines like Isnard, to examine the interdependence of receipts and payments of the various classes under a general ceteris paribus condition, which includes the composition of each class, the price-level, the quantity of money, etc.

If x, y, z are the total money receipts of the primary producers, of the manufacturing class and of services respectively, we have

(1) $x = a + b$ where a denotes receipts from manufacturing class and b receipts from services.
(2) $y = c + d$ where c denotes receipts from primary producers and d receipts from services.
(3) $z = e + f$ where e denotes receipts from primary producers and f receipts from the manufacturing class.

On the contrary we have

payments by primary producers	(4)	$x' = c + e$
payments by manufacturing class	(5)	$y' = a + f$
payments by 'services'	(6)	$z' = b + d$

As therefore, by definition, payments of each class are equal to its receipts we have[21]

$$(7) \qquad\qquad a + b = c + e$$

$$(8) \qquad\qquad c + d = a + f$$

$$(9) \qquad\qquad e + f = b + d$$

But up to this point, money for Lang is the medium of exchange; to be able to calculate receipts or payments from the quantities of goods, which each class has available for sale or buys, we need to know their exchange value in terms of a common measure. This unit of value or accounting unit may be different from the medium of exchange; and it is in terms of such units that receipts and payments must be equal. Lang takes as the unit of exchange value 'that quantity of food and other products of nature, which a person belonging to the manufacturing class needs on the average for the satisfaction of his immediate personal wants per year'.[22] This is the unit of value and is equal to one.

If we assume that the total population of a country is made up of V persons belonging to the class of primary producers, X belonging to the manufacturing class and that Y offer services, we shall have[23]

$$(10) \qquad\qquad A = V + X + Y$$

The receipts of the primary producers consist of the value of what they sell to the other two classes; these consist of X units sold to the manufacturing class, since each of its members needs by definition a unit of food; of the value of raw materials sold to industry say, mX; and of the value of food sold to members of the 'service class', say fY. As he assumes that each member of this class consumes more than a member of the industrial class he sets $f > 1$. We thus have

$$(11) \qquad\qquad B = X + mX + fY$$

where m is the relation of exchange value of materials to that of food. The receipts of the service class, D, are

$$(12) \qquad\qquad D + gB + e(X + mX)$$

where gB is what they receive from primary producers and $e(X + mX)$ is what they receive from the manufacturing class. The receipts of the industrial class are

$$(13) \qquad\qquad C = (1 - g)B + kB$$

where $(1 - g)B$ is what they receive from primary producers and kB their receipts from services.

In the same way, Lang gives the equations for the payments by the various classes, which can be deduced from receipts above:

(14) $B' = (1 - g)B + gB$ payments by primary producers
(15) $D' = fY + kB$ payments by services and
(16) $C' = (X + mX) + e(X + mX)$ payments by
                                          manufacturing class.[24]

All these results we have summarised in Table 7.1:

TABLE   7.1

Payments by	Primary producers	Payments to Manufacturing class	Services	Total payments
Primary producers	—	$(1-g)B$	gB	$B' = B$
Manufacturing class	$X + mX$	—	$e(X + mX)$	$C' = (1 + e)(1 + m)X = C$
Services	fY	kB	—	$D' = fY + kB = D$
Total receipts	$B = X + mX + fY$	$C = (1 - g)B + kB$	$D = gB + e(X + mX)$	

The requirement is that $B' = B$, $C' = C$ and $D' = D$. There is no need for the receipts of, say, primary producers from services to be equal to their payments. But if a class gives more money to one class it will give less to the other.[25]

For Lang, B or the receipts of the primary producers is of first importance; it generally increases with the increase in the population of the industrial class or the owners of services; or when the relation of the exchange value of materials compared to that of food increases, when the population is steady, or owners of services need more food than they used to need.[26] Given the values of m, f, g, e, k, the receipts or payments of each class can be calculated.

The gross national product is made up of the gross product of the three classes. The gross product of the primary producers is made up of (a) the value of the product which is used for reproduction, like seeds etc. This is equal to, say, U. (b) The value of the product which primary producers keep for their own consumption. As their needs are assumed to be the same as those of the industrial class, the value of their consumption is equal to V. (c) The value B of their 'superfluous' product which they exchange and which was calculated above.

In the same way he calculates the total product of the industrial class; as for services, he calculates as their value what they receive. From the gross national income he distinguishes the net national income, which is the remainder after allowance for the depreciation of capital and for double-counting has been made.[27] This net income he divides by the population of the country to find the net income per capita.[28]

Lang had up to this point separated the unit of value from money; now he asks 'What is the money *price* of this unit of value?' To answer the question he seeks to determine the total value of circulation of goods. This is made up:

(a) *of inter-class circulation*: The value can be found from either the payments or receipts of *all* three classes.

Thus, in Table 7.2, if:

TABLE   7.2

Payments by	Payments to			Total payments
	Primary producers	Manufacturing class	Services	
Primary producers	—	$(1-g)B$	gB	B
Manufacturing class	$(1-g+k)B$	—	—	$(1-g+k)B$
Services	$(g-k)B$	kB	—	gB
Total receipts	B	$(1-g+k)B$	gB	$(2+k)B$

The value of goods circulating among the classes is $(2+k)B$.

(b) *of intra-class circulation of goods;*[29] A portion of manufacturing goods circulates among industrial workers and a portion of primary products circulates among primary producers; but Lang does not think that owners of services have any use for the services of one another. Thus if the value of manufactures circulating be μN and that of primary products be πB, we shall have as the total value of all goods circulating

$$(17) \qquad P = (2 + k)B + \pi B + \mu N$$

If x is the money price of the unit of value, Z the quantity of money (coins and credit) circulating and y the average velocity of the circulation of money, we have[30]

$$(18) \qquad yZ = Px$$

This is the Fisher equation in its most explicit form. From this we get the money price for the unit of value

$$(19) \qquad x = \frac{yZ}{P}$$

'What therefore an increase in the quantity of money or the velocity of circulation does, when the real value of goods is not increased simultaneously, is to cause an increased money price of the unit of value and an increase of all money prices, in so far as they are determined by the money price of the unit of value.'[31]

If both the quantity of money and its velocity are constant, x and P are inversely related. Thus if P' is the new total value of commodities circulating and x' the new price, we shall have[32]

$$P'x' = Px, \text{ or } P' : P :: x :: x'$$

This result, Lang for the first time in the history of mathematical economics, writes by using the finite difference notation. Thus since $P'x' = Px$ where $x > x'$, $P' > P$ and $x' = x - \triangle x$ and $P' = P + \triangle P$, we have:

$$(20) \qquad \triangle P = \frac{P \triangle x}{x - \triangle x}$$

If the quantity of money is increased by $\triangle Z$ and 'if all the other relations remain the same as they used to be, only the money price of the unit of value rises'[33] and as

$$y(Z + \triangle Z) = P(x + \triangle x)$$

$$y\triangle Z = P \triangle x$$

$$(21) \qquad \triangle x = \frac{y}{P} \triangle Z$$

which is directly comparable with (19).

Thus this is the clearest possible statement of the quantity theory.

Having established the way money price is determined, Lang turns to examine the repercussions of its applications. We have already seen that he had assumed that primary producers gave to 'services' a portion g of the value of their 'superfluous products' B in payment of rent, interest and taxes; if the price of the unit of value is x, gB has a money value of gBx; now, he says,[34] assume that the contributions of producers for services increase in *money terms* by an amount a. One of three things may happen, if we assume that B remains unchanged:

(a) Either the money price x changes, while the contribution in real terms remains unchanged. Then

$$gB(x + \triangle x) = gBx + a$$

and the change in price is

$$\triangle x = \frac{a}{gB}$$

(b) Or price may remain unchanged, and primary producers will have to make up the increased contribution by increasing the portion g of their total amount of goods B which they have available for exchange. Then

$$(g + \triangle g)Bx = gBx + a$$

and the increase in real terms against primary producers is

$$\triangle g = \frac{a}{Bx}$$

(c) Or, what is more plausible, both the price x and g change. Then

$$(g + \triangle g)B(x + \triangle x) = gBx + a$$

and
$$\triangle x = \frac{\lambda - x\triangle g}{g + \triangle g}$$

where $\lambda = \frac{a}{B} > x\triangle g$ by definition, since x increases together with g.

It may be noticed immediately that the greater $\triangle g$ becomes, the smaller $\triangle x$, i.e. the change in price is smaller, ceteris paribus. When $\triangle g = \frac{\lambda}{x}$, $\triangle x$ becomes zero. On the contrary when $\triangle g = 0$, $\triangle x$

becomes a maximum equal to $\dfrac{\lambda}{g} = \dfrac{a}{gB}$ as in the first case.

This is a very broad outline of Lang's views. He has many interesting things to say about the effects of a change in the quantity of money on the receipts and payments of each of his classes since such a change creates a disequilibrium which must be adjusted; he also examines the effects of a change in the population on the composition of his classes and on his system in general. His work is entirely unknown. The only one to attempt a very cursory review of his work is Ross M. Robertson who accuses him of insisting on classifying population of a country illogically into agriculture, manufacture and 'officials'.[35]

7.3   GEORG VON BUQUOY

We have already seen that Canard had in his treatment of the 'latitude' found that there was a price such that the seller could not exceed without diminishing his profits. This is, of course, the point where marginal cost equals marginal revenue and it was von Buquoy, who first determined it but by taking as the independent variable not price but the 'depth of ploughing' of a field.[36]

He considers that both the revenue and the costs of cultivating a field are functions of the depth of ploughing. Thus if x is the depth of ploughing, y the total revenue from crops and Y the total costs of cultivation we have

(1) $$y = f(x)$$

(2) $$Y = F(x)$$

But although he writes his functions in this general way, he says that if they are plotted (Figure 7.1), with the 'depth of ploughing' on the abscissa and total revenue or cost on the ordinate, the locus of the first equation will be such that with increasing depth, total revenue will increase but at an always decreasing rate while the locus of the second will show costs increasing at an increasing rate; the first curve beyond a certain value of the abscissa flattens out, while the second becomes infinite when the value of the abscissa becomes infinite.[37] Buquoy does not plot his curves but he has fully described them so that the plotting is quite straightforward.[38]

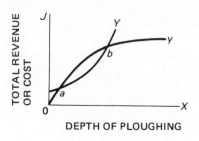

FIG. 7.1

The net revenue is the remainder, when from total revenue, total costs are subtracted:

(3) $f(x) - F(x)$

and the problem is to find that value of x which will make (3) a maximum. Differentiating in respect of x we get[39]

(4) $f'(x) - F(x) = 0$

(5) $f'(x) = F'(x)$

where $f'(x)$ is the marginal revenue and $F'(x)$ is the marginal cost.[40] Therefore the depth of ploughing must be such that its marginal revenue will be equal to its marginal cost if the net revenue is to be maximised.[41]

7.4   JOHANN HEINRICH VON THÜNEN

Von Thünen's first volume of *Der isolirte Staat in Beziehung auf Landwirthschaft und Nationalökonomie* appeared in 1826.[42]

In it Von Thünen seeks to examine the influence which costs of transportation have on the location of agriculture and on the methods of cultivation followed. To do this he imagines an isolated State surrounded by uncultivated wilderness. In the centre of the State lies the unique city, which is the source of all goods, other than the products of agriculture in the widest sense including forest and animal products. The land round the city is assumed to be of uniform fertility throughout and subject to uniform climatic conditions. All agricultural holdings are of equal size and no particular place in the state enjoys any special advantage in the form of access to a method of transportation, such as nearness to a river or a road, not open to the others, as by assumption there are no navigable rivers, or roads or railways in the State. Under such ideal conditions, the only factor which varies for every farmer in the State is the distance of his farm from the city, at which he has to sell his products and from which he has to procure the necessary non-agricultural goods. Under these circumstances, various zones of cultivation will be established round the town, each characterised by the production of certain products. In general those products which have a great weight or occupy a great space in comparison to their value, will be produced nearer the town than those which in relation to their value have smaller transport costs. 'On these grounds alone,' he writes,[43] 'there will appear around the city clearly separated concentric circles, in which this or that product will be the main product.'

To determine these concentric circles he attempts, by using his experience from his farm and assuming that the costs of transportation in the Isolated State are similar to those from his farm to the nearby town, to determine the relation between the price in the city and the net value which the farmer receives per unit of his commodity after the transportation costs have been deducted. Thünen gives two similar formulae for this relation; the first formula uses a numerical value for the price existing in the town;[44] in the second formula,[45] Thünen uses a symbol to denote the price in the city and this is thus the generalised form of the first formula.

Let a be the price per bushel of corn existing in the city, and b the net value per bushel for the farmer; let, further, the costs of transportation per mile be $\frac{1.63}{5}$ in money units[46] and $\frac{2.57}{5}$ bushels of corn,[47] for a cart the gross carrying capacity of which is $\frac{2400}{84}$ bushels of corn. The horses drawing the cart consume $\frac{30}{84}$ bushels of corn per mile-distance from the town.

If the farm is situated x miles from the town, the cart can only carry

(1) $\qquad\qquad \dfrac{2400 - 30x}{84}$ bushels

which at a units of money per bushel sell for

(2) $\qquad\qquad (\dfrac{2400 - 30x}{84})a$ units of money.

The net money revenue of the farmer is, however, his gross receipts (2) minus his money cost, which for x miles is $\frac{1.63}{5} x$. Thus the farmer receives in money

(3) $(\frac{2400 - 30x}{84})a - \frac{1.63}{5}x$ units of money

having given away in all

(4) $\frac{2400 - 30x}{84} + \frac{2.57x}{5}$ bushels of corn

where $\frac{2.57x}{5}$ are his costs in bushels of corn.

To find b, i.e. what the farmer gets for each bushel of corn, Thünen divides (3) by (4) and arrives at the formula[48]

(5) $b = \dfrac{(12,000 - 150x)a - 136.92x}{12,000 + 65 \cdot 88x}$

For a given a, x and b are inversely related, and we may find a distance x for which what the farmer receives is zero. This Thünen calculates[49] for $a = 1.5$ units of money and finds that at $x = 49.95$ miles, $b = 0$. The limits of his Isolated State are therefore at a distance of approximately 50 miles from the city, for beyond this, even if production was absolutely free, it would not pay to transport the product to the city.

But the farmer has many expenses to meet out of what he gets for his product; the remainder after these expenses have been met is what Thünen calls the rent of land. For given costs and given fertility of land, there is a certain value of b at which the rent is zero and this forms the limit of this kind of cultivation.[50] For land to be cultivated further than this point, if fertility has remained unchanged, a new method of cultivation or a new product must be adopted, which by the lowering of costs makes the rent of land again positive.

On this basis and assuming that the price in the city is given, Thünen calculates the distance from the town of the various zones. There will in turn be: the free zone,[51] the zone of forest economy, three zones of corn cultivation in which the form of cultivation becomes increasingly less intensive, and the zone of animal breeding. Thünen illustrates these zones in what he calls a 'pictorial representation',[52] which together with three more are to be found at the end of his book (Figure 7.2).

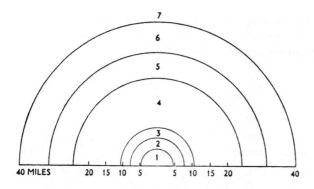

FIG. 7.2. Thünen's Isolated State when prices and yields are given.

Up to this point Thünen had considered that the price in the city *a* was given. Now he chooses[53] to examine how changing prices affect the distance at which each form of cultivation ends, at which it gives, that is, zero rent. Thus for the fifth circle: having found that the value of *b* which produces zero rent is 0.38, Thünen substitutes in equation (5a) this value for *b* and solving for *x* he finds:

$$(6) \qquad x = \frac{182(a - 0.38)}{2.3a + 0.38 + 2.1}$$

Using this equation, he finds that the rent will be zero, and consequently this form of cultivation will cease, when:

a is equal to	at *x* miles
1.5 units of money	at 34.7
1.35	at 31.7
1.20	at 28.6
1.05	at 25
0.90	at 20.9
0.75	at 16.1
0.60	at 10.4

Instead of drawing these figures on conventional coordinates, Thünen chooses an ingenious alternative which we reproduce as Figure 7.3. The table of values given above is represented by the curve *ABC* where the radius from the centre represents the distance. For each price *a* a corresponding radius is drawn and the locus of all the points at the end of the radii is curve *ABC*. If one wishes to know the circle of production at any particular price *a*, one can simply read the length of the radius at this price from curve *ABC* and then draw a circle from the centre at this radius.[54]

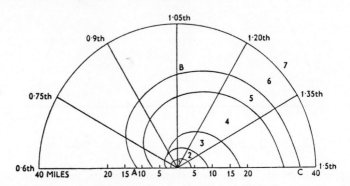

FIG. 7.3   Table showing distances of the various concentric circles in the Isolated State under different prices (in German 'Thaler').
1. Free economy zone.
2. Forest economy zone.
3. Continuous rotation of crops (Fruchtwechselwirtschaft). ⎫
4. Rotation of crops with breaks in cultivation   ⎬ Zones of cor
    (Koppelwirtschaft).   cultivation
5. Rotation of crops with breaks in cultivation   ⎭
    (Dreifeldwirtschaft).
6. Animal breeding zone.
7. Uncultivated area.

   In the two figures we have discussed so far fertility was considered as given. In another figure Thünen examines how changes in the fertility of the soil affect his concentric circles, other things being equal. And lastly in a fourth figure, which is the least mathematical of all, he shows how a navigable river affects the location of his various zones.

   Some formulae are also given by Karl Heinrich Rau in his *Grundsätze der Volkswirthschaftshehre*, published in 1826. Among these is a formula of the equation of exchange. This is similar to that given by Lang and includes the average velocity of circulation. Rau, in his analysis of this formula, expressly says that price will vary in proportion to the quantity of money only when the velocity of circulation and the quantity of goods are kept constant.[55] Friedrich Hermann also gave some simple formulae of production in his *Staatswirthschaftliche Unteruschungen*.[56]

NOTES

1. *Das Steuerwesen nach seiner Natur und seinen Wirkungen untersucht* (Darmstadt und Giessen, 1804). Fisher and Jevons mention in their bibliographies another earlier work by Kröncke, *Versuch einer Theorie des Fuhrwerks mit Anwendung auf den Strassenbau* (Giessen, 1802), but I have found little in the book of interest in economic theory. The book is a road-engineering book and the only economic questions dealt with there are of a practical nature like the calculation of costs of building a new road.
2. Kröncke, op. cit., Introduction, p. xv.
3. Petty, Locke and Cantillon are the authors to whom mainly is due 'perception of this fact and its insertion into the analytic engine'. Schumpeter, op. cit., p. 316.
4. Kröncke, op. cit., p. 194.
5. Ibid., p. 195.
6. 'Dieses Kapital *r* dient bloss dazu, die Werthe für die gegebenen oder genommenen Sachen auszugleichen.' Kröncke, op. cit., p.195.
7. The country could invest the money not needed.
8. Kröncke, op. cit., pp. 127–31.
9. Kröncke, op. cit., pp. 127–31.
10. Ibid., pp. 17–47. On pp. 55–9 Kröncke skilfully applies ideas from the theory of probability to calculate the height of the premium, which must be added to the rate of interest as an insurance against default by the debtor. He also shows how the value of a factor which gives return over a number of years can be found by discounting at compound interest its returns. Ibid., pp. 62–80. His ideas on taxation, though interspersed with a lot of mathematics, are much less interesting. He thus advocates the 'per capita tax' as more equitable by linking the level of taxation with the individual's wealth and personal safety and maintaining that the value of the second is infinitely larger than that of the first so that contributions should really be in proportion to the safety afforded to each individual by the State. Kröncke, op. cit., pp. 392–3.
    Kröncke also gave a definition of *wealth* and *national income*. If, he says, the total resources of a country $A, B, C \ldots$ have values a, b, c, etc., $a + b + c + \ldots = \pi$ is the national wealth. If these resources produce A', B', C', etc. quantities which have values a', b', c', etc. then $a' + b' + c' + \ldots = \Sigma$ is the yearly national income. Kröncke, op. cit., p. 206.
11. Kröncke, op. cit., p. 206.
12. It was published in Kharkov (Charkov) in Russia in 1811. The substance of the part on Lang has been printed as an article by the author under the title 'Joseph Lang and Macroeconomics', in *Economica 1958*, pp. 319–25. The author is indebted to the editors of *Economica* for leave to reprint the substance of this.
    On Lang, see also W. Jaffé, 'A.N. Isnard', op. cit., p. 20 n.; G.H. Bousquet, 'Joseph Lang' in *Revue Économique*, (1958), pp. 268–74; G.H. Bousquet, 'Le Système Mathématique', op. cit., pp. 967–8.

13. Lang, op. cit., p. ix.
14. Ibid., p. 54.
15. Isnard called it 'superflu', Lang calls it 'Balanz'.
16. Lang, op. cit., pp. 3 *et seq.*
17. Isnard, op. cit., vol. I, pp. 19 *et seq.*
18. Lang, op. cit., p. 11.
19. Ibid., p. 11.
20. Ibid., pp. 13 *et seq.*
21. Lang's results may be illustrated by the following matrix (Table (7.1n) – which is not Lang's but our own construction.

TABLE   7.1n

| | Payments to | | | |
Payments by	*Primary producers*	*Manufac-turing class*	*Services*	*Total payments*
Primary producers	—	c	e	$c+e=x'$
Manufacturing class	a	—	f	$a+f=y'$
Services	b	d	—	$b+d=z'$
Total receipts	$a+b=x$	$c+d=y$	$e+f=z$	$x+y+z=x'+y'+z'$

22. Lang, op. cit., p. 22.
23. Ibid., pp. 55 *et seq.*
24. Ibid., pp. 55–62.
25. Ibid., p. 20.
26. Ibid., p. 62.
27. Ibid., pp. 66–7.
28. Ibid., p. 84.
29. Ibid., p. 116.
30. Ibid., p. 117, where $Px = [(2 + k)B + \pi B + \mu N]x$.
31. Ibid., p. 119.
32. Ibid., p. 172.
33. Ibid., pp. 173–7.
34. Ross M. Robertson, 'Mathematical Economics before Cournot', *Journal of Political Economy* (1949) p. 534.
35. Lang has also written *Über den obersten Grundsatz der Politischen Ökonomie* (Rigal 809), a copy of which I have been unable to trace.
36. *Die Theorie der Nationalwirthschaft, nach einem neuen Plane und nach mehreren eigenen Ansichten dargestellt* (Leipzig, 1815) p. 54. See also on Buquoy, Reichardt, op. cit., pp. 77–8.
37. Buquoy, op. cit., p. 54.
38. These two curves have a shape similar to their shape in modern theory where the independent variable is output; but the y curve instead of flattening out, turns downwards.

39. Buquoy, op. cit., p. 54. He mentions that while the first derivative must be zero, the second must be negative.
40. In our figure, x will be at that point where the tangents to the two curves become parallel.
41. Buquoy does not use the terms marginal cost and marginal revenue but uses the term net revenue.
42. Hamburg 1826. The second part of the *Isolirte Staat* dealing with the problem of the natural wage appeared in two sections, the first in 1850 and the second in 1863; it does not, therefore, fall within the scope of the present work.
43. Thünen, op. cit., p. 2.
44. Ibid., pp. 10–11.
45. Ibid., pp. 285–6.
46. Golden 'Thaler'.
47. Both these results were derived from the costs of transportation from Thünen's farm to the nearby town.
48. Thünen, op. cit., p. 286 in conjunction with p. 11. Thünen gives an approximation of (5) as:

$$(5a) \quad b = \frac{(182 - 2.3x)a - 2.1x}{182 + x}$$

49. Ibid., p. 8.
50. Thünen actually gives a formula for b when rent is zero on pp. 34–5 of the *Isolirte Staat*.
51. Where perishable foodstuffs and milk as well as such things as potatoes, carrots, etc. are produced.
52. Thünen, op. cit., p. 282. Thünen himself, however, did not draw these diagrams, as is evident from the beginning of his notes on p. 282. 'Diese, *von einem meiner Freunde gezeichneten, bildlichen Darstellungen*'. [my italicising.]
53. Ibid., p. 286.
54. The other curves in Fig. 7.3 are similarly drawn. Thünen actually discusses the level at which the price of corn will settle in the city 'The price of corn, he writes, must be so high that the rent of that farm, whose delivery of corn to the market though the most expensive is necessary for the satisfaction of the need for corn, does not fall below zero.' Thünen, op. cit., p. 179.

    On von Thünen see also: E. Schneider, "Einführung in die Wirtschaftstheorie", IV Teil, (Mohr, 1962) pp. 145–64.
55. Rau, op. cit., 4th edn, p. 305 n. See also ibid., p. 256.

    On Rau, see also: E. Schneider, op. cit., pp. 130–1.
56. München (1832) pp. 80–8, 168 n., 187 n., 190 n.

8 The British Authors

We have already reviewed the work of H. Lloyd who was among the earliest mathematical economists. For some fifty years, however, while important developments were taking place in other parts of Europe, the appearance of Lloyd's book was not followed, as far as we know, by any other contribution to mathematical economics from any British author, apart from the contribution of Samuel Gale, who was an American and with whom we deal at the end of this section.

The new break was made by Samuel Turner in 1819 in *A letter addressed to the Right Hon. Robert Peel with reference to the expediency of the resumption of cash payments at the period fixed by law*. Having given[1] the equation of exchange in the form

(1) $$a = bc$$

where a is 'the value of commodities of any country exchanged in a given portion of time, as a year', b is 'the quantity of precious metals circulating in that country'[2] and c 'the circulating power or the number of times that b changes hands within that given portion of time',[3] he extends this formula to apply, as he says, to the whole world. He then defines the 'natural price' of a to be bc, a process which one cannot justify since a has already been defined as the value of commodities.[4] By analogy, the 'natural or real price' of a portion $\frac{a}{f}$ will be equal to $\frac{bc}{f}$. The reasoning which follows is no less confused. If, he says, taxes of value $\frac{bc}{g}$ are imposed on articles equal to $\frac{a}{f}$, these articles will have to be sold above their natural price, at a price equal to $\frac{bc}{f} + \frac{bc}{g}$. It is indeed very difficult to make any sense of this statement, unless one understands that $\frac{a}{f}$ is now a quantity and not the value of commodities.

If the remainder of the goods which were left untaxed is $\frac{a}{r}$ these would have to sell below their 'natural price' $\dfrac{bc}{r}$, for $\dfrac{bc}{r} - \dfrac{bc}{g}$, if

there was no increase in money,[5] since the amount $\dfrac{bc}{g}$ had been

withdrawn to pay for the taxed articles. 'How', he asks then,[6] 'would the grocers or manufacturers of that portion of the annual produce of the lands and labour of any country which before taxation sold at

$\dfrac{bc}{r}$, be able to fulfil their engagements in money, in case the same

produce sold only at $\dfrac{bc}{r} - \dfrac{bc}{g}$.' His remedy is an increase in the

circulating medium, which could be either coin or paper money. He therefore extends formula (1) to include not only coin b but also the quantity of paper money p.

(2) $$a = (b + p)c$$

Turner was followed by an anonymous author who, writing under the initials 'E.R.', published in 1822 *An Essay on Some General Principles of Political Economy, on Taxes upon Raw Produce and on Commutation of Tithes.* There, he gives a mathematical treatment of the incidence of taxation on land. E. R. A. Seligman, who discovered this work, says in comparing it with Lloyd's:[7] 'The mathematics used in the work of 1771 is of extreme simplicity when compared to that of the essay of 1822 which has escaped the attention of both Jevons and Irving Fisher in their respective bibliographies.'

T. Perronet Thompson, made two contributions. The first was an examination of the effects of an excessive issue of bills by the state, if the issue continues over a period of time. This was made in an article in the *Westminster Review* under the title 'The Instrument of Exchange'.[8] Perronet Thompson's argument is broadly this: Let us assume that when the payment of taxes is made uniformly and p is the daily produce of taxes, the Government issues an amount of irredeemable bills every day, such that it not only puts into circulation an amount of bills equal to what had been withdrawn from circulation but in excess of this. Let therefore the daily issue of bills, each nominally for a bushel of wheat be $(p + s)$ where s is the daily *excess on the 'superfluous issue'* as Thompson calls it. Our author, as a supporter of the quantity theory, then says that the price level is determined by the total quantity of bills in circulation when the number b occupied in the discharge of taxes is deducted. If, thus, we have a number of bills, A, including those occupied in the discharge of taxes, just adequate to keep prices at par, so that $A = 4000$ and $b = 1000$, the quantity of bills, $A - b$, which determines prices is 3000. If this number is increased to 5000, prices will increase, and the currency depreciate, by $\frac{2}{5}$. The fraction z which expresses the depreciation of the currency will be:

$$(1) \quad z = 1 - \frac{4000 - 1000}{3000 + 2000} = 1 - \frac{A - b}{A - b + st} = \frac{st}{A - b + st}$$

st is the increase in the currency, where s is the 'superfluous' issue and t the number of days it has continued.

But the depreciation of the currency works against the State for the fall in the value of money affects the real value of the proceeds from the issue of bills. Thus, though it nominally issues bills of a value of st bushels of wheat, it really can buy only $st(1 - z)$ bushels; it therefore loses stz bushels on the 'superfluous' issue; but it will also lose on its legitimate issue of bills, to replace those withdrawn through the payment of taxes. If the issue of such bills has lasted for t days the loss on them is ptz. The net result from a 'superfluous' issue which has lasted for t days is

$$(2) \quad st - stz - ptz$$

and for a given s and p, (2) is a function of t and z; but z itself is a function of t when A and b are given.

The problem which Thompson tackles[9] is for what value of t, the net result for the government becomes zero and therefore

$$(3) \quad st = stz + ptz$$

Substituting z and solving

$$(4) \quad t = \frac{A - b}{p}$$

which shows in how many days the net result for the Government will become zero, if superfluous issues continue; any further superfluous issues, result in negative net receipts for the Government.

In the same article, Thompson, discussing what a proper scale of taxation should be[10] says that this scale 'should be nothing at a certain income and approach to some reasonable percentage as to an asymptote'.[11] He returned to the same subject in a 'Postscript to the article on the Instrument of Exchange' in the *Westminster Review* of 1830[12] where he plots the curve (Figure 8.1) representing the above scale as:

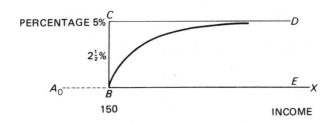

FIG. 8.1

The equation of the curve is $y = M \times \dfrac{x - a}{x}$ where x, the income, is the abscissa measured from a point A outside the curve, a the level of income after which taxation is to start, and $M = $ line BC is the fixed percentage to be levied uniformly on the excess of x over a. Y, therefore, the curve, represents the percentage of the tax on the whole income. This approaches asymptotically M as $x \to \infty$.

The second contribution of Thompson was his perception of the approach through time to a dynamic equilibrium, achieved through an analogy with the finite series of mathematics. Discussing in his book *An Exposition of Fallacies on Rent, Tithes, etc.*[13] Ricardo's objection against the recovery of taxes on wages, as the rise in the price of goods would again operate on wages and 'the action and reaction first of wages on goods, and then of goods on wages, will be extended without any assignable limits',[14] Thompson observes that 'the supposition that any absurd conclusions will arise is founded on inattention to the nature of infinite series. Because a series is endless in its numbers of terms, it does not follow that its amount is infinite.[15] If a man was to proceed to calculate all the successive actions and reactions of wages and prices upon each other, he might find himself engaged in what mathematicians call the method of approximation; which, though he could never positively arrive at its end, he might carry to as minute a fraction of a farthing as would satisfy the most scrupulous accountant. But there exists a palpable cause which would prevent the effect of these actions and reactions not only from being infinite, for that they could never be, but from rising above a certain amount. And this cause is, the impossibility of money prices rising above what can be conducted by the circulating medium. The nature of the process is the opposite of that by which an excess of circulating medium causes a depreciation of the currency and increase of money prices'.[16]

W. Whewell refers to the same question in his 'Mathematical Exposition of some Doctrines of Political Economy' which was read before the Cambridge Philosophical Society in 1829 and published as a book in the same year.[17] If, he says, Ricardo had considered his arguments mathematically, the absurdity which, he thinks, exists in rising prices and wages outside any limit would disappear. For 'Let wages rise to the whole amount of the tax; say $\frac{1}{10}$; and let this rise in wages produce a rise of $\frac{1}{20}$ in the price of manufactured goods; (not so much as $\frac{1}{10}$, because only a part, say $\frac{1}{2}$, of the *value* of goods is wages;) and let this rise of $\frac{1}{20}$ in the price of goods produce a rise of $\frac{1}{40}$ in wages (not so much as $\frac{1}{20}$, because only a part, say, $\frac{1}{2}$ of the labourer's *consumption* is manufactures;) and so on. Then it is manifest that the whole rise in wages is

$$\frac{1}{10} + \frac{1}{40} + \frac{1}{160} + \text{, etc.}$$

and that the whole rise in goods is

$$\frac{1}{20} + \frac{1}{80} + \frac{1}{320}, \text{ etc.}$$

And the simplest principles of systematic arithmetic inform us, that these are not quantities having 'no assignable limit', but that according to these suppositions, the whole rise in wages will be $\frac{4}{30}$, and the whole rise of manufactured goods $\frac{2}{30}$. And if the result of these suppositions had been determined by expressing the conditions algebraically, we should have had the same result directly and immediately, without even the process which we have had to introduce, of summing a geometrical series.'[18]

The above passage shows clearly how ill-founded is Whewell's description by most of those who reviewed his work as that of a mere translator of existing doctrine into mathematical language, an author whose 'effort does not go beyond stating in symbols what had already been stated in words and therefore does not really constitute mathematical economics'.[19]

It is a fact, however, that he himself sought to distinguish between the moral axioms and fundamental assumptions of Political Economy on the one hand and the task of deducing conclusions from these on the other. It is to this latter task that the use of mathematics may provide considerable help, especially when there are complex and confused calculations to be made.

'Such a system of calculation must of course borrow the elements and axioms which are its materials, from that higher department of the Science of Political Economy, which is concerned with the moral and social principles of men's actions and relations. These materials thus received, stated in the simplest manner, must be subjected to the processes of a proper calculus, and we may thus obtain all the results to which the assumed principles lead, whatever be the complexity of their combination.'[20] It is, therefore, clear that he does not see the task of mathematical economics as simply a task of translation.

Nor is this first attempt of his lacking in originality. Having set out the following six axioms:[21]

(1) Rent = produce − return to capital with profits;
(2) Land will be cultivated if produce ⩾ profits;
(3) There is always a limiting soil;
(4) The increase of price is proportional to the deficiency of supply;
(5) Price = cost of production + profits;
(6) Partial Taxes do not affect the rate of profits;

he discusses the differences between the followers of Ricardo who maintained that all taxes on the produce of land are ultimately paid by the consumer and the followers of the view that such taxes are principally paid by the landlord and points out under what conditions each view would be correct.

Thus, he shows, that the tax will fall wholly on rent, when there is no limiting soil,[22] while the existence of marginal soil means that the tax is 'the sum of the diminution of rent, the diminution of return to capital, and the increase of price'.[23]

Whewell also is credited with giving, in his first memoir of 1829, a mathematical statement of the flexibility of price from which the coefficient of demand elasticity can be derived.[24]

Whewell presented a second memoir to the Cambridge Philosophical Society in 1831; this is, however, purely an exposition of Ricardo's doctrines with the help of mathematics and presents no interest from the point of view of this book.[25]

The last British author in our survey is D. G. Lubé, whose book *An Argument against the Gold Standard with an Examination of the Principles of the Modern Economists* was published in London in 1832 and contains some mathematical passages of no interest. Thus the relative value of each commodity is represented, thirty years after Valeriani, as $\frac{d}{s}$ where d is the demand and s the supply.[26] The value of money he represents[27] in the form $\frac{a}{c}$ where $a = b + d + f + g$ is the total of merchandise and c the amount of money; he, thus, has no place in his equation for the velocity of circulation, which had already been treated by Kröncke, Rau and Lang. Finally his argument[28] that the gold standard imposes an arbitrary limit on currency, as the production of gold cannot keep pace with increased demand, is based on an examination of the relation of money as such and as a commodity on lines similar to those followed by Ceva and Spinelli a century before.

The American, Samuel Gale, also published a book containing a considerable amount of mathematics. This was his work *An Essay on the Nature and Principles of Public Credit* (London 1784); this deals with an examination of methods of treatment of the Public Debt, incurred chiefly through financing of one or more wars and is essentially an application of the theory of compound interest and annuities.

If a nation carries a war at a half-yearly expense S, over a number of half-years T, and R is the rate of increase of the unit of money due to its interest, the final value of expenses at the end of T years will be, when these expenses are paid to the Treasury at the beginning of each half-year:

Loan S			
at beginning of 1st half-year	becomes after	T half-years	$R^T S$
at beginning of 2nd half-year	becomes after	$T - 1$ half-years	$R^{T-1} S$
. . . . .	. . . .	. . . .	.
at beginning of $T - 1$ half-year	becomes after	2 half-years	$R^2 S$
at beginning of T half-year	becomes after	1 half year	RS

Therefore the total value of this annuity at the end of T years will be the sum of the geometric progression and will be equal to

$$\frac{R^{T+1} - S}{R - 1} \times S$$

This is the public debt at the end of T half-years.[29] Such calculations are repeated by Gale throughout the book,[30] whenever he uses mathematics. It seems therefore that, in view of the very interesting and important contribution made by earlier Italian and German authors, whose work we have described, a claim advanced by E. R. A. Seligman, who discovered Gale, on his behalf that 'the books by Gale are by all means the most comprehensive and detailed examples of early mathematico-economic literature and will repay careful examination',[31] appears to have no foundation.

NOTES

1. Turner, op. cit., p. 12.
2. Ibid., p. 12.
3. Ibid., p. 12.
4. Ibid., p. 13.
5. Presumably, therefore, we have (1) $\frac{a}{f} = \frac{bc}{f} + \frac{bc}{g}$, (2) $\frac{a}{r} = \frac{bc}{r} - \frac{bc}{g}$ and (3) $\frac{a}{f} + \frac{a}{r} = a = bc = \frac{bc}{f} + \frac{bc}{r}$.
6. Turner, ibid., pp. 15–16, The same mathematical argument is also included in another work by Turner, *Considerations upon Agriculture, Commerce and Manufactures of the British Empire* (1822), pp. 34–7.
7. E. R. A. Seligman, 'On Some Neglected British Economists', *Economic Journal* (1903) p. 352, reproduced also in *Essays in Economics* (1925) by the same author.
8. Thompson, *Westminster Review*, vol. I (1824) pp. 171–205, reprinted separately in 1830 and also in 1842.
9. Thompson, op. cit., p. 187.
10. Ibid., p. 204 n.
11. Ibid., p. 204 n.
12. Ibid., vol. XII (1830) pp. 525–33. The figure is on p. 527.
13. Thompson (London, 1826) p. 39.
14. Ibid., p. 39; Ricardo, *Principles*, p. 301.
15. Thompson remarks that the most familiar example is the series $\frac{1}{2} + \frac{1}{4} + \frac{1}{8} + \ldots$, whose sum ad infinitum is 1 and which is the foundation of the sophism of Achilles and the tortoise. Ibid., p. 39.
16. Thompson, *An Exposition of Fallacies on Rent, etc.*, pp. 39–40.
17. The paper is also included in vol. III of the *Transactions of the Cambridge Philosophical Society* (1830) pp. 191–229. We refer to the book edition.
18. Whewell, op. cit., pp. 2–3.
19. Schumpeter, op. cit., p. 448 note 7. W. S. Jevons in his preface to the 2nd edn of his *Theory* describes Whewell as belonging to those economists who used mathematics abundantly but have built upon the sand.
20. Whewell, op. cit., pp. 3–4.
21. Ibid., p. 15. Axiom (4) is written as 'Increase of price $\propto$ diminution of supply'.
22. Whewell, op. cit., p. 19.
23. Ibid., p. 17.
24. Ibid., p. 21. See also, J.P. Henderson, *William Whewell's Mathematical Statements of Price Flexibility, Demand Elasticity and the Giffen Paradox* (The Manchester School of Economic and Social Studies, 1973)

pp. 329–42; J.L. Cochrane, *William Whewell's Mathematical Statements* (The Manchester School of Economic and Social Studies 1975) pp. 396–400; J.P. Henderson, Rejoinder, ibid., pp. 401–3.

25. Whewell, 'Mathematical Exposition of Some of the Leading Doctrines in Ricardo's *Principles of Political Economy and Taxation*' read in 1831 and published in vol. IV of the *Transactions of the Cambridge Philosophical Society* (1833) pp. 155–98. Whewell returned to the same subject in vol. IX (1856) of the *Transactions* (part I, pp. 128–49 and part II, pp. 1–7), where he examines questions of demand, supply, price and international exchanges and uses the concept of demand elasticity to identify various classes of goods, including goods like diamonds, whose demand changes in the same direction as their price.

   On Whewell, see also: R. D. Theocharis, 'William Whewell' in *International Encyclopedia of the Social Sciences* (New York, 1968) pp. 531–2; J.L. Cochrane, The First Mathematical Ricardian Model in *History of Political Economy*, 1970, pp. 419–31; S. Rashid, 'William Whewell and Early Mathematical Economics', *Manchester School of Economic and Social Studies*, 1977, pp. 381–91.

26. Lubé, op. cit., p. 66.

27. Ibid., p. 95.

28. Ibid., pp. 187–92.

29. Gale, op. cit., pp. 23 *et seq.*

30. E. R. A. Seligman, 'On Some Neglected British Economists', *Economic Journal* (1903) p. 352 n.

31. Ibid., p. 352 n.

9 Augustin Cournot

9.1 INTRODUCTION

Antoine-Augustin Cournot was born[1] on 28 August 1801 at Gray, a French town in the Franche-Comté. The family background was essentially rural, but an uncle of his was a public notary. It was this uncle, with his conservative leanings, who exercised a considerable influence on Cournot.

Cournot started his education in his native town; he was a great reader of scientific works as an adolescent, and in his *Souvenirs* he lists the work of Laplace *Exposition du Système du monde* among the books which he read at this time.[2]

In 1820 he entered the Royal College in the neighbouring town of Besançon to prepare for the entrance examination to the École Normale, which he entered in the succeeding year together with Auguste Walras, who was destined to become a notable economist in his own right apart from being the father of Léon Walras.[3]

His stay at the École Normale was, however, short for it was closed in 1822 by the Government because of the alleged republican feelings of its students and Cournot had to transfer to the Sorbonne from which he graduated in Mathematics in 1823. His teachers included Laplace, Lagrange and Poisson, who befriended him and helped him considerably in his later career.

In the same year of his graduation he became private secretary to Marshal Gouvion Saint-Cyr and tutor of his son. He helped the Marshall to write his memoirs and also edited them, when they appeared in 1831, a year after the Marshal's death.[4] His employment with the Marshal's household, which extended until 1833, proved invaluable to him for he had the chance to come into close contact with many influential people in the fields of politics and business. In the meantime he had been working for the Doctor's degree which he gained in 1829[5] and had been contributing scientific articles, which had made him known to a wider circle of scientists.[6]

For a year after 1833 he was engaged in the translation of two works[7], one on mechanics and one on astronomy, until he was appointed, on the recommendation of Poisson, Professor of Mathematical Analysis in the University of Lyon. He held the chair for only one year, for in 1835 he was appointed, again on the recommendation of Poisson, Rector of the Academy of Grenoble. In 1836 he was provisionally appointed to the post of 'Inspecteur Général des Études', an appointment which became permanent in 1838, the year of his marriage and the publication of his first book, the *Recherches sur les principes mathématiques de la théorie des richesses*.

Parallel to the office of the Inspector-General, he held other educational offices during his career as an official, chiefly the membership of the 'Commission des hautes études' and the presidency of the 'Concours d'agrégation des mathématiques'.

In 1854 he returned to academic life, this time as Rector of the Academy of Dijon, a post which he kept until his final retirement in 1862. The remaining years till his death on 30 March 1877 he spent in Paris engaged in philosophical meditation and writing.

He was an extremely reserved man; in his *Souvenirs* there is scarcely any mention of his family. 'Il est muet,[8] sur son frère, ses neveux et nièces, il ne fait même pas allusion à sa soeur Judith qu'il aimait beaucoup, et à laquelle étant à Paris, il rendait visite chaque jour.' One of his biographers, Giacalone-Monaco, thinks that he was in addition an opportunist because 'on account of his love for quietness and his conservative spirit, he followed the current'.[9]

Cournot was an economist, a philosopher and a mathematician. He published three mathematical works. The *Traité élèmentaire de la théorie des fonctions et du calcul infinitésimal* appeared in two volumes in 1841. It is an exposition of the theory of the calculus, viewed as an integral part of the theory of continuous functions, an idea which was quite novel for its time as Cournot observes in the preface of the book[10]. This was followed in 1843 by the *Exposition de la théorie des chances et des probabilités*, which is a systematic exposition of the calculus of probabilities and its application to statistics. Lastly, he published in 1847 a book under the title, *De l'origine et des lim ites de la correspondance entre l'algèbre et la géométrie*, where he attempts to find up to what point, after submitting geometric questions to algebraic processes, algebra and geometry correspond and to ascertain the rules to which such correspondence obeys.[11]

Cournot's philosophical works, which have been influenced throughout by his ideas on probability, began to appear in 1851 when the *Éssai sur les fondements de nos connaissances et sur les caractères de la critique philosophique* appeared. This was followed by the *Traité de l'enchaînement des idées fondamentales dans les sciences et dans l'histoire* (1861) and the *Considérations sur la marche des idées et des évènements dans les temps modernes* (1872). His last philosophical work *Matérialisme, Vitalisme, Rationalisme* appeared two years before his death, in 1875[12].

It is, however, as an economist that his fame, though lately acquired, will most probably survive among future generations. Cournot started and finished his career as an author with an economic work. The *Recherches sur les principes mathématiques de la théorie des richesses* appeared, as already mentioned, in 1838, and the *Revue Sommaire des doctrines économiques* in 1877, the year of his death. A third work the *Principes de la théorie des richesses* which is essentially a repetition of the *Recherches* without the mathematics, appeared in 1863.

By far the most important of these works is the *Recherches*, not only because it contains the great majority of Cournot's leading ideas on economic analysis, to which he was again to return in his later works, but also because it is the first consistent and generally success- ful attempt to apply mathematical analysis to a wide range of economic problems.

But though Cournot is sometimes considered as the father of mathematical economics, it is a fact that, as we have seen, long before the appearance of the *Recherches*, there were important attempts to employ mathematical analysis in the discussion of economic problems.

Indeed the *Recherches* must be seen as the culmination of a process which had started long before Cournot. As we have shown so far, there have been notable contributions to mathematical economics as early as the beginning of the 18th century which cannot be considered as isolated phenomena, for as we have already indicated in the intro- duction one can find on the one hand contributions from people who had used the same method, although they were not in direct connec- tion with one another, while on the other hand there are many examples of authors who had known of the work of their predecessors in mathematical economics and had been able to build on it.

9.2 THE ORIGIN OF THE *RECHERCHES*

It has been a matter of considerable interest among all those who ever wrote about Cournot's economic work how he, an accomplished mathematician, was induced not simply to turn to the study of economics but actually to appear for the first time before the wider public as an author of an economic treatise.

In fact, very little is definitely known. His *Souvenirs* do not give any indication and there was nothing apparent, before the actual publication of the book, to indicate that Cournot's mind was working towards such a direction. *Les Recherches*, writes La Harpe[13], 'surgissent un beau jour sans aucune apparence de préparation'. Of necessity, therefore, the answer to the question is restricted to the field of conjecture.

There are two opposing views. The first[14] believes that Cournot started with the express intention to apply mathematical analysis to wider fields. It points out that in the days of Cournot questions in the pure theory of mathematics were unpopular: the fashion was to attempt the extension of the application of the theory of mathematics to as many practical fields as possible. Why Cournot actually chose the field of economics for his applications was either due to the fact that, as Cournot's special field was the theory of probabilities, he found a very fertile field in social questions[15] or the fact that economic questions had always interested him. 'Sa biographie explique, dans une large mesure, l'intérêt qu'il portait aux questions sociales; les conflits sociaux et politiques l'ont intéressé dès son plus jeune âge.'[16]

The second view starts from the opposite end. Cournot did not start with the express intention of extending the application of mathematics. His study of economics was a side interest. But having read Smith, Ricardo and Say, as he himself admits, he must have found their analyses vague and confusing. A logician like Cournot, preoccupied with generalisations and very skilful in the employment of the calculus could not but be tempted to attempt to put their arguments into mathematical form, as Whewell had done before him[17]. There is a more ambitious view. Cournot's reading of Smith, Malthus and Say showed him that economic science was assuming 'the dignity of a science of laws'[18], and, as he was already influenced by A. Comte's ideas of a science of 'social physics', the idea must have come to his mind that by developing the mathematical approach he could evolve a science of 'economic physics' ('physique économique').[19]

It may well, of course be, that it was Canard,[20] who having given with his ideas a lead to Cournot in monopoly theory, played a decisive role in directing his steps towards Economics.

Cournot himself seems to imply that it was the aim of expanding the application of mathematics, which made him primarily attempt this application to *certain economic topics*; but it was the vagueness of the doctrine then current which drove him to the more ambitious work of developing the mathematical principles of the theory of wealth. 'There is', he writes at the end of his preface[21], 'a large class of men, and, thanks to a famous school, especially in France, who, after thorough mathematical training, have directed their attention to applications of those sciences which particularly interest society. Theories of the wealth of the community must attract their attention; and in considering them they are sure to feel, as I have felt, the need of rendering determinate by symbols familiar to them, an analysis which is generally indeterminate and often obscure, in authors who have thought fit to confine themselves to the resources of ordinary language.'

9.3 SCOPE AND METHOD

i) Generalia

The aim of the *Recherches* is not to develop a theory of wealth but to apply the mathematical method to those parts of the theory which Cournot thinks are susceptible to such a treatment. 'I have not set out to make a complete and dogmatic treatise on Political Economy; I have put aside questions to which mathematical analysis cannot apply, and those which seem to me entirely cleared up already',[22] he writes.

The *raison d'être* of the book is therefore the method Cournot has chosen to use and this governs not only the topics which Cournot decides to examine, but also the length at which he decides to deal with each question.

This method is not aiming at finding directly numerical results; its aim is to ascertain what form of relation exists between two or more economic quantities and to apply there the theory of functions. The determination of the relation may be vague but nonetheless the theory of functions will be applicable. Thus the relation between quantity demanded and price may be represented by the function $D = F(p)$. It is sufficient to know some of its properties – in this case e.g. that it is decreasing and continuous – in order to find by means of analytical symbols 'relations equally general which would have been difficult to discover without this help.'[23]

This conception of the role of mathematics in economic theory struck, Cournot thought, at the roots of the argument of those authors, who although theorists of repute, mistakenly thought that 'the use of symbols and formulas could only lead to numerical calcula tions, and as it was clearly perceived that the subject was not suited t such a numerical determination of values by means of theory alone the conclusion was drawn that the mathematical apparatus, if no liable to lead to erroneous results, was at least idle and pedantic'.[24]

There was another class of people Cournot thought, who greatl contributed to the prejudice against the use of mathematical analysis These were the authors, like Canard, who had already used thi method. In a sweeping generalisation Cournot rejects all attempts which had already been made, as having approached the subject from a false point of view. That he is not justified in the criticism he made i evident from what we have already said about earlier contributions t mathematical economics; that he was ignorant of such contribution as those of Beccaria, Vasco, Lang and Thünen is evident from thi passage of his preface: 'The attempts which have been made in thi direction have remained very little known, and I have been able t learn only the titles of them, except one, *Les Principes de l'Économi Politique*, by *Canard*, a small work published in the year X (of th French Republic, A.D. 1801) and crowned by the *Institut*.'[25]

But although Cournot believes that mathematical analysis can b usefully applied to economic theory[26], he does not appear to hav reached the point of maintaining that such analysis is indispensabl for economic reasoning. It is true that when speaking of authors lik Ricardo, Cournot says that they 'have not been able to avoid algebra and have only disguised it under arithmetical calculations of tiresom length'[27] but his action in stripping his *Principes de la Théorie de Richesses* (1863) of all mathematics and in publishing the *Revu Sommaire* in the form it has appeared at a time when L. Walras ha already spoken so highly of the contribution of the *Recherches*, poin clearly towards the view that Cournot considered the role of mathe matics as subsidiary.

(ii) The role of pure theory

Closely connected with Cournot's views on the use of mathematics i economic analysis are his conception of pure theory and his views o the role which pure theory has to play in the development of th science of economics.

The science of wealth must be cultivated for its own sake irres pective of any practical considerations. Impassioned polemics, pre ferences for any system or party and moral judgments do not fall within the scope of such a theory. 'Our part', he writes[28], 'is to observe, and not to criticise, the irresistible laws of nature.'

Pure theory must, he believes, be based on one or more fundamental ideas which are definite and invariable. Only such ideas are 'susceptible of rigorous treatment in combinations'[29] and 'can become the object of theoretical deductions'.[30]

The relations of complex reality must be reduced to an abstraction of a number of fixed terms[31], to a model as we may say today.

The results derived from pure theory, should be tested in the light of experience. Though his *Recherches* is a treatise of pure theory, Cournot often goes out of his way to suggest possible applications of statistical methods to his results and in some cases, he even simplifies these results to facilitate such application.

(iii) Particular methods used

In his application of mathematical analysis Cournot uses extensively the theory of arbitrary functions and illustrates his argument by diagrammatic representations and analogies from the fields of astronomy, mechanics and hydrostatics.

By applying the probability law of great numbers, Cournot is able to assume that his functions are continuous, they do not pass, that is, suddenly from one value to another but take in passing all intermediate values[32]. This assumed continuity of the function enables him to assume that within short ranges and as an approximation, his functions are linear, and to use extensively Taylor's theorem for the expansion of a function by assuming at the same time that squares and higher powers of a small increment may be ignored.[33]

Linear models are, thus, very useful as a first approximation because they simplify the analytical expressions of the laws which govern the movement of economic quantities.[34]

Cournot applies extensively the differential calculus to determine maximum and minimum values of various economic quantities. This is the first treatise in economics that the calculus is applied consistently and systematically in all stages of the argument. The *Recherches* has at the same time the distinction of being the first treatise where diagrams have been used extensively as an accepted form of exposition of economic argument. Practically nothing, which had been published before Cournot's book, can equal his treatment in these fields.

9.4.   THE PURE THEORY OF PRICE

Cournot deals mainly with three subjects in his *Recherches sur les principes mathématiques de la théorie des richesses*. These are the pure theory of price, the theory of the rates of exchange and international trade and his theory of Social Income.

His pure theory of price may be divided into two sections. The first section, which we shall examine here, sets forth Cournot's ideas about the nature of value and price and their changes and elaborates what Cournot has called the law of demand. The second section, with which we shall deal immediately after the first section, examines the problems connected with price determination under different market forms, where competition is restricted.

(i) Value and price

Cournot, as we have already seen, believes that abstract and invariable ideas must provide the foundations of pure theory: Such an idea for the theory of economics is, he thinks, the idea of wealth ('richesses'), if it is identified with the abstract idea of value in exchange. The idea, therefore, must be completely detached from considerations of time, place and forms of society or market structure; it would mean what one would get in exchange in an ideal state, where there would be no friction to overcome and exchange could be effected instantaneously and at will. For the same reasons the abstract idea of exchange must be detached from personal considerations and must not be identified with utility, for utility is variable according to the individual and therefore unsuitable as a foundation of pure theory.[35]

Such a value in exchange could however exist only as an idea. What we get in exchange in actual life is bound to be affected by the peculiar circumstances which characterise the real situation. 'In the act of exchange,' Cournot writes[36], 'as in the transmission of power by machinery, there is friction to be overcome, losses which must be borne, and limits which cannot be exceeded. The proprietor of a great forest is only rich on condition of managing his lumbering with prudence, and of not glutting the market with his lumber; the owner of a valuable picture gallery may spend his life in the vain attempt to find purchasers.'

He does not believe, however, that his theory based on such an ideal conception of wealth is an idle speculation, because this idea is not 'too far from corresponding with the actual objects which make up wealth in the existing social status'[37] and, in fact, he says 'the influence of a progressive civilization constantly tends to bring actual and variable relations nearer and nearer to the absolute relation, which we attain to from abstract considerations'.[38]

The very idea, however, of value in exchange implies the necessity of comparison between two things; the idea of value is a relative one and to seek for absolute values is to fall into a logical contradiction.[39] There can be absolute changes in one or both of the terms making up the ratio of value and these, once accomplished, will affect the value of the ratio but the idea of an absolute *change* in one of the terms of the ratio must be clearly distinguished from the idea of the ratio itself. 'There are no absolute values, but there are movements of absolute rise and fall in values.'[40]

The introduction of a common measure enables all these values to be expressed in terms of this common measure; all the ratios expressing values now have a common denominator and it is easy to change this standard of value to a different one by simple multiplication. Thus if:[41]

$$P_1, P_2, P_3, \text{ etc.,}$$

be the values of certain articles, with reference to a gram of silver and the standard of value is changed to a myriagram of wheat, where a is the price of the myriagram of wheat in terms of a gram of silver, the values of the above articles will now be given by

$$\frac{1}{a} P_1, \frac{1}{a} P_2, \frac{1}{a} P_3 \text{ etc.}$$

If the common denominator of all values remains unchanged, it will be reasonable to believe that all changes in value are due to changes in the numerators of the ratios. Thus if monetary metals did not experience absolute variation at all in their value, we would be in a position to study the variations in the various values as a result of absolute variations in the values of the goods themselves. But the precious metals, though they in ordinary circumstances and in the short run experience only slight variations, do not fulfil the necessary conditions of perfect fixity. Cournot however thinks that, 'if no article exists having the necessary conditions for perfect fixity, we can and ought to imagine one, which, to be sure, will only have an abstract existence'[42] in the same way as astronomers imagine a mean sun. Cournot has thus conceived the idea of a fixed accounting unit of value as an entirely separate idea from that of the money circulating and its functions. By doing this, he has been able in all his later developments to ignore the role of money.[43]

(ii) The law of demand[44]

The determination of price is the result of the play of the forces of supply and demand. Of these two, Cournot believed that it was demand which played the essential part; 'supply is the necessary counterpart of demand and consequently the accessory fact'.[45] That is why, while he devotes a whole chapter (chapter IV) to the discussion of demand, his discussion of supply is hidden away as a discussion of costs in the chapter on Monopoly.

Cournot is the author who for the first time put in clear mathematical terms the notion that, ceteris paribus, quantity demanded and price are functionally related.

It was customary to say, and indeed much of the energy of the Italian mathematical School had been devoted to this, that 'the price of goods is in the inverse ratio of the quantity offered, and in the direct ratio of the quantity demanded'. This was in Cournot's estimation an absurd principle, for the fact 'in general, that 100 units of an article have been sold at 20 francs is no reason that 200 units would sell at 10 francs in the same lapse of time and under the same circumstances'[46].

The quantity demanded refers always to a definite price and their relation may be generally written as

$$D = F(p)$$

where D indicates the sales or demand of a commodity during a given period, which Cournot takes as a year[47], in a given market[48], and p the average price of the same commodity during the year. In this case he considers price as the independent variable, but later in the treatment of oligopoly he gives the form of the function as $p = f(D)$ when the quantity becomes the independent variable.

Cournot makes it clear that his demand function depends on 'the *ceteris paribus* condition' and that this is only an approximation to the ideal treatment of general equilibrium, a treatment which he thinks is beyond the powers of mathematical analysis. 'We have studied,' writes in a later section of his book[49], 'how, for each commodity by itself, the law of demand, in connection with the conditions of production of that commodity, determines the price of it and regulates the incomes of its producers. We *considered as given and invariable the prices of other commodities* and *the incomes of other producers*; but in reality *the economic system is a whole of which all the parts are connected and react on each other.'* And he adds[50]: 'It seems as if, for a complete and rigorous solution of the problems relative to some parts of the economic system, it were indispensable to take the entire system into consideration. But this would surpass the powers of mathematical analysis and of our practical methods of calculation, even if the values of all the constants could be assigned to them numerically.'

Cournot's demand function is the total demand function. Although he does not expressly show how such a function could be built up by summing the individual demand functions, he points the way towards this by discussing the factors on which the form of the function depends. These factors are the utility of the article, the nature of its services, the habits and customs of the people, the average wealth, the scale on which wealth is distributed[51] and the prices of other commodities.

Statistical observation may furnish 'the means of drawing up between proper limits a table of the corresponding values of D and p; after which, by the well-known methods of interpolation or by graphic processes, an empiric formula or curve can be made to represent the function in question'.[52] Such a table will generally show that 'the sales or the demand generally . . . increases when the price decreases'.[53] But though this is the rule, there are objects where 'a great fall in price would almost annihilate the demand'.[54] These are 'objects of whim and luxury which are only desirable on account of their rarity and of the high price which is the consequence thereof'.[55]

Cournot has, moreover, in addition to the concept of the downward sloping demand curve and its exceptions, developed the concept of the elasticity of demand, without actually giving it this name. The demand of an article might be in the inverse ratio of the price; but this is an exceptional case. Usually and especially in connection with most manufactured products the demand is elastic or as he puts it 'it increases or decreases in much more rapid proportion'.[56] In other cases demand is less elastic 'which appears (a very singular thing) to be equally applicable both to the most necessary things and the most superfluous'.

Cournot makes another assumption, which, as we have seen, recurs in his mathematical treatment; this is that of the continuity of the demand function, from which it follows that there may be a linear approximation to it within short ranges.[57]

Such an assumption, he feels, is legitimate to make when there is a great number of consumers. 'The wider the market extends, and the more the combinations of needs, of fortunes, or even of caprices, are varied among consumers, the closer the function F(p) will come to varying with p in a continuous manner. However, little may be the variation of p, there will be some consumers so placed that the slight rise or fall of the article will affect their consumptions, and will lead them to deprive themselves in some way or to reduce their manufacturing output, or to substitute something else for the article that has grown dearer.'[58]

The demand curve is not only downward sloping and continuous; as the price in the function F(p) has been taken to mean the average price during a year, the curve of F(p) is 'in itself an average of all the curves which would represent this function at different times of the year'.[59]

Thus the demand curve has in general the form *anb* in the following Figure 9.1:[60]

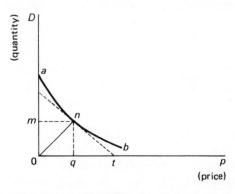

FIG. 9.1

The total revenue pF(p), is represented by rectangles under *anb* such as *omnq*, corresponding to the various prices.

There are two limits when $p = 0$ and when p becomes infinite[61]. Between these two limits there is a maximum revenue corresponding to a certain price, which may be found if[62]

(1) $$\frac{dp\mathrm{F}(p)}{dp} = 0$$

or by denoting by F' the differential co-efficient of function F

(2) $$\mathrm{F}(p) + p\mathrm{F}'(p) = 0$$

The price *oq* which maximises total revenue is found from Figure 9.1 at such a point *n* on the curve *anb*, such as *on* = *nt*, where *nt* is the portion of the tangent to the curve at the point *n*, which lies between *n* and the abscissa.[63]

Cournot points out that equation (2) might indicate either a maximum or a minimum.[64]

The additional condition for maximisation is

(3) $$2F'(p) + pF''(p) < 0$$

If on the contrary

(3a) $2F'(p) + pF''(p) > 0$, then revenue will be at a minimum.

In his discussion of the problem of maximisation of the total revenue, Cournot further elaborate his concept of the elasticity of demand. For, he says, we could examine by statistical observation what happens to the total revenue $pD = pF(p)$, if there is a small change in price.

If the price becomes $p + \triangle p$, where $\triangle p$ is a small fraction of p, the annual consumption would become $D - \triangle D$. Then if[65]

(4) $$\frac{\triangle D}{\triangle p} < \frac{D}{p},$$

the increase in price will *increase* the total revenue $pF(p)$; in other words, we would say today that demand is inelastic.

The contrary would happen if

(5) $$\frac{\triangle D}{\triangle p} > \frac{D}{p}$$

when total revenue would *decrease* as a result of a rise in price and demand would be elastic.

Under his particular conditions, the maximum revenue is derived when elasticity is equal to unity or

$\frac{\triangle D}{\triangle p} = \frac{D}{p}$, which is easily comparable with the result from equation

(2), remembering that $\frac{\triangle D}{\triangle p}$ is positive as is $-F'(p)$.

It is, therefore, according to Cournot, of importance to know whether 'the two values p and $p + \triangle p$ (assuming $\triangle p$ to be a small fraction of p) fall above or below the value which makes the product under consideration a maximum'.

Cournot thinks that commercial statistics should separate economically important goods into two categories in accordance with their demand elasticity or, as he puts it, 'according as their current prices are above or below the value which makes a maximum of $p\mathrm{F}(p)$'.[66]

The above is a further proof of the greatness of Cournot; *long before Marshall himself, he fully elaborated the concept of the Marshallian elasticity of demand*[67].

Cournot points out that $p\mathrm{F}(p)$ might have several maxima and pass through minimum values between, depending on the shape of the demand curve. He proves that whenever $\mathrm{F}''(p)$ is negative or when the curve $D = \mathrm{F}(p)$ 'turns its concave side to the axis of the abscissas, it is impossible that there should be a minimum, or more than a maximum. In the contrary case, the existence of several maxima or minima is not proved to be impossible'.[68]

On this question, however, Cournot thinks that in actual practice, it is improbable that the function $p\mathrm{F}(p)$ will present such a problem 'inside of the limits between which the value of p can vary'.[3] The question therefore is always whether within the limits of the oscillation of p, 'the function $p\mathrm{F}(p)$ is increasing or decreasing for increasing values of p'.[69]

(iii) The conditions of supply

Cournot's discussion of the costs of production and their relation with the supply of a commodity does not occupy a separate chapter. It is spread throughout his discussion of the determination of price under different market forms.

The cost of production is a function of the quantity; and the general form $\varphi(D)$ denotes[70] the total cost of producing a quantity D.

By differentiating this function in respect of D, we get

$$(1) \qquad \frac{\mathrm{d}[\varphi(D)]}{\mathrm{d}D} = \varphi'(D)$$

This shows the way in which total cost changes in response to a very shall change in the quantity produced and is what will be later called the *marginal cost*. It is in terms of this cost that Cournot carries out the discussion.

The total cost is an increasing function of the quantity produced for 'it would be absurd that the *absolute* expense of production should decrease as production increases'.[71] This means that though the marginal cost $\varphi'(D)$ may be decreasing or increasing in response to D, it must always be positive.

He further points out[72] that the marginal cost must always be smaller than price, i.e.

(2)
$$p > \frac{d[\varphi(D)]}{dD}$$

(3) $pdD > d[\varphi(D)]$, where pdD is the increase in gross receipts and $d[\varphi(D)]$ is the increase in costs. 'Whatever', he writes[73], 'may be the abundance of the source of production, the producer will always stop when the increase in expense exceeds the increase in receipts.' This last sentence he elaborates later in the discussion of free competition, where the *condition of equilibrium for each producer is that his marginal cost will be equal to the price*[74] or

(4) $p = \varphi'_k(D_k)$, where p is the price and $\varphi'_k(D_k)$ indicates the marginal cost of each individual producer (k) corresponding to a quantity produced, D_k.

The function $\varphi'(D)$ may be increasing or decreasing or constant; this is another way of saying that returns are diminishing, increasing or constant[75] and Cournot believes that what actually happens to marginal costs is closely linked with 'the nature of the producing forces and of the articles produced'.[76]

In the case of agriculture and mining, marginal cost increases with D increasing. 'This comes from better organization of the work, from discounts on the price of raw materials in large purchases, and finally from the reduction of what is known to producers as *general expense*.'[77] But even in this case returns may become diminishing beyond a certain limit through higher prices for raw materials and labour.[78]

In the case of agriculture and mining marginal cost increases with D; siding with Ricardo, Cournot considers that it is this fact which is the reason of agricultural rent even under conditions which cause 'between producers a competition which can be considered as un-limited'.[79]

But though he considers that diminishing returns will, even under conditions of free competition, give rise to the phenomenon of rent, he goes further and says that even under increasing returns this pheno-menon will arise but only provided that there is restriction in supply. He writes[80]

Investments made under the condition that as D increases, $\varphi'(D)$

decreases, can only yield a net income or a *rent* in the case of a monopoly properly so-called, or of a competition sufficiently limited to allow the effects of a monopoly collectively maintained to be still perceptible.

Thus Cournot, apart from his clear formulations of the cost curve and the concept of marginal cost, has been able to generalise the idea of rent.[81]

In addition to the cases of increasing and decreasing marginal cost, Cournot visualises two more cases, the first where the cost is 'constantly proportional to the production'[82] and marginal cost is a constant, so that

(5) $\varphi'(D) = g$ where g is constant,

and the case where the total cost is constant and marginal cost zero, and therefore

(6) $\varphi'(D) = 0$

This would be the case with a theatrical production where the cost remains the same irrespective of the number of tickets sold.[83]

(iv) The static equilibrium price under free competition

We have already mentioned that, for Cournot, the equilibrium production for each individual producer, under conditions of what he calls 'unlimited competition', is where his marginal cost is equal to the price. Thus for any given price p, the quantities $D_1, D_2 \ldots D_n$ produced by the first, second etc. producers respectively, are such that[84]

for the first producer $p = \varphi'_1(D_1)$
for the second $p = \varphi'_2(D_2)$
                 . . . .
for the nth $p = \varphi'_n(D_n)$ where the marginal costs
                                           $\varphi'_k(D_k)$ are assumed to
                                           be increasing.[85]

Each individual quantity is therefore a function of price and the total quantity offered $D_1 + D_2 + \ldots + D_n$ is also a function of the price. We may therefore write in general

(2) $D_1 + D_2 + \ldots + D_n = W(p)$ which gives us our total supply function, expressing the quantity that would be offered at any assigned price.[86]

The total demand function is as we have already seen (3) $D = F(p)$ and the *condition of equilibrium is that the total quantity demanded should be equal to the total quantity supplied*[87] and therefore

$$(4) \qquad W(p) = F(p)$$

Cournot proceeds to plot the two curves[88], and it can be immediately seen that the equilibrium price and quantity given by the solution of equation (4) are those provided by the intersection of the traditional supply and demand curves. The figure is reproduced here as Figure 9.2.

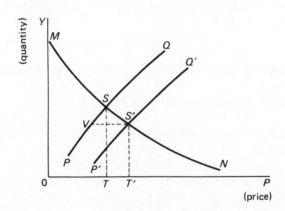

FIG. 9.2.

MN is the demand curve, of which the equation is $y = F(p)$, 'a curve of which the characteristic feature is that its tangent always makes an obtuse angle with the positive axis of abscissas, p',[89] which in other words is downward sloping. PQ is the supply curve of which the equation is $y = W(p)$, a curve which is upward sloping.[90] The intersection of the two curves provides the equilibrium OT, or what Cournot calls the root of equation $F(p) = W(p)$.

Curve $P'Q'$ shows how the supply curve would shift after the imposition of a specific tax equal to VS'. The equilibrium price will now be OT' and though this is greater than OT, the increase in price TT', will be, owing to the shape of the demand curve, smaller than the increase in cost VS'. 'In all cases', he concludes, 'the rise in price will be less than the increase in costs.'[91]

One cannot but admire the way in which Cournot has approached and solved this problem; there is little that modern analysis of price determination under free competition and static conditions of partial equilibrium, can add or has added to his performance.

Indeed it was the analysis of Cournot and his definition of Unlimited Competition as 'the state of affairs in which no single producer is able to influence appreciably the prices of the market', which enabled, as Hicks observed, 'Walras and Marshall to overcome the difficulties which had baffled Jevons, those difficulties which arise from differences in the wants of different buyers of a particular commodity. In the hands of Walras, this conception of perfect competition was converted into a special technique of using prices as economic parameters. Although of course this technique was used by Marshall as well, its very consistent employment is highly characteristic of Walras' work'.[92]

9.5 COURNOT AND THE PURE THEORY OF MONOPOLY

(i) The theory of monopoly before Cournot.[93]

Monopoly has occupied authors since early times. It is not our aim to deal extensively with these authors but only to provide some highlights. Aristotle deals with two cases in his *Politics*[94] and the Scholastic authors in the middle ages concentrated their attention on it in connection with their preoccupation with the 'just price'.[95] All condemn monopoly as iniquitous and monopoly price as an unjust price.

Of interest is the observation of Nicole Oresme that the price of monopolised salt could be set by the prince arbitrarily at any level he likes.[96] C. Summenhart also gave in 1500 an interesting classification of monopolies.[97]

Joannes Maior in his treatment of monopoly links price with quality and points out that if there is to be price uniformity there must be quality uniformity. Finally D. Bañez pointed out that the monopolist is obliged by the fact that he owns a large quantity to dispose of it, but in such a case the price does not depend on him but on what the buyers are willing to pay to take the quantity off his hands.[98]

The humanists and jurists also condemned monopolies[99] and J.J. Becher tried to classify market forms according to the degree of competition.[100]

The English pamphleteers argued vehemently on the definition of monopoly and its merits[101] and the idea is extended by some to cover, as indeed it had been done by some of the scholastic authors, the case where not one but few sellers can control the price.

Galiani argues that the monopoly price is not at the discretion of the monopolist. It is a joint result of the desires of the buyer and of the valuation of the seller.[102] The other Italian authors of the 18th century had little to add to the theory of monopoly and the same is true of the physiocrats.

Condorcet also deals with the possibility of collusive practices in monopoly conditions and Condillac points out that the aim of the monopolist is to maximise his benefit.[103] The most original contribution and a notable exception to the dreary repetition of the established ideas is Canard's view, already described, that, under a monopoly, profits would be at a maximum leading to maximum profits.

The Classical School is no exception. No significant contribution to the theory of monopoly has been made by them. They simply stress the view that the monopolist is in a position to impose the highest price.[104]

(ii) Cournot's theory of monopoly

Such was the state of the theory of monopoly until the appearance of Cournot's *Recherches*. With the exception of Canard who tried to apply his own particular analytical apparatus to the problem of price determination under monopoly conditions, there was practically no analysis of the problem.

Cournot dealt with the problem in chapter v of his *Recherches*. His analysis, as we shall show, has been so successful that very little has been added to the pure theory of monopoly even since.

We have already seen from the section on 'The law of demand' that Cournot had given as the condition of maximizing revenue, where there are no costs:

$$(1) \qquad \frac{\mathrm{d}p\mathrm{F}(p)}{\mathrm{d}p} = 0 \quad \text{which leads to}$$

$$(2) \qquad \mathrm{F}(p) + p\mathrm{F}'(p) = 0$$

If there is a monopoly, as in the case of the proprietor of a mineral spring with exclusive salutary properties,[105] he will seek to maximise his revenue by applying (2) above which gives as the maximising price

$$(3) \qquad p = \frac{\mathrm{F}(p)}{-\mathrm{F}'(p)}$$

and the total revenue of the monopolist is

$$(4) \qquad\qquad pF(p) = \frac{F(p)^2}{-F'(p)}$$

Cournot points out that, if the quantity which would correspond to the maximising price it is not possible to be forthcoming, because only a lesser quantity can be produced, then only this quantity will be offered. We have already described in discussing the 'law of demand', how Cournot introduces a figure by which he shows how the price which maximises total revenue can be determined. This is of course the monopoly price.

Cournot uses a second figure which is more general and under which monopoly price is determined alongside the price under other market forms[106] (see Figure 9.3).

He plots the right-hand side of equation (3) on the Y axis. Under his assumptions the monopoly equilibrium is determined when $p = \dfrac{-F(p)}{F'(p)}$. This is found at the point where the curve $\dfrac{-F(p)}{F'(p)}$ is intersected by the line $y = p$, a 45° line drawn from the origin. In Cournot's figure this is line (2), while line (1) is the duopoly case, where the price is smaller 'as the result of competition is to reduce prices'.[107]

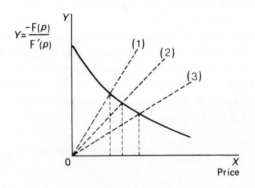

FIG. 9.3

Cournot's $\dfrac{-F(p)}{F'(p)}$, in terms of which the analysis is carried out, can be shown to be related to the modern concept of demand elasticity. For if (i) $A = \dfrac{-F'(p)}{F(p)}$ is 'the relative rate of change of the quantity demanded in response to the change in price', $\dfrac{-F(p)}{F'(p)}$ is the inverse of this, $\dfrac{1}{A}$. Under the usual definition of demand elasticity

(ii) $\eta = -\dfrac{p}{F(p)} \cdot \dfrac{dF(p)}{dp} = -\dfrac{p \cdot F'(p)}{F(p)} = pA$. From (i) we get

(iii) $\dfrac{\eta}{A} = p$, from which it follows that where $p = \dfrac{-F(p)}{F'(p)} = \dfrac{1}{A}$, $\eta = 1$. At the point, therefore, where according to Cournot, revenue is a maximum demand elasticity is equal to unity.

As already indicated, Cournot's total cost of production $\varphi(D)$ is a function of the quantity $D = F(p)$

Under monopoly, if there are costs, the net receipts to be maximised are[108] $pF(p) - \varphi(D)$ and the maximising condition is

(5) $$\frac{dpD}{dp} - \frac{d\varphi(D)}{dp} = 0$$

(5a) $$\frac{dpD}{dp} = \frac{d\varphi(D)}{dp}$$

This is the first explicit formulation that *the monopoly price is determined so as to maximise profits and this is achieved when the marginal revenue is equal to marginal costs.* But it should be pointed out that here, contrary, to the oligopoly case, Cournot's marginal analysis is made in terms of infinite changes in the price and not in the quantity.

Cournot gives equation (5) in the form[109]

(6) $$D + \frac{dD}{dp}\left(p - \frac{d\varphi(D)}{dD}\right) = 0$$

Cournot denotes the change in cost in response to a change in quantity as $\varphi'(D) = \dfrac{d\varphi(D)}{dD}$. He uses a figure similar to Figure 9.3 to show how the monopoly price can be determined when there are costs (this is Figure 9.8 below)[110].

From (6) we get

(6a) $$F(p) + F'(p)(p - \varphi'(D)) = 0$$

(6b) $$p - \varphi'(D) = -\frac{F(p)}{F'(p)}$$

The monopoly price is found (in Figure 9.8) where the curve $\dfrac{-F(p)}{F'(p)}$, denoted by MN, is cut by the curve $p - \varphi'(D)$, which he also plots as curve $P'Q'$.

Cournot points out that if $\varphi'(D) = 0$ then we have the case given by equation (2) above; and if $\varphi'(D) = g$ where g is a constant, then equation (6) becomes

$$(6c) \qquad\qquad D + \frac{dD}{dp}\{p - g\} = 0$$

Cournot discusses the effect on the monopoly price of a change in the various conditions of costs.

He also discusses the effects of taxation on the price which is established under a monopoly[111]. These results will depend on whether the tax is a fixed tax or a direct levy proportional to the income of the seller (when there will be no effect on monopoly price or quantity) or whether the tax is a specific tax on the good (when there are repercussions as this means an additional cost to the producer).

(iii) The theory of monopoly after Cournot

The theory of monopoly was developed independently by Cournot's Contemporaries Charles Ellet and J. Dupuit.

Ellet developed the idea that the monopoly price (or the toll in his case) is determined where the monopoly profit is a maximum and therefore its rate of change is zero[112]; and he showed how the price which gives a maximum profit could be determined.

Dupuit also gave a solution to the problem of monopoly price when there are no costs similar to Cournot's. This determines the maximum revenue from the fixing of the toll of a bridge[113].

But unfortunately the work of Cournot and of his contemporaries Ellet and Dupuit on monopoly price was not quickly appreciated. The only noteworthy development was Menger's treatment of monopoly on lines compatible with the Austrian Theory of Value[114].

It was only when Walras reproduced in his *Eléments d' Économie Pure* 1874 Cournot's analysis that it came to the foreground.[115]

The development of the theory thereafter is carried in terms of the analysis of Cournot. As however the authors dealing with the subject use various diagrams and curves, we could distinguish:

(a) Those who use curves of total revenue and total cost and show under what conditions, revenue will be maximised. The main representatives here are Dionysius Lardner and R. Auspitz and R. Lieben[116].

(b) Those who use average revenue and average cost curves and show under what conditions total net revenue is maximised. The main representatives here are Edgeworth and Cunynghame.[117] Of special interest is A. Marshall's use of rectangular hyperbolas to determine the monopoly price[118].

(c) Those who use marginal revenue and marginal cost curves. Precursors here include D. Lardner, A. Marshall and S. Chapman[119] but the first to trace the marginal cost and marginal revenue curves in the analysis of the problem of monopoly was T.O. Yntema[120].

It is worth noting, however, that a common characteristic of all approaches is that, apart from presentational innovations, they in reality do nothing more than reproduce Cournot's original treatment of 1838.

9.6   COURNOT AND THE THEORY OF OLIGOPOLY

(i) Early theories of oligopoly

It is a common assumption that the theory of oligopoly starts with Cournot's *Recherches sur les Principes Mathématiques de la Théorie des Richesses*. Thus E.H. Chamberlin in discussing the state of 'duopoly' theory as it appeared to him in 1924–6, writes:[121] 'The "literature" consisted in a chapter by Cournot, an article by Edgeworth, a few pages or paragraphs or even lines here and there and a few footnotes, including the inevitable one by Marshall.'

There is only an occasional reference[122] to Thomas More's use of the word 'oligopolium' in his *Utopia* (1518), where he had argued that an increase in the number of sheep might not lead to a fall in their price because, though there was not 'monopolium', as the sheep did not belong to a single person, there was an 'oligopolium' as the sheep belonged to a few rich people who could afford to wait until they got the desired price.

It is the aim of this section to show that there are other contributions to the theory of oligopoly which are earlier than Cournot's and which can be considered as precursors of certain modern theories in this field.

(a) Verri's theory of oligopoly.

Verri in his *Meditazioni Sulla Economia Politica* which, as we have seen, was published for the first time in Livorno[123] in 1771 deals with both the problem of monopoly and of oligopoly. He visualises there[124] a town where the food is in the hands of a single seller, who could offer for sale a small quantity and thus fetch a high price.

He then proceeds to ask what will happen if food were in the hands of two sellers. It is conceivable that they might make an agreement and then 'we would find ourselves in the first case',[125] the case that is of monopoly.

Verri has two versions of what will happen if there is not an agreement among the sellers. In the first editions of the 'Meditazioni', he simply says that, if a rivalry should arise between them and a struggle as to which of them 'will collect more promptly the universal commodity'[126] should ensue 'it will be seen that the offers are redoubled and that both will bring to the market a quantity sufficient for the daily consumption' with a consequent fall in price.

To the argument of Verri, G.R. Carli, his annotator, had this to say:[127] 'the two sellers of the same commodity will make offers proportional to their needs. The fall in price is in proportion to the increase in the offers; but the number of these offers is proportional to the needs of those offering and the competition or rivalry to lower the price arises from the *fear of losing* what they in turn seek'.

Verri's first version was repeated in successive editions of the *Meditazioni*. But in the edition of 1781, which was printed in Milan and reproduced in Paris in 1784, there is a further elaboration of Verri's ideas.[128] The most profitable course for the two sellers would be, he says, to divide, for the purpose of selling, the town into two equal parts. But as man always desires more, the sellers will be driven to some form of competition. 'Each will soon begin to speculate', he writes, 'through calculating how much profitable a cut in price would be, whether the portion which he would seize from his rival is enough to surpass in utility the general diminution in price.'[129]

This is a rather obscure passage and raises many questions. The first refers to the assumptions of each duopolist about his rival's behaviour. If he can hope to 'seize a portion of his rival's market', as Verri pictures him to think, he must presumably assume that, for a time at least, his rival's price will remain at a higher level than his own. That this will be only temporary and that the duopolist includes in his calculations the possibility that the rival will react by lowering the price is evident from the expression '*general* diminution in price'.

Verri assumes that such calculations will be made by both sellers; he does not, however, say whether a position of equilibrium will be reached; presumably as long as it pays each seller to undercut his rival, he will do so and equilibrium will be reached when price settles at the free competition level. Verri's approach through price adjustments is thus similar to what is described in current oligopoly theory as the 'Bertrand Case'.[130]

There is another obscure point. Verri says that each seller will undercut his rival as long as the *utility* from the increased quantity is greater than the loss of utility from the diminished price. Whether this utility is a subjective measure Verri does not say. But as 'utilitá' may mean also profit, Verri's condition may simply mean that the profit from increased sales at the new smaller price is greater than the profit from lower sales at a higher price,[131] which is another way to say that the expected new revenue is bigger than the last one.[132]

If there are more than two sellers, the share of each in the market will become proportionately smaller. 'If a third, a fourth, a fifth seller and so on present themselves in the market offering the same particular commodity, the share which each separately would be able to sell will always become smaller.'[133] As his share of sales is now smaller, 'the loss from the lowered price will always become smaller',[134] but it will be more easily offset by an extension of sales as a result of the lower price.[135] Each seller thus is expecting an increase in his revenue, if he lowers the price and 'the competition to accumulate more promptly the universal commodity thus being born, they will multiply their offers'.[136]

It has already been mentioned that Verri considers collusion among oligopolists as conceivable. But he remarks now that 'the more they increase in number, the more difficult it is for them to make an agreement',[137] and the more price will fall. This result he had anticipated in his 'Riflessioni sulle leggi vincolanti principalmente nel commercio de' grani'.[138] 'As the number of sellers increases indefinitely, it is easy', he writes there[139], 'to understand that it is with difficulty, increasing in proportion to the increase in the number of sellers, that those agreements and conspiracies which prosper among a small number of sellers, are attempted.' This is because, even if an agreement is concluded, there is always the temptation for any one seller to break it in attempting to secure a profit at the expense of the other sellers. 'A sole seller, seeking a quicker profit than his other companions, breaks promptly the conspiracy', by lowering the price of the good he sells, 'and thus inviting all buyers to deal with him rather than with the others; and because of this, there are born in the other sellers the necessity and emulation to lower their own prices'[140] in order to dispose of their goods.

(b) Giammaria Ortes and economic power

Giammaria Ortes, who as we have seen, was one of the early contributors to mathematical economics,[141] was another early contributor to the theory of oligopoly. In his *Calcolo sopra il valore delle opinioni umane* (1757)[142] he contributes a theory of economic conflict in terms of power, which may be applicable to both the cases of oligopoly and bilateral monopoly.[143]

Ortes starts from the assumption that each man has a certain power at his disposal and that he is also afraid of other men's power. This fear is the greater the smaller he conceives his power to be in comparison to that of his rivals. The power of every individual is used in society to ensure the satisfaction of his needs and the final result of an individual action will depend on the comparative power of the individual. 'If there are two people trading', he writes,[144] 'the more powerful will subdue the weaker and will become the sole arbiter of the above named choice.' If there are three people, the result will depend on whether a combination of the forces of the two is smaller, equal or greater than the force of the third. If any two of them together are stronger than the third, each of them will be afraid of the other two; but if the force of one is equal to the force of the other two together, then he can be considered as the more powerful, and even more so when his power is greater than the others' combined power.[145] Similar calculations are made if there are four or five people.

If, however, there is a great number of people, every man, no matter how more powerful than another he is, when they are compared together, 'will have equal power to the other, when both are compared to the united force of all'.[146] In such a case, 'as all are equally powerful and equally afraid, no one will oppose the other', and the result will be indeterminate.

(c) Melchiorre Gioja's theory of collusion.

Gioja in his *Nuovo Prospetto delle Scienze Economiche*, took up Verri's theory of oligopoly and further extended it.[147]

Gioja considers that when there are only two or three sellers it is not simply conceivable but it is the natural thing that they will 'agree together to impose the law on the buyers'. The causes for this tendency are principally the following 'and not the laws and regulations as Smith, Beccaria and the French economists preached':[148]

1. The common interest of sellers of the same good, 'interest which becomes bigger in proportion to the diminution of their numbers'.[149]
2. The odiousness with which the merchant, 'who breaks off from the league to sell at a lower price than the others', is treated.[150]
3. The fear of merchants that their selling at a lower price may be interpreted as a sign of financial weakness.

Gioja, however, considers that, in spite of the above forces making for collusion, it is conceivable that someone from the members of the coalition may start making speculations 'whether it is advisable to free himself from the coalition and lower a little the price in order to attract to himself all buyers and be recompensed for the loss produced by the lowering of price, with the gain procured by the bigger sales'.[151] This is exactly Verri's argument; the only difference is that Verri's vague 'utility' has been replaced with the more precise terms 'loss' and 'gain'.

If the seller decides that it will pay him to break off the coalition and lowers his price, he will spread, Gioja continues, among the other sellers 'the fear that they will be unable to sell, fear which forces them to lower the prices in order to attract to themselves a part of the customers'. The greater the number of sellers, the more difficult it is for collusive agreements to prosper and Gioja attempts to classify the forces working against collusion as: (a) the ideas, opinions and sentiments of each seller; (b) the fear of being unable to sell or of being too late in selling; and (c) the different needs which force each seller to sell.[152]

Gioja draws attention to the wide existence of oligopolistic practices. He enumerates the following manifestations 'of the tendency of sellers to restrict themselves into a small number':[153]

1. The reluctance to accept apprentices and to communicate scientific secrets.
2. The opposition to the entry of new enterprises.
3. The collusive projects which heads of businesses make whenever they meet together.
4. The laws directed against the foreigners.[154]

(ii) The oligopoly theory of Cournot

(a) Duopoly equilibrium where there are no costs

Cournot gives to chatper VII of the *Recherches*, in which he discusses the theory of oligopoly, the title 'Of the competition of producers'.

It has already been mentioned that Cournot, in order to illustrate the case of monopoly had imagined a unique proprietor of a mineral spring. He now imagines two owners of two springs, 'of which the qualities are identical, and which, on account of their similar positions, supply the same market in competition'.[155]

As the product is not differentiated and sells in the same market, there can be but one price. As we have seen, Cournot had defined the quantity demanded, D, as a function of its price p. Inversely one can define p as a function of the quantity demanded, so that

$$p = f(D)$$

The total quantity of sales D will be made up of the separate quantities sold by the two producers. Thus if D_1 and D_2 are the two quantities produced by the two sellers respectively, we shall have

(1) $$D = D_1 + D_2$$

If neither of the producers has any costs, the net revenue of the first will be his sales at the current price, that is, pD_1 and the net revenue of the second will be pD_2. As $p = f(D)$, and given (1) above, the net revenue of the first will be

(2) $$pD_1 = D_1 f(D_1 + D_2)$$

and that of the second will be

(3) $$pD_2 = D_2 f(D_1 + D_2)$$

Cournot makes now two crucial assumptions:

The first is that there is no collusion between the sellers. '*Each of them independently* will seek to make this income as large as possible.'[156] This is essential, 'for if they should come to an agreement so as to obtain for each the greatest possible income, the results would be entirely different, and would not differ, so far as consumers are concerned, from those obtained in treating of a monopoly'.[157]

It is, however, the second assumption which is of the most crucial importance. The assumption is that either of the sellers seeks to maximise his revenue by assuming that his *rival's quantity will remain unchanged.*[158] 'Proprietor (1) can have no direct influence on the determination of D_2: all he can do, when D_2 has been determined by proprietor (2), is to choose for D_1 the value which is best for him'.[159] This last sentence has led many to the conclusion that it is the essence of the theory of Cournot that oligopolists act through quantity adjustments. But Cournot, having given the function $p = f(D) = f(D_1 + D_2)$, could not but be aware that, given the rival's quantity D_2, there was a quantity D_1 and a corresponding market price p which would maximise A's revenue. Of course there can be only one price in the market, but A might by announcing the price, which would maximise his revenue on the assumption that the rival's quantity would remain constant, force his rival to accept this price.[160] That Cournot did not exclude price adjustments is evident from this passage which immediately follows the passage already quoted.[161] 'This he will be able to accomplish by properly *adjusting his price*, except as proprietor (2), who, seeing himself forced to accept this price and this value of D, may adopt a new value for D_2, more favourable to his interest than the preceding one.'

The confusion arose from the fact that in the analytical demonstration Cournot chose to differentiate with respect to D_1, and D_2. Thus the first's revenue will be maximised, when D_2 is assumed constant, by

(4) $\quad \dfrac{d(D_1 p)}{dD_1} = p + D_1 f'(D) = 0$ which may be written as[162]

(4a) $\qquad\qquad f(D_1 + D_2) + D_1 f'(D_1 + D_2) = 0$

Similarly the second seller's revenue will be a maximum, for constant D_1, when

(5) $\dfrac{d(D_2 p)}{dD_2} = p + D_2 f'(D) = 0$, which may be as written as

(5a) $\qquad\qquad f(D_1 + D_2) + D_2 f'(D_1 + D_2) = 0$

Equations (4a) and (5a) form a system of equations, the solution of which gives

$$D_1 = D_2$$

as 'ought to be the case, as the springs are supposed to be similar and similarly situated'.[163]

The addition of (4a) and (5a) leads to the result[164]

(6) $\qquad\qquad\qquad D + 2p\,\dfrac{dD}{dp} = 0$

As $D = F(p)$ and $\dfrac{\mathrm{d}D}{\mathrm{d}p} = F'(p)$, the solution of (6) in respect of p gives

$$(6a) \qquad\qquad p = \frac{F(p)}{-2F'(p)}$$

Cournot arrives at the same result by using a graphical illustration. Equation (4) above shows the quantity of the first producer which maximises his revenue, when the quantity of his competitor is given. For every given rival quantity there corresponds a quantity D_1 which maximises the first seller's revenue. The locus of all points, which show the optimum values of D_1 for given values of D_2, is curve $m_1 n_1$ which is the plot of equation (4) above. Similarly the plot of equation (5) shows the optimum values of D_2 for the second seller, corresponding to given values of D_1, and is shown as curve $m_2 n_2$ in the following reproduction of Cournot's figure (Figure 9.4).[165]

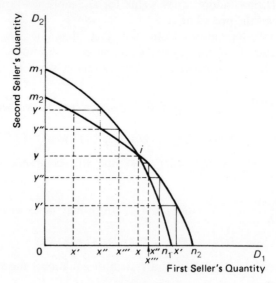

FIG. 9.4

It is, of course, obvious that the intersection of the two curves, will provide the solution and furnish the equilibrium quantities $D_1 = x$ and $D_2 = y$. But further than this, Cournot discusses whether the equilibrium will be stable by using dynamic process analysis.

'If proprietor (1)', he writes[166], 'should adopt for D_1 a value represented by ox', proprietor (2) would adopt for D_2 the value oy', which, for the supposed value of D_1, would give him the greatest profit.' But this would lead (1) to adopt for D_1, the value ox'', which forces (2) to adopt oy'' and so forth, until the equilibrium is reached at the point of intersection i; symmetrical results are obtained if one started from a value ox' on the other side of point i. Thus, says Cournot,[167] 'the state of equilibrium corresponding to the system of values ox and oy is therefore *stable*; i.e. if either of the producers, misled as to his true interest, leaves it temporarily, he will be brought back to it by a series of reactions, constantly declining in amplitude, and of which the dotted lines of the figure give a representation by their arrangement in steps'. We have already seen that other authors had used dynamic analysis,[168] but Cournot is the first to have demonstrated dynamic stability so clearly and, as far as we know, to have used the term 'stable' in this context.

But the stability of equilibrium depends on the condition that $om_1 > om_2$ and $on_2 > on_1$. For Cournot demonstrates that the opposite,[169] where $om_2 > om_1$ and $on_1 > on_2$, though leading to an intersection of the two curves, is an unstable equilibrium, as any deviation from it leads to reactions, which take the quantities further and further away from the point of equilibrium.

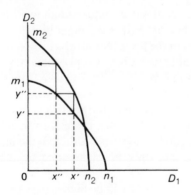

Fig. 9.5

Thus in the Figure 9.5 $m_1 n_1$ is the first seller's reaction curve and $m_2 n_2$ that of the second. If (1) fixes his quantity at ox', the second's best quantity is oy'', which will in turn force (1) to adopt ox'', which is further then ox' from the equilibrium quantity and so on.

Cournot proves that it is the first set of conditions and the first of these two diagrams which hold in his own version of duopoly.[170]

(b) The comparison between monopoly and duopoly results

We have already seen that, in the case of monopoly, Cournot had
given the equation, determining the monopoly price when there were
no costs, as:

(7) $F(p) + pF'(p) = 0$

Equation (6), which determines the equilibrium price for similar
conditions of duopoly, can be written as:

(8) $F(p) + 2pF'(p) = 0$

As it is only the price, as given by equation (7), which renders
revenue a maximum, it follows that the total revenue, when price is
determined by equation (8) is smaller. This latter total revenue is
shared equally by the two sellers because, as we have seen, the
quantities which they produce in equilibrium are equal. The share
therefore of each seller under dupoly is smaller than what would have
been, 'if the two proprietors had come to an understanding'[171] to
impose the monopoly price and share the resultant greater revenue
equally.

But no producer, without an understanding with his rival, can fix
the quantity of his at half the quantity which would produce
maximum revenue, in the hope that his rival will do the same. For then
'the other will be able to fix his own production at a higher or lower
rate *with a temporary benefit*'.[172] Of course, this will force the first
producer to react, thus bringing about a whole chain of reactions,
which will take them farther and farther from the monopoly quantity.
The condition of monopoly, when there are two sellers, is not therefore 'one of stable equilibrium; and, although the most favourable for
both producers, it can only be maintained by means of a formal
engagement'.[173]

The price under monopoly will be higher than the equilibrium price
under duopoly. For from (7) we get

(7a) $p = \dfrac{F(p)}{-F'(p)}$

while from (8) we have

(8a) $2p = \dfrac{F(p)}{-F'(p)}$

Cournot assumes that $y = -\dfrac{F(p)}{F'(p)}$ can be plotted[174] for every real and positive value of p. As we have already explained in the section on monopoly, the monopoly price will be found where $y = p$; the price under duopoly will be found where $y = 2p$. While therefore the monopoly price will be found to correspond to the intersection of y by a 45° line, drawn from the origin, the duopoly price will be found where in Figure 9.6 the line $y = 2p$, drawn from the origin, meets the curve y. It can be seen that the monopoly price p, is bigger than the price under duopoly, p''.

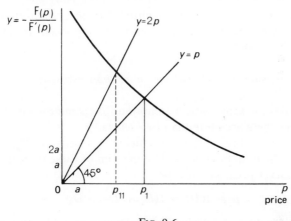

FIG. 9.6

(c) The determination of duopoly equilibrium when there are costs

The extension of the analysis from the case of no costs to that of costs is quite straightforward and follows the same lines as in the treatment of monopoly.

The cost of each producer is assumed as a function of his quantity. Thus if φ_1' (D_1) and φ_2' (D_2) are their respective marginal costs, the equation which maximises the first's net revenue $p_1D_1 - \varphi_1(D_1)$, on the assumption that D_2 is constant, is

(9) $$f(D) + D_1f'(D) - \varphi_1'(D_1) = 0$$

and that of the second, on the assumption that D_1 is constant is

(10) $$f(D) + D_2f'(D) - \varphi_2'(D_2) = 0$$

Equations (9) and (10) thus imply that each seller in order to *maximise his net expected revenue must equate his marginal expected revenue with his marginal cost.* Their simultaneous solution determines the values of D_1 and D_2 in equilibrium.

If (10) is subtracted from (9) we get

(11) $$D_1 - D_2 = \frac{1}{f'(D)} [\varphi'_1(D_1) - \varphi'_2(D_2)]$$

As $f'(D)$ is essentially negative, we have[175]

$$D_1 > D_2 \text{ when } \varphi_2'(D_2) > \varphi_1'(D_1) \text{ and vice versa.}$$

This means that the *producer with the smaller marginal cost will in equilibrium produce a higher quantity than the producer with the higher marginal cost.*[176] This is another important result which Cournot clearly points out.

(d) The extension of the theory to more than two sellers

Cournot uses the same basic assumptions to extend the discussion to cases where there are more than two sellers.[177]

If there are three sellers producing respectively D_1, D_2, D_3 quantities, the total quantity will be the sum of these three quantities and the market price will now be

$$p = f(D) = f(D_1 + D_2 + D_3)$$

If there are no costs, each will seek to maximise his revenue, pD_1, pD_2, pD_3 on the assumption that the *sales of the other two will remain unchanged.*

The quantities which will be produced in equilibrium are determined by the conditions

$$\frac{dpD_1}{dD_1} = 0, \frac{dpD_2}{dD_2} = 0, \frac{dpD_3}{dD_3} = 0$$

which give the following system of equations:

(12)
$$\begin{aligned}
f(D) + D_1f'(D) &= 0 \\
f(D) + D_2f'(D) &= 0 \\
f(D) + D_3f'(D) &= 0
\end{aligned}$$

The solution of this system gives the quantities which will be produced in equilibrium by each producer. If this system is compared with the system in the case of duopoly, given by equations (4) and (5) above, we shall see that it differs from that because the additional equation $f(D) + D_3f'(D) = 0$ has been added. Had there been four sellers, the system would have been the same as (12) above, except for the fact that an additional term $f(D) + D_4f'(D) = 0$, would have been added.

The solution of (12) gives $D_1 = D_2 = D_3$. If we add together its equations, we shall find[178] instead of (6) above

$$\text{(13)} \qquad D + 3p\,\frac{\mathrm{d}D}{\mathrm{d}p} = 0$$

from which the price may be found.

Similarly if there were four sellers, we would find that in equilibrium their quantities would be equal and that

$$\text{(13a)} \qquad D + 4p\,\frac{\mathrm{d}D}{\mathrm{d}p} = 0$$

And in general where there are n sellers

$$\text{(13b)} \qquad D + np\,\frac{\mathrm{d}D}{\mathrm{d}p} = 0$$

a formula which is equally applicable where $n = 1$.

But equation (13) may be written in the form

$$\text{(14)} \qquad 3p = -\frac{F(p)}{F'(p)}$$

If we again plot[179] the curve $y = -\dfrac{F(p)}{F'(p)}$, which we have used to compare the price under monopoly and duopoly, we shall find that the price in the case of three sellers is found at the point of intersection of y by the line $y = 3p$. It can be seen that the price op'', is smaller than in the two previous cases, where the price was respectively op' and op'' (Figure 9.7).

If there are four sellers the price is found at the point where y is interested by the line $y = 4p$. This price is smaller than the price in the case of three sellers. In general it is seen that the larger the number of sellers the smaller the price[180]. And if the number of sellers is infinite the price tends to become zero, a remarkable result, as there are no costs in this case.

There finally remains for discussion the case where there are many sellers and their costs are not zero.

It has already been seen from equations (9) and (10) above that, where there are two sellers, whose respective marginal costs are

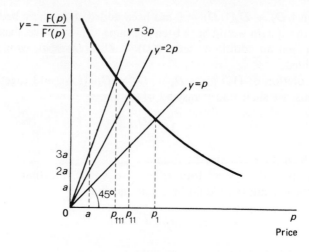

FIG. 9.7

$\varphi_1'(D_1)$ and $\varphi_2'(D_2)$, the condition that each seller seeks to equate his marginal expected revenue to his marginal cost leads to the system

$$(9) \qquad f(D) + D_1 f'(D) - \varphi_1'(D_1) = 0$$

$$(10) \qquad f(D) + D_2 f'(D) - \varphi_2'(D_2) = 0$$

If instead of two we had n sellers producing $D_1, D_2 \ldots D_n$ quantities at total costs $\varphi_1(D_1), \varphi_2(D_2), \ldots \varphi_n(D_n)$ and marginal costs $\varphi_1'(D_1), \varphi_2'(D_2), \ldots \varphi_n'(D_n)$, the above system would be replaced by a system of n equations, the simultaneous solutions of which would determine the equilibrium quantity of each producer.[181]

$$f(D) + D_1 f'(D) - \varphi_1'(D_1) = 0$$

$$f(D) + D_2 f'(D) - \varphi_2'(D_2) = 0$$

$$(15) \qquad\qquad .\qquad .\qquad .$$

$$f(D) + D_n f'(D) - \varphi_n'(D_n) = 0$$

Because of the different cost functions, the equilibrium quantities will not now be equal, but as already noticed in the case of duopoly, those producers with smaller marginal costs will produce greater quantities.[182]

If we denote by $\Sigma \varphi_n'(D_n)$ the sum of the marginal costs of the n producers, the summation of (15) gives[183]

(16) $$np + D \frac{dp}{dD} - \Sigma \, \varphi_n'(D_n) = 0$$

Multiplying (16) by $\frac{dD}{dp}$ we get equation

(16a) $$D + \frac{dD}{dp}(np - \Sigma\varphi_n'(D_n)) = 0$$

It can be seen that where the sum of marginal costs is zero, (16a) becomes identical with (13b), the general equation for the determination of market price when there are no costs.[184]

Equation (16a) can also be written in the form

(16b) $$np - \Sigma\varphi_n'(D_n) = - \frac{F(p)}{F'(p)}$$

This equation is used by Cournot to derive a variation[185] of the figure he had used to compare the prices under monopoly and oligopoly when there were no costs.

If the curve $y = \dfrac{-F(p)}{F'(p)}$ is plotted as before, the price will be determined where this curve is intesected by the curve $y = np - \Sigma\varphi_n'(D_n)$, which is shown as curve PQ in Figure 9.8.

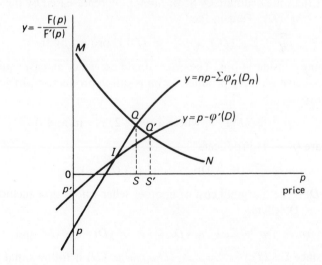

FIG. 9.8

And since, as we have seen, the price under monopoly is determined by the equation $F(p) + pF'(p) - \varphi'(D)F'(p) = 0$ the price under monopoly will be found where the curve $y = -\dfrac{F(p)}{F'(p)}$ is intersected by the curve $y = p - \varphi'(D)$, which is shown as curve $P'Q'$ in the above figure.

Cournot's intention is to show that the price under monopoly is higher than under oligopoly. When $p = 0$, the monopoly curve becomes $y = -\varphi'(D)$, while the oligopoly curve $y = np - \Sigma\varphi_n'(D_n)$ becomes $y = -\Sigma\varphi_n'(D_n)$.

But, as already explained, $\varphi'(D)$ represents the marginal cost of the monopolist, while $\Sigma\varphi_n'(D_n)$ is the sum of the marginal costs of all sellers under oligopoly. It is obvious that this latter quantity is greater than the marginal cost of a single seller[186] and

$$\Sigma\,\varphi_n'(D_n) > \varphi'(D)$$

Cournot then proceeds to give a very complicated proof that the two curves cross one another below the curve MN, and that therefore the price under monopoly OS' is greater than OS, the price under oligopoly.[187] A simplified version of his proof is as follows. For the two lines to intersect below MN, the ordinate QS of oligopoly, given by the intersection of curve MN by $y = np - \Sigma\varphi_n'(D_n)$, must be greater than the ordinate $Q'S'$ of monopoly represented by the curve $y = p - \varphi'(D)$. That in fact

$$np - \Sigma\varphi_n'(D_n) > p - \varphi'(D) \text{ is proved by the}$$

following considerations. The price should exceed or at least equal the marginal cost of every producer, who is still in production. In general therefore

(a) $p > \varphi_k'(D_k)$ where $k = 1, 2, \ldots$ n, and if

there are $(n - 1)$ producers

(b) $(n - 1)p > \Sigma\,\varphi'_{(n-1)}(D_{(n-1)})$

If $\varphi'(D)$ is the marginal cost of another seller who is now included in the $(n - 1)$ sellers,

(c) $(n - 1)p > \Sigma\varphi'_{(n-1)}(D_{(n-1)}) + \varphi'(D) - \varphi'(D)$ and

since $\Sigma\varphi_n'(D_n) = \Sigma\varphi'_{(n-1)}(D_{n-1}) + \varphi'(D)$ it follows that

(d) $(n - 1)p > \Sigma\varphi_n'(D_n) - \varphi'(D)$ and

$$np - \Sigma\varphi_n'(D_n) > p - \varphi'(D)$$

(iii) **Charles Ellet, the contemporary of Cournot**

Ellet who made a notable contribution to the subject of monopoly independently of Cournot, discussed also the case where two railway lines compete for the railway traffic of light goods.

He visualises two parallel railway lines, each running to a city. The cargo has to be carried a certain distance overland to reach either railway line, and it is obvious that *ceteris paribus* each producer will travel to the railway line nearest to him. But of course, there are also those producers who are at an equal distance from both lines and who are dealing 'alternately and indiscriminately at both places'.[188] It is obvious that, if a railway line charges more than the other, it will pay some producers who are nearer the first line to take their products to the second line, for the higher overland cost is more than compensated by the lower cost of railway carriage.

Let the two competing lines be as in the following diagram (Figure 9.9):[189]

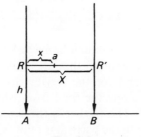

FIG. 9.9

The destinations of the two lines are A and B and the question is to decide the overland distance x, which is the maximum distance from which cargo will come to join the line at point R. At the point a people will be indifferent as to the choice of line, given of course equal conditions at the two markets A and B, and provided that it costs them an equal amount to send their goods to either of them. If h is the distance by railway which the goods have to travel to market A, b is the charge per ton per mile on line A and b' that on line B, and β is the cost of overland transportation per ton per mile, the cost of transporting goods to A is

$$hb + x\beta$$

and that of transporting goods to B is

$$h'b' + (X - x)\beta$$

where X is the total distance between the two lines and h' the distance which the goods have to travel by rail to B.

A producer would therefore be indifferent as to the choice of line if he were at such apoint that

(1) $$hb + x\beta = h'b' + (X - x)\beta$$

If for any reason the market at A is superior to that at B, it will pay to send goods to A even if the costs of transportation were higher. This superiority of market is used by Ellet to mean not simply differences in current prices but 'to embrace many other considerations and to indicate the excess of value to the holder of the property, which the commodity will possess by being delivered at one point instead of another'.[190] If M is 'the value of the superiority of the market at A',[191] condition (1) above would become

(1a) $$hb + x\beta = h'b' + (X - x)\beta + M$$

which gives[192] as the distance $Ra = x$

(2) $$x = \frac{X\beta + h'b' - hb + M}{2\beta}$$

Ellet makes now the same assumption which he had made in the discussion of monopoly, namely that the quantity of tonnage and consequently the demand for the services of each line is 'proportional to the distance along the road from which the commodity is brought to the line'.[193] The farther is the distance which goods can travel from the interior to the particular railway point, the more is the demand of railway services at this point. If we assume that the proportionality factor is equal to unity, equation (2) becomes the demand equation, where x is the quantity demanded. It is obvious from this equation that when all other conditions are given, which of course *includes also the rival's charge b' as given*, the quantity demanded is a decreasing function of the charge of the line, in this case the charge b of line A.

Ellet now splits the charge b into the fixed freight δ, which includes every charge to which the article is liable, with the exception of the variable part, and the variable profit or toll c, which is 'the profit to the proprietors of the work on the article conveyed'.[194] He further assumes that the demand of railway services is a function of the toll, since this is the variable part of the railway freight.

The total net revenue is for line A:

(3) $$cx = \frac{X\beta + h'b' - h(\delta + c) + M}{2\beta} c \text{ since } b = \delta + c$$

Differentiating the above equation and equating the result with zero, Ellet finds that the toll which will give the maximum net revenue to the line at this point is[195]

$$(4) \qquad c = \frac{X\beta + h'b' - h\delta + M}{2h}$$

and the total charge which the line should charge at this point is

$$(5) \qquad b = \delta + c = \frac{X\beta + h'b' + h\delta + M}{2h}$$

To reach this result, Ellet had however to assume among other things that the charge b' of the rival line would remain constant or in other words that the line A would fix its charge on the assumption that B would not change its own charge. This is similar to Cournot's approach with the difference that Cournot had assumed that in the case of duopoly the rival company's quantity rather than its price would remain constant. The real difference between them is this however: Cournot had examined simultaneously the conditions for equilibrium for both producers; Ellet examines the position of equilibrium of one line only. But the other line, if it also sought to maximise its profits, will find that the change in the charges of its rival affects its own profit and will have to make a consequent adjustment in its own charges, which will in its turn affect the first line's charges. The real question which Cournot answered and Ellet did not, is whether under their peculiar assumptions a position of stable equilibrium will be reached.

(iv) The development of the theory of oligopoly after Cournot

Cournot definitely left his mark on the theory of oligopoly as he had also done on the theory of monopoly. Practically every author, who wrote on the subject after him, felt that it was imperative for him to refer to Cournot's solution and to criticise or defend him. It would not be an exaggeration to say that to this very date Cournot and his treatment of oligopoly continue to be in the forefront of the controversy still raging round the solution of oligopoly.

The development of the theory of oligopoly after Cournot has been marked by two tendencies of approach to the problem. The first is the 'behaviourist' approach; after Cournot, it has endenvoured to establish behaviour norms by postulating certain appropriate fundamental assumptions. Its adherents differ in both the tools they have used and in the fundamental assumptions they have chosen. The second approach, the 'institutionalist' approach, believes that any attempt to formulate an economic theory of oligopolistic behaviour is doomed; its adherents advocate the introduction of a number of institutional factors, exogenous to the economic system. It is obvious that this second approach cannot be subjected to a uniform treatment as it can be broken up into as many case studies as there are institutional factors.

By far the most important is the 'behaviourist' approach. It is not the purpose to trace its development. The controversy created by Bertrand, Edgeworth and Pareto against Cournot's oligopoly analysis as well as its defence by K. Wicksell, L. Amoroso and others have been extensively covered.[196]

But it is a proof of the resilience of Cournot's analysis that his approach to the problem of oligopoly is still the basic approach; and it was by using his assumptions that attempts to create dynamic Oligopoly Models covering up to *n* sellers were made[197] and later extended and developed to cover other behavioural norms and assumptions.[198] The resilience of Cournot's oligopoly approach is not without explanation.

Cournot's crucial assumption is that at the beginning of each period each seller assumes that his competitor's quantity will remain unchanged in the coming period.

There are two questions to be asked: Is this assumption realistic in the sense that it represents the frame of mind in which oligopolists make decisions? And secondly, does this assumption lead to realistic results?

As in the Theory of Games, one could also make a very strong case that in oligopolistic situations the desire for 'playing safe' is reigning. This idea of 'playing safe' actually corresponds to what actually happens in a large section of the business world. The idea of 'playing down' one's expected profits and swelling expected losses to be taken care of, is the basis of prudent management as evidenced by the accounting practice to provide for future losses both certain and uncertain but not to take into consideration expected profits; and to value the stock at the lower of the cost or market price.

This desire for 'playing safe' will make oligopolists very reluctant to take steps, which they feel will provoke instant retaliation by their rivals. A policy of price undercutting makes sense, as Wicksell pointed out, only when the seller has a definite advantage over his competitor. Under normal conditions the two sellers would have to find a 'modus vivendi', under which the price would be stabilised and only quantity adjustments, brought about through non-price competition, would take place.

Advertising campaigns therefore have the aim to adjust the quantity which each firm sells to that level, at which it is thought that profits will be maximised. A firm planning an advertising campaign in a nearly saturated market will consider that a certain time will be needed before its rivals are able to retaliate through advertising. This period of time may be long or short, but what is of importance is that the firm in question considers that it will be a step ahead of its rivals. An estimate of what the rivals will sell is necessary for the calculation of the firm's expected revenue curves. The firm may of course assume that during the period it is ahead of its rivals, their sales will actually decline or will remain unaffected. This latter situation will be the worst of the two possibilities envisaged and the first firm may well, in its desire to be on the 'safe side', assume that the quantity of its rival will remain unchanged in the coming period.

There is however a more important aspect. When dynamic analysis is used it can be seen that, under suitable assumptions, which are within the Cournotian spirit, after the lapse of a very small number of periods we shall draw quite near the equilibrium position. A seller therefore, who sees that, if he persists for two or three periods in this pattern of attitude, he will get quite good predictions, will not hasten to change the basis of his prediction. This argument is reinforced by the fact that in actual life displacements from the oligopolistic equilibrium will not be far from it. An advertising campaign, once an oligopolistic market is almost saturated, cannot displace the combination of quantities of the two sellers far from the equilibrium position. The deviations therefore of the expectations of an oligopolist, under the assumption that his rival's quantity will remain unchanged, from the results actually obtained will be very small indeed. From the businessman's point of view the basis for the prediction will be quite satisfactory in view of his experience of general economic uncertainty.

That the Cournot assumption itself leads to realistic results is evident from the above. The most important result is stability itself, which is characteristic of oligopolistic situations. Apart from the case of collusion, mainly two explanations have been offered for the stability of the system. The first explanation is that offered by the *kinked demand* theory; but, this theory explains too much, for it provides not only for the stability of the price but also for the absolute stability of the quantity. A seller may not change the quantity he is already selling at the kink, for this will automatically mean changing the price which is *a priori* excluded by the theory.

The other explanation is that given in terms of *price leadership*. But this theory cannot explain the stability in the case where the oligopolists are not very different in economic power.

Cournot's analysis provides a framework within which stability of the system can be achieved with assumptions which may be acceptable in certain situations.

9.7   THE OLIGOPOLY OF COMPLEMENTARY GOODS IN THE ANALYSIS OF COURNOT

We have so far covered the two main forms of monopolistic market structure with which Cournot has dealt. In both, one or a few sellers dealing in a homogeneous product were facing purchasers, whose competition was assumed to be unlimited.

There is a third type of imperfection in selling which Cournot discusses.[199] In this he assumes that there is a number of monopolists each dealing in a factor of production, of which he has the monopoly. Each factor contributes to the production of a single commodity, the marketing of which is subject to free competition. There is thus an unlimited number of sellers of the final product and consequently of buyers of the various factors.

Thus the various monopolists of factors of production are facing an unlimited number of buyers. This is therefore not a case of bilateral monopoly, as is sometimes[200] described, for in that situation a unique seller faces a unique purchaser of the same commodity.[201] We may describe the various monopolists of factors as sellers in a group, dealing in a differentiated but related product, for each variety of which a different price is possible.

Competition among the sellers in the group is provided, not by the possibility of substitution, for this is excluded by Cournot's assumption that the factors contribute to the final product in a fixed proportion, but by the attempt of each seller so to adjust his price as to maximise his revenue.

The crucial assumption of Cournot, in addition to the fixed proportionality of factors, is that each seller adjusts his price in the belief that the other sellers of factors *will not change their prices*. The equivalent assumption in the case of simple oligopoly was, as we have seen, that each seller adjusted his quantity in the belief that the quantities of the other sellers would remain unchanged.

The attempt of Cournot to discuss the problems involved in the competition of monopolised factors is the first which has ever been made. We have been unable to find any reference in the previous economic literature, though in the development of the theory of monopoly, there were frequent references to the monopoly of a single factor.[202]

(i) The equilibrium of two monopolised factors, the production of which involves no costs

Cournot assumes that there are two factors, (a) and (b), 'which have no other use beyond that of being jointly consumed in the production of the composite commodity (ab)'.[203]

It is also assumed that there are no additional costs involved in the production of (ab), except for the reward of the two factors, which is paid to their owners. It is further assumed that the production of each factor costs nothing to its owner.

There is an additional assumption: This is that the two factors are used in the manufacture of the commodity in a fixed proportion $m_1 : m_2$. For every unit of (ab) produced, m_1 quantity of (a) is used and m_2 of (b), so that

$$m_1 + m_2 = 1$$

If the price of (a) is p_1 and that of (b) is p_2, the total cost of producing a unit of (*ab*) is

$$m_1 p_1 + m_2 p_2$$

Cournot implicitly accepts that the price of (ab) is equal to its cost, an assumption fully justified, since as we have seen he assumes perfect competition of (ab). We have therefore

(1) $$p = m_1 p_1 + m_2 p_2$$

The quantity of the commodity demanded at price p is given by the demand function

(2) $$D = F(p) = F(m_1 p_1 + m_2 p_2)$$

But if the producer of (ab) wants to produce the quantity D' he will have to use $m_1 D$ of (a) and $m_2 D$ of (b). If D_1 is the quantity of (a) demanded and D_2 is the quantity of (b) demanded, it is possible to define each as a function of its own price and the price of the other factor.

D_1 is found by successive substitution[204] to be

(3) $$D_1 = m_1F(m_1p_1 + m_2p_2) \text{ and } D_2$$

(4) $$D_2 = m_2F(m_1p_1 + m_2p_2)$$

Each of the two monopolists will seek to maximise his respective revenue p_1D_1 and p_2D_2. This, as already mentioned, is done by each seller through price adjustments in the belief that the others' price will remain constant. The conditions to be satisfied are

(5)
$$\frac{d(p_1D_1)}{dp_1} = 0 \qquad \text{for the seller of (a) and}$$

$$\frac{d(p_2D_2)}{dp_2} = 0 \qquad \text{for the seller of (b).}$$

The development of these equations leads to the system

(6)
$$F(m_1p_1 + m_2p_2) + m_1p_1 \, F'(m_1p_1 + m_2p_2) = 0$$
$$F(m_1p_1 + m_2p_2) + m_2p_2 \, F'(m_1p_1 + m_2p_2) = 0$$

The solution of the system gives as a result that the price of each will in equilibrium be such that the profits of the two sellers are equal.

(7) $$m_1p_1 = m_2p_2 = \frac{1}{2}p$$

The equilibrium price of the first will be equal to

(7a) $$p_1 = \frac{p}{2m_1}$$

and the equilibrium price of the second seller will be

(7b) $$p_2 = \frac{p}{2m_2}$$

The solution of equations (7a) and (7b) presupposes the solution of p. The addition of the two equations of system (6) gives[205]

(8) $F(p) + \frac{1}{2} pF'(p) = 0$ \qquad which can be written as

(8a) $$\frac{1}{2} p = - \frac{F(p)}{F'(p)}$$

If we plot the equation $y = - \dfrac{F(p)}{F'(p)}$, with which we are already familiar from the discussion of the cases of monopoly and oligopoly, the price in this case will be found at the point of intersection of y by the line $y = \frac{1}{2}p$. 'If the interests of the two producers had remained undistinguished',[206] and we had a case of pure monopoly, the price would have been determined by the intersection of y by the line $y = p$.

Thus in Figure 9.10 the price $ox_{\prime\prime}$ of the composite commodity produced from the monopolised factors is higher than the monopoly

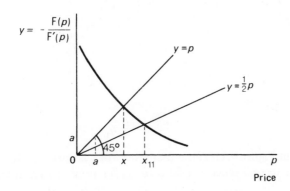

FIG. 9.10

price ox. 'The composite commodity', writes Cournot[267], 'will always be made more expensive, by reason of separation of interests than by reason of the fusion of monopolies. An association of monopolists, working for their own interest in this instance will also work for the interest of consumers, which is exactly the opposite of what happens with competing producers.'

We have so far found the static equilibrium values of p_1 and p_2 by the solution of the system of equations (6). To prove that the equilibrium is stable Cournot plots the reaction curves of the two sellers. The reaction curve of the first is given by the first equation of (6). It shows the optimum price which he must adopt to maximise his revenue for every given price of the second seller. Similarly the reaction curve of the second seller is given by the second equation of (6).

According to the form of the function F, the two reaction curves, m_1n_1 for the first and m_2n_2 for the second seller, will have one of the following two forms in Figure 9.11.[208]

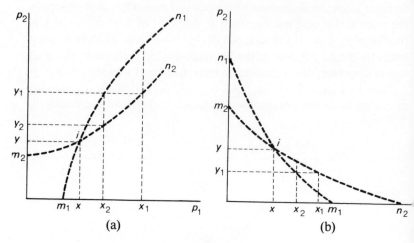

F<small>IG</small>. 9.11

When in Figure 9.11(a) the first seller fixes his price at ox_1, the best which the second seller can do is to fix his price at oy_1, in answer to which the first adopts ox_2 and so on; there is thus a successive approach to the equilibrium values ox and oy, which correspond to the point of intersection of the two curves. A similar process will take place when the reaction curves have the shape of Figure 9.11(b).[209].

(ii) The equilibrium of more than two monopolised factors with no costs

Following an argument similar to that used in the respective case of simple oligopoly, it can be seen that when there are three factors and three monopolists, there will be an additional equation to system (6). In general if there are n factors and n monopolists, where

$$(9) \qquad p = m_1p_1 + m_2p_2 + \ldots + m_np_n$$

we shall have a system of n equations similar to (6). The solution of this system will give

$$(9a) \qquad m_1p_1 = m_2p_2 = \ldots = m_np_n = \frac{1}{n}p$$

Equation (8) is now replaced by

(10) $F(p) + \dfrac{1}{n} pF'(p) = 0.$ This can be transformed into

(10a) $\dfrac{1}{n} p = - \dfrac{F(p)}{F'(p)}$. The price is found where, in Figure 9.12, the

curve $y = - \dfrac{F(p)}{F'(p)}$ is intersected by the curve $y = \dfrac{1}{n} p$, from which

'we should conclude that the more there are of articles thus related, the higher the price determined by the division of monopolies will be, than that which would result from the fusion or association or monopolies'.[210]

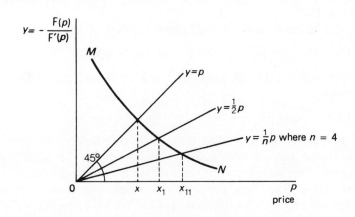

FIG. 9.12

(iii) The equilibrium of monopolised factors with costs

Cournot also examines the case where each of the two monopolists of factors has to undertake certain expenses for the provision of the factor. If thus the total cost of the first factor is a function of its quantity and is denoted by $\varphi_1(D_1)$ and that of the second by $\varphi_2(D_2)$, the net revenue of the first monopolist, which he will seek to maximise, is $p_1 D_1 - \varphi_1(D_1)$ and that of the second is $p_2 D_2 - \varphi_2(D_2)$.

The first seller so adjusts his price as to make his marginal revenue equal to the change in cost corresponding to a very small change in price. The same procedure is followed by the second seller and both assume that the price of the other factor will remain constant. The conditions of the maximum revenue are

$$\frac{d}{dp_1}(p_1 D_1) = \frac{d}{dp_1}\{\varphi_1(D_1)\} \quad \text{for the first seller}$$

(11) $$\frac{d}{dp_2}(p_2 D_2) = \frac{d}{dp_2}\{\varphi_2(D_2)\} \quad \text{for the second seller}$$

This system can be developed[211] into

$$F(p) + m_1 F'(p) [p_1 - \varphi_1'(D_1)] = 0$$

(12)

$$F(p) + m_2 F'(p) [p_2 - \varphi_2'(D_2)] = 0$$

where $\varphi_1'(D_1) = \dfrac{d}{dD_1}\varphi_1 (D_1)$ is the marginal cost of the first mono-

polist and $\varphi_2'(D_2)$ that of the second. The results derived from this system by Cournot follow the same lines as in the previous cases examined.

It can be immediately derived from (12) that

(13) $m_1 [p_1 - \varphi_1'(D_1)] = m_2 [p_2 - \varphi_2'(D_2)]$

If this is multiplied by D, and since[212] $m_1 D = D_1$ and $m_2 D = D_2$, (13) becomes

(13a) $D_1 [p_1 - \varphi_1' (D_1)] = D_2 [p_2 - \varphi_2' (D_2)]$

This means that the product of the difference between the price of each factor and its marginal cost multiplied by the equilibrium quantity of the same factor will be equal to the similar product of the other factor. This does not mean, however, that their respective profits will be equal; for the total profit of (a) is the product of D_1 by the profit per unit which is the difference between price and *average cost*. Thus this total profit will be

$$D_1 \left(p_1 - \frac{\varphi_1 (D_1)}{D_1}\right)$$

If the marginal cost of (a) in equilibrium is greater than the average cost $\dfrac{\varphi_1 (D_1)}{D_1}$.

(14) $D_1 \left(p_1 - \dfrac{\varphi_1 (D_1)}{D_1}\right) > D_1 [p_1 - \varphi_1'(D_1)]$

If at the same time

$$\varphi_2'(D_2) < \frac{\varphi_2(D_2)}{D_2} \text{ it will follow that}$$

(14a) $D_2 [p_2 - \varphi_2'(D_2)] > D_2 \left[p_2 - \dfrac{\varphi_2(D_2)}{D_2}\right]$

A comparison of (14) with (14a) shows[213] that the net profit of the first seller is greater than that of the second seller.

Cournot also demonstrates that the market price of the final product will in equilibrium be higher than if there had been a fusion of monopolies, by following the procedure with which we are already familiar.[214]

(iv) The determinateness of the prices of monopolised factors

Cournot was thus able to show that under his peculiar assumptions, determinate solutions of the prices of factors could in general be found. He, however, pointed out that even under his assumptions, there could be exceptional cases, 'which cannot have any application to actual events',[215] and which allowed of no determinate solution.

The first exception, to which we have already drawn attention, is where the form of the demand function is such that the reaction curves of the two monopolists, represented by (6) above, do not intersect. (See Fig. 9.3n.)

There is, however, another case, originating from a peculiarity on the supply side of the factors, where though the reaction curves intersect, the solution is indeterminate.[216] It is quite conceivable, argues Cournot, that the supply of one or more of the factors has a fixed maximum limit; as he has assumed that each factor is needed in a fixed proportion for the production of the commodity, this limitation in the supply of the factor is reflected in a limitation in the quantity of the commodity produced. If therefore $\triangle$ is the limit of the commodity, the price cannot be so low that a quantity D greater than $\triangle$ will be demanded. There is a lower limit to the price below which it cannot fall, for then $D > \triangle$. If this lower limit is π so that $\triangle = F(\pi)$, the actual price p must exceed π and then $D < \triangle$.

But as we have seen $p = m_1 p_1 + m_2 p_2$; in this case however the prices of the two factors must be such that the resultant price is higher than π. The limit below which the price cannot fall is

$$(15) \qquad \pi = m_1 p_1 + m_2 p_2$$

This limit is represented by Cournot by line $h_1 h_2$, in Figure 9.13.[217]

If p is to exceed π, as required, the combination of p_1 and p_2 must lie to the right of $h_1 h_2$. If the form of the reaction curves is such that they intersect to the left of $h_1 h_2$, as in the figure, the prices corresponding to the point of intersection are unattainable. 'The values of p_1 and p_2 are indeterminate, being subject only to this condition, that the points which would have the values of these variables for coordinates fall on the part $k_1 k_2$ of the line, which is intercepted between the

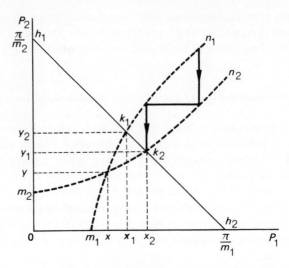

FIG. 9.13

curves m_1n_1 and m_2n_2.'[218] Thus p_1 will vary between the limits ox_1 and ox_2 and p_2 between the limits oy_1 and ov_2. But this indeterminateness, Cournot concludes,[219] will not be found in actual life where the price of everything is completely determined.[220]

(iv) Charles Ellet and later developments

Charles Ellet in his *Laws of Trade*[221] discusses also a case of such correlated oligopoly. He visualises two railway lines, enjoying a monopoly of transportation, but forming a continuation of one another, so that the first feeds the second. Ellet proceeds to prove that it is more disadvantageous to the railway customers when each line sets its charge independently, rather than jointly.

Ellet had established that the best toll for the monopolist, which would maximise his profit, would be half that toll, which would exclude entirely the commodity from coming to the line from the interior.[222] The first company will impose half the maximum toll p; the toll available to the second company is now $\frac{p}{2}$ and the optimum toll for it is half this, that is $\frac{p}{4}$. The first company now finds that, given the second's charge for toll, its optimum toll will be half of $\frac{3}{4}p$, i.e. $\frac{3}{8}p$. Thus the consequence of the second company's toll of

$\frac{p}{4}$ was "to cause the first company to reduce its toll down to one half the amount taken by the second company, and thus give opportunity to the second again to increase its exactions. And the ultimate result would be, if there were much disparity between the lengths of the lines, to cause $\frac{2}{3}$ of the whole toll which might be levied without excluding trade, to be charged upon the two lines'.[223]

Ellet thus provides a dynamic explanation of the approach towards an equilibrium toll, which he supplements with a mathematical solution of the static equilibrium.

As a matter of fact Ellet's argument could easily be put into modern dynamic form. If c_t and c_t' are the tolls of the first and second line at time t, and p is the toll which would exclude the commodity from transportation by rail, we shall have

$$(1) \quad c_t = \frac{p - c_{t-1}'}{2} \quad \text{and (2)} \quad c_t' = \frac{p - c_{t-1}}{2}$$

The solution of these equations will give

$$(3) \qquad c_t = p\left[\frac{1}{3} + \frac{1}{4}\left(\frac{1}{2}\right)^t - \frac{1}{12}\left(-\frac{1}{2}\right)^t\right] \text{ which tends}$$

to $\frac{p}{3}$ as t tends to infinity.

$$(4) \quad c_t' = p\left[\frac{1}{3} - \frac{1}{4}\left(\frac{1}{2}\right)^t - \frac{1}{12}\left(-\frac{1}{2}\right)^t\right] \text{ which also tends}$$

to $\frac{p}{3}$ as t tends to infinity. The equilibrium will thus be stable and the total toll will in equilibrium be

$$(5) \qquad\qquad , \qquad c_t + c_t' = \frac{2p}{3}$$

Zeuthen used an approach identical to Ellet's with the sole difference that he called Ellet's 'toll' the 'excess price', but there is no indication that Zeuthen knew of Ellet's work. His approach was derived directly as an adaptation of the solution of Cournot. The development of the theory of oligopoly of complementary goods after Cournot is marked by the fact that it is Cournot's theory which always serves as the starting point.

Edgeworth introduces the assumption that one or both sellers will not simply assume, as Cournot had suggested, that the other seller's price will remain constant but will try to guess how the other will react to his own change of price and will fix his own price after taking this factor into account.[224]

Other contributors to the theory are H.L. Moore and A. Marshall who criticised Cournot[225] and A.L. Bowley, K.W. Wicksell and F. Zeuthen who lean towards Cournot's view.[226]

9.8   THE THEORY OF SOCIAL INCOME

The solution of the problem of price determination was effected by Cournot under *ceteris paribus* conditions, which included the condition that incomes remain unchanged. But Cournot, as we have already seen, felt that this was only an approximation and that the ideal thing would be 'to take the entire system into consideration'.[227] This, however, he estimates beyond the powers of mathematical analysis and he chooses to make another approximation and investigate how changes in the *prices of consumers' goods* directly affect individual incomes and by implication the national income. But his is a pedestrian approach; he will not examine how changed prices affect production and how this affects in turn the national income. His vision stops at the first stage, at the point, i.e., where a changed price has swollen or deflated the pocket of the producer.

The author of the *Recherches* defines social income[228] or national income as 'the sum total of individual incomes, of rents, of profits and of wages of every kind, in the whole extent of the national territory'[229] and it includes 'the annual amount of the stipends by means of which individuals or the state sustain those classes of men which economic writers have characterised as unproductive, because the product of their labour is not anything material or salable'.[230] This definition is a fairly satisfactory one, and I can find little support for Fisher's contention that Cournot's treatment forms 'one of those innumerable and futile attempts to define the income of the community'.[231] Nor can I find any support for the argument that Cournot was inconsistent in his definition. He, writes Fisher, 'first describes social income as the sum of individual incomes, the latter term being self-explanatory. He then redefines it as the sum of commodities 'for consumption'. He thinks he bridges over the gap between these two descriptions of income on the theory that the price of any commodity 'for consumption' consists of parts, ascribable to the different agents of production'.[232] What, in fact, Cournot did was to choose to investigate how changed prices of consumers' goods affect the national income, but this does not show that he believed that it is only this kind of goods which makes up the national income.

The total revenue, accruing to the various owners of factors of production on the sale of a certain quantity of goods, makes up a part of the national income in money terms. If this good is a consumers' good and D is the quantity which is annually sold at a price p per unit, 'the product pD will express the sum to the extent of which this commodity cooperates in making up the social income'.[233] Thus if we use Cournot's figure (1) slightly altered (Figure 9.14), at price p_o, the

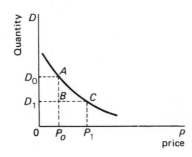

FIG. 9.14

contribution to the national income in money terms is the rectangle $0p_oAD_o$. If the price increases to p_1, the new total revenue will be[234] p_1D_1 or the rectangle $0p_1CD_1$. Now, this is made up of the rectangles

$$0p_oAD_o - D_oD_1BA + Bp_op_1C \qquad \text{or}$$

$p_1D_1 = p_oD_o - p_o(D_o - D_1) + D_1(p_1 - p_o)$ and therefore the decrease in revenue as a result of the new price is

$$p_oD_o - p_1D_1 = + p_o(D_o - D_1) - D_1(p_1 - p_o).$$

$p_o(D_o - D_1)$ is the decrease in the revenue due to the fact that a por-
    tion $D_o - D_1$ previously bought at p_o is no longer
    bought at p_1

$D_1(p_o - p_o)$ is the increase in revenue due to the fact that the new
    quantity D_1 is sold at a price increased by $p_1 - p_o$.

$p_oD_o - p_1D_1$ is therefore the total decrease in the revenue of the
    producers.[235]

This result Cournot proceeds to interpret in another way. Those consumers who continue to buy the quantity of good D_1 at the increased price p_1 paying thus p_1D_1 while previously they would have paid only p_oD_1 for this quantity, 'are really in just the same situation as to fortune as if the commodity had not risen and their incomes had been diminished by $(p_1 - p_o)D_1$'.[236] $P_oD_o - p_1D_1$ represents the diminution in the *nominal income*, and their joint effect gives $(p_1 - p_o)D_1 + p_oD_o - p_1D_1 = p_o(D_o - D_1)$ which, Cournot thinks, represents the *'real diminution of the social income'*,[237] a result which shows the reduction in quantity from D_o to D_1 at constant prices.

But though Cournot has calculated the loss to those consumers who still buy the article, he has not calculated the loss to those who stop buying it. This was criticized by Pareto,[238] who showed that under Cournot's assumptions, the 'way taken to pass from one state (of price) to another'[239] affects the calculation of Cournot's 'real diminution of income'.

Thus if R_o, R_1, R_2 denote the real income at three points of time, we should have according to Cournot's formula, a 'real diminution of income' when we pass

from p_o to p_1 $R_o - R_1 = p_o(D_o - D_1)$

from p_1 to p_2 $R_1 - R_2 = p_1(D_1 - D_2)$ from which we

get $R_o - R_2 = p_oD_o + (p_1 - p_o)D_1 - p_1D_2 = p_o(D_o - D_1) + p_1(D_1 - D_2)$,

or in terms of Figure 9.15.

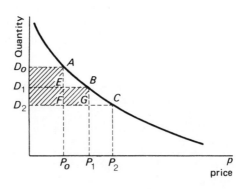

FIG. 9.15

the real diminution will be equal to the sum of the rectangles D_oD_1EA and D_1D_2GB. If however we pass directly from p_o to p_2 the real diminution will be only $p_o(D_o - D_2)$ or the rectangle D_oD_2FA, which differs from the sum of the rectangles in the previous case by the rectangle *EFGB*. This is due to the fact 'that when one passes from p_oD_o to p_1D_1 the consumers who buy still at p_1D_1 are taken into consideration, while they are not considered when one passes directly from p_oD_o to p_2D_2'.[240]

Pareto has other objections to the notion of Cournot that $p_o(D_o - D_1)$ indicates the 'real diminution in income'. If $p_o = 0$ this diminution is zero, which would be a ridiculous result, because 'if air which we now have freely became a scarce good for which we would have to pay, the real diminution of social income would be zero'.[241] In the same way if $D_o = D_1$, the real diminution would again be zero, which would mean that, 'if the price of bread increases but its consumption remains the same as before, the real diminution of income would be zero'.[242] It is because of these objections that Pareto concludes that we must 'recognise that what the author calls real variations of social income are not an index which can teach anything about the real situation'.[243]

Equally serious are the objections against Cournot's belief that a change in the income of the community generated through a change in the price of a commodity will be approximately equal to only the immediate change in the incomes of the producers of the commodity.

Thus, as we have seen, a change in price from p_o to p_1 will generate a reduction in the income of the producers of the commodity equal to $p_oD_o - p_1D_1$. The incomes of all other persons, Cournot argues, may be considered unchanged because the perturbation which originated from the change in income of the producers of the commodity 'leaves intact the sum total of the funds applicable to the demand for the other commodities', or alters it 'by a quantity which is negligible in comparison with the variation $p_oD_o - p_1D_1$ which is experienced by the incomes of the producers of A'.[244]

This may be true in the statistical distribution of error, from which Cournot was obviously influenced, but it ignores the fact that the effects of a change may be cumulative and their importance quite considerable.

9.9 THE THEORY OF INTERNATIONAL TRADE

Cournot's contribution to the theory of international trade consists of three parts. In the first he develops a 'highly ingenious'[245] theory of foreign exchanges; the second deals with the effects of trade between markets, which were previously isolated, on prices. Finally, the third part seeks to apply Cournot's ideas about social income and its variations to the theory of international trade.

(i) The theory of foreign exchange

The structure of the whole of Cournot's book has been greatly influenced by Cournot's belief that 'any demonstration ought to proceed from the simple to the complex'.[246] This can be seen not only in his treatment of the various market forms but also in his treatment of the theory of foreign exchange.[247]

Our author starts from the simplifying hypothesis that there are only two centres between which exchange takes place and that both of them have adopted the same monetary unit, which is one gram of fine silver, 'or, what amounts to the same thing, that the ratio of each monetary unit to a gram of fine silver be permanently established'.[248]

The par of exchange is therefore unity and there will be no movement of silver as long as the 'cost of exchange', i.e. the difference of the actual rate from unity, does not exceed the cost of transportation of this weight of fine silver or, if there is no free trade in precious metals, 'the cost of transportation plus the expense of smuggling',[249] a conception which is reminiscent of Beccaria's and Silio's earlier treatment of this problem.

On the assumption that the exchange takes place without any real transportation of money and that the two places balance their accounts, we shall have

(1) $m_{12}\, c_{12} = m_{21}$ or $c_{12} = \dfrac{m_{21}}{m_{12}}$ where c_{12} is the rate of exchange

at place (1) on place (2) and c_{21} is the opposite,[250] and m_{12} is the total of the debts per year of place (1) to place (2) and similarly for m_{21}, which denotes the debts of (2) to (1).

In general, the equilibrium condition is (2) $c_{21} = \dfrac{1}{c_{12}}$ and we therefore need to know only the one-way rate of exchange to determine the rate of exchange the other way.

If there are r centres, there will be $r(r - 1)$ rates of exchange; but as in general $c_{ik} = \dfrac{1}{c_{ki}}$, where i and k are the centres of exchange, the number of these coefficients is reduced to $\dfrac{r(r - 1)}{2}$.

When there are, however, more than two centres, there is the possibility of arbitrage between centres. In equilibrium therefore we have

(3) $c_{ik} = c_{il} \times c_{lk}$ where i, k, l are three places of exchange. If this relation is disturbed 'banking transactions continually tend to re-establish it'.[251]

It is evident therefore that of the three ratios c_{ik}, c_{il}, c_{lk} only the two are independent; if we have r centres of exchange, there are, in equilibrium, only $r - 1$ unknown ratios.

With the same assumptions as before, we have for three centres three equations, each showing that what one centre owes to all the others is, at this first centre, equal in value to what the others owe to it:

$$\begin{aligned}
(4) \qquad m_{12} + m_{13} &= m_{21}c_{21} + m_{31}c_{31} \\
m_{21} + m_{23} &= m_{12}c_{12} + m_{32}c_{32} \\
m_{31} + m_{32} &= m_{13}c_{13} + m_{23}c_{23}
\end{aligned}$$

Of this system of equations, only two are independent and their solution gives the values of the two ratios from which that of the third may be found.[252] A similar procedure is followed for the solution, when there are r centres.

This is the third attempt after Isnard and Lang[253] at a general equilibrium solution of an economic problem and may well have provided the starting point of Walras' thoughts in this respect, since the *Recherches* was, as Walras says, one of the first books which he read as an undergraduate.[254]

Up to this point Cournot had assumed that no actual transportation of metal takes place.

If the cost of transportation of a unit of metal is p_{21} the point beyond which the first country will begin importing metal will be where

(5) $c_{12} = 1 + p_{21} = \gamma_{12}$. This is the maximum rate for the first country on the second, and beyond this point the rate of exchanges becomes a constant. At the same time, the rate in the second country, which exports silver, will reach its minimum at $c_{21} = \dfrac{1}{1 + p_{21}} = \gamma_{21}$ and become a constant. The unknown quantity c_{21} is now replaced by the known constant γ_{21} and the system of equation (4) is reduced by one equation and one unknown and can still be solved.[255]

Cournot also deals with a special problem of foreign exchange under bimetallism, which is reminiscent of the earliest contributions to mathematical economics. The rate of exchange is expressed in terms of silver and is denoted as before by c_{ik}; this shows how many units of silver are payable in country k for a unit of silver paid in country i. It is further assumed that p_i and p_k are the ratios of gold to silver in the two countries respectively.

A quantity of gold h is exchanged in country i for a quantity of silver hp_i, which at the rate of exchange in force will fetch hp_ic_{ik} in country k. If instead we choose to send this quantity directly to country k, a quantity $\epsilon_{ik}h$ will only arrive, ϵ_{ik} being the allowance for the cost of actual transportation and smuggling. In country k this quantity is exchanged for silver equal to $p_k\epsilon_{ik}h$.

Transportation of actual gold will therefore take place only if

$$(6) \qquad p_k\epsilon_{ik}h > p_ic_{ik}h \text{ or } \frac{p_k}{p_i} > \frac{c_{ik}}{\epsilon_{ik}}$$

As, however, gold flows to country k, p_k becomes smaller while p_i, owing to the scarcity of gold, becomes larger. Equilibrium, in the sense that no metal is transported, will be reached when[256]

$$(7) \qquad \frac{p_k}{p_i} = \frac{c_{ik}}{\epsilon_{ik}} \text{ or } \frac{c_{ik}}{\epsilon_{ik}} > \frac{p_k}{p_i}$$

The more ϵ_{ik} approaches unity, the more we shall approach the position

$$(8) \qquad \frac{p_k}{p_i} = c_{ik} \quad \text{Given therefore the ratio of}$$

exchange and the price of gold at one centre, the equilibrium price of gold at the other centre may be found.[257]

That these two ratios tend to draw closer together, through arbitrage operations is a subject elaborated by previous writers. Cournot is interested only in examining their relation with the actual rate of exchange. It can however be seen immediately that, as in equilibrium $c_{ik} = 1$,

$$p_k = p_i$$

(ii) The theory of price determination under international trade

The discussion of price determination under international trade is conditioned by Cournot's belief that problems arising out of the trade between nations can be approached and discussed as problems arising from the communication of two markets which were previously isolated.[258] In his argument he visualises the cost schedules of the two countries as given. But this is due, as we shall see, to his *ceteris paribus* analysis and not to any explicit acceptance of the fact, which according to Mill distinguished international from internal trade, that is the comparative lack of mobility of factors of production from one country to another.[259]

Cournot's analysis of the theory of price under international trade follows the pattern of his analysis of price in a closed economy. The analysis is static and the method used is that of partial equilibrium. He wants to examine how equilibrium of the price of a *single* good is established through the interplay of its supply and demand, when such supply and demand are considered as functions of only the cost and the price of the good respectively. All other conditions are assumed to remain unchanged. His approach is therefore entirely different from Mill's approach.

Viewed from this point of view, not only is it not difficult to explain the differences in the results of the two methods, but also to accept the view that such an approach as Cournot's, which was followed by among others Barone,[260] is 'quite indispensable to a study of the *direct* effects of international trade and of measures of trade policy, such as tariffs'[261] and is 'an essential preliminary to a more far-reaching analysis'.[262]

Cournot visualises two markets which had previously been in isolation and which are now allowed to trade. If competition is free, 'an article capable of transportation must flow from the market where its value is less to the market where its value is greater, until this difference in value, from one market to the other represents no more than the cost of transportation'.[263]

It has already been seen that Cournot had established that the internal price, under conditions of partial equilibrium, would obey the equation

$W(p) = F(p)$ where p is the price of the good, $W(p)$ its supply function and $F(p)$ its demand function.

If, therefore, $F_a(p_a)$ is the downward sloping demand function, and $W_a(p_a)$ the upward sloping supply function of the first country, before communication, the *ceteris paribus* equilibrium price of this particular commodity, p_a, is determined by

(1) $$W_a(p_a) = F_a(p_a)$$

In a similar way, the equilibrium price, p_b, of the second country will, before trade, be such that

(2) $W_b(p_b) = F_b(p_b)$ where the first is the supply

function and the second the demand function.

If e denotes the costs of transportation and

(3) $p_b > p_a + e$

the removal of the barriers to communication will mean that the commodity will flow from the first country to the second. This will have as a result a higher price, p_a', in the exporting country with a consequent increase in domestic production and diminution in domestic consumption.

On the contrary, the price, p_b', in the importing country will fall with a consequent expansion in domestic consumption and contraction in domestic production, with the gap between the two met through imports.

The flow will continue until the price in the importing country does not exceed that of the exporter by more than e, and total demand is therefore equal to total supply.[264] The basic equilibrium equation is thus

(4) $W_a(p_a') + W_b(p_a' + e) = F_a(p_a') + F_b(p_a' + e)$

Whether the new total production will exceed the production of both countries before they had been allowed to trade, depends on whether conditions are such that the increase of production of the exporting country can more than compensate for the diminution of production in the importing country. It is conceivable, though improbable, that communication may lead to an actual diminution of total production.[265] The condition, which Cournot demonstrates, must hold for this *not* to happen is

(4) $F'_b(p_b) W'_a(p_a) - F'_a(p_a) W'_b(p_b) < 0,$

where the functions F' and W' show the rates of change of quantities demanded and supplied in the two countries in response to the change in their respective prices.[266]

It is also conceivable that the total money revenue accruing to producers after communication, will be smaller than before, not only where there has been a diminution in total material production but also when there has been an actual increase. This will happen in the case where, on the one hand, the price in the exporting country before communication is above that price where revenue is a maximum, while on the other hand, the price in the importing country is below that which would render revenue a maximum. Communication then means a still further movement from the price at which the maximum revenue is to be found in the exporting country and thus

$$p'_aF_a(p'_a) < p_aF_a(p_a)$$

Similarly, for the importing country, the lowering of price means

$$p'_bF_b(p'_b) < p_bF_b(p_b)$$

It becomes immediately apparent by adding the two inequalities that in this case the new total revenue is smaller than the previous one.[267]

The same chapter contains a discussion of the effect on price of an imposition of 'a tax on exportation or importation' which the author considers as equivalent to an increase in the cost of transportation.[268] Unfortunately, through an oversight in his solution, he arrives at the result[269] that such a tax will cause a fall in the price of the commodity in the exporting market, which may be smaller or larger than the tax itself and a rise or fall in the price of the importing market, according to the circumstances. A correct solution shows that given Cournot's premises, the tax always raises the price in the importing market and causes it to fall in the exporting market but in both cases by an amount smaller than the tax.[270]

(iii) The effect of international trade on national income.[271]

Cournot's treatment of this subject is a continuation of the techniques he had used in his theory of Social Income. The limitations of his analysis, to which we drew attention, and especially Cournot's unsatisfactory way of calculating real changes in income are in part responsible for the peculiarity of his results. But it is, essentially, his attempt to analyse the effects of trade in a system of partial equilibrium which led him to results directly contradictory to those given by the theory of comparative costs.

(a) The principle of the compensation of demands

Cournot's aim is to study in isolation the effects which the removal of barriers, affecting only a single commodity, has. Given free competition, there will be importation into the country with the higher price from that with the lower price. But whereas under the theory of comparative cost, such a movement would lead to a re-orientation of every factor of production, which could be more profitably employed elsewhere, so that in the end each country would specialise in producing these goods in which its comparative advantage is greater, Cournot believes that he cannot simply assume but must actually prove, through what he calls the 'principle of the compensation of demands',[272] that it is only the direct and immediate impact of such a movement on the incomes of producers which counts.

This principle seeks to establish that the increase in the income of the producers of the exporting country does not affect the income of producers of other commodities in the same country. And similarly the diminution of income of the producers of the given commodity in the importing country does not affect the incomes of other producers in that country.

Thus if in the exporting country we had for the commodity M (see Table 9.1):

TABLE   9.1

	Price	Quantity consumed	Quantity exported	Quantity produced
Before trade	p_a	D_a	—	D_a
After trade	p'_a	$\triangle$	E	$D'_a = \triangle + E$

where $p'_a > p_a$, $D_a > \triangle$ and $D'_a > D_a$, the increase in the income of the producers will be

(5) $$p'_a D'_a - p_a D_a$$

This extra income plus the amount released because certain domestic buyers no longer buy the commodity at the higher price,

(6) $$p_a(D_a - \triangle)$$

could conceivably be devoted to increasing the demand for other domestic commodities in general. What actually happens, however, Cournot maintains,[273] is that this extra purchasing power is diverted to buying imports of exactly equal value to exports,

(7) $p'_a E$ and to financing the expenditure of those domestic buyers who continue to buy the commodity and who now need an extra amount equal to

(8) $$(p'_a - p_a)\triangle$$

Since (5) + (6) = (7) + (8), nothing is left to finance the demand for other commodities, the implication being that there is no change in the income of their producers[274] but only a change in the income of producers of M which is reflected in the national income.[275]

Cournot, thus, in this reasoning concedes that the importation of commodities other than M will largely counterbalance the increase in the income of producers of M. What effect this importation will have on incomes and prices of the same commodities produced at home is not considered by Cournot; nor for that matter does he examine how factors would be reallocated and how this reallocation would affect incomes and prices.

It would be quite legitimate for Cournot to *assume* that other incomes and prices remain unchanged. But the peculiarity of the 'Principle of the compensation of demands' is that, by showing only a part of the picture, he seeks to establish that prices and incomes do remain unchanged and believes that his result can form the basis for policy recommendations. 'We believe', he writes,[276] 'that this question',[277] when considered in its theoretical aspect, can be reduced to very simple terms, of which the mere statement, by overthrowing false systems, opens the way to the practical knowledge which essentially concerns the destiny of nations. It is on this account that the considerations which we are here examining appear to us something more than mere intellectual exercises or chimerical abstractions.'[278]

(b) Changes in income

Given the 'principle of compensation of demands', the calculations of changes in income are similar to those for the Social Income.

Since the increase in the nominal income of the exporting country is

$$(5) \qquad p'_a D'_a - p_a D_a,$$

the 'real change in the social income' is found[279] by deducting from the nominal income the excess which consumers in the country had to pay for commodity M, i.e.

$(9)\, (p'_a - p_a)\triangle$ \qquad This 'real change' in income is therefore

$$(10)\, p'_a (D'_a - \triangle) - p_a (D_a - \triangle) = p'_a E - p_a (D_a - \triangle)$$

since $D'_a - \triangle = E$.

\qquad Since $p'_a > p_a$ and[280] $E > D_a - \triangle$

$$(11) \qquad p'_a E > p_a (D_a - \triangle) \text{ and the change in real}$$

income in the case of the exporting country is always positive.[281]

In the case of the importing market, if for the commodity M we had (see Table 9.2)

TABLE   9.2

	Price	Quantity consumed	Quantity imported	Quantity produced
Before Trade	p_b	D_b	—	D_b
After Trade	p'_b	$D'_b + E$	E	D'_b

where $p_b > p'_b$, $D_b > D'_b$ and $D'_b + E > D_b$, there would be a diminution in money income, since $p_b D_b > p'_b D'_b$. This would be equal to

$$(12) \qquad p_b D_b - p'_b D'_b$$

To find the 'real change in income' Cournot deducts[282] from (12), what consumers of M in B, who had been buying it before trade began, gain through the fall in price

$$(13) \qquad (p_b - p'_b)D_b$$

The net result is equal to:

$$(14) \qquad p'_b(D_b - D'_b)$$

This Cournot calls 'the decrease in real income' of the importing country, which is due to the importation of M.[283]

(c) The criticism of Cournot's analysis of international income effects

These results were in direct contradiction with the doctrine of classical writers. They, using the theory of comparative costs, were able to determine each country's advantage in terms of its imports.[284] Cournot presents imports as diminishing a country's real income. This is not only due to his method but also to his definition of such 'real changes'; he feels free to ignore in part the effects of foreign trade on the income of the consumers. 'In deducing the real increase,' he writes,[285] "due to exportation of commodity M, we have not considered the loss experienced by that class of home consumers who stop buying the dearer commodity, and who thus make a use less to their liking of a part of their incomes. This loss ... is not capable of measurement and does not directly affect the national wealth in the commercial and mathematical sense of this term.' Similarly, in examining the effects of importation, he wrote[286]: 'We do not consider, as an amount to be deducted from this actual diminution of income, the advantage resulting to consumers, who buy as a consequence of the reduction, from their thus being able to use a part of their incomes more to their liking. This advantage is incapable of valuation.'[287]

Cournot was, however, aware that his results would arouse a spate of criticism and he sought to forestall it in part.

He first concedes that if the commodity is 'exotic', the natural conditions of production of which, that is, do not exist in the country of importation, then the national income of this country does not experience any change since 'the quantities D_b and D'_b become equal to zero or insignificant';[288] in the country of exportation, however, there is always a nominal and real increase in income.

To the argument that each of the markets A and B 'should be considered as importing and exporting at the same time'[289] and then there would be 'no apparent reason why the wealth of the former should be affected by the establishment of communication, in any way differently from the wealth of the latter',[290] he concedes that no country can only export and never import and that 'it would probably happen that the removal of barriers, by causing exportation of certain commodities M, N, P, from A to B, would cause the exportation of certain commodities of a different kind $R, S, T, \ldots$ from B to A'.[291] But he objects that he did not set out to examine this; 'Our supposition', he writes, 'was that there was no change in the facility of communications between markets A and B, except with reference to commodity M'; and he adds[292]: 'Doubtless the quantity E of commodity M cannot pass from A to B, without having an equal value imported, directly or in some roundabout way from B to A; but we have considered this foreign demand which the act of importation necessitates on market B, and we have shown that this increase in the foreign demand was more than offset by the impoverishment of the home producers of commodity M in consequence of importation, and by the reduction of the total fund which home consumers could apply to the collective demand for commodities $R, S, T, \ldots$ other than M .... We have therefore accounted for all the data of the problem.' But Cournot's critics were not satisfied that he had accounted for all the data of the problem; their criticism aims to show that Cournot failed to measure correctly the advantages from foreign trade. Some approach the problem from the side of consumption, others from the side of production.

The first to find fault with Cournot's calculations was Carl Heinrich Hagen in his book *Die Nothwendigkeit der Handelsfreiheit für das Nationaleinkommen, mathematisch nachgewiesen.*[293] He criticises Cournot because in his calculations he used the gross revenue pD without deducting costs. But his main criticism is that when a branch is diminishing its activity 'the funds which are no longer used, flow to other activities',[294] and, on the contrary, when a branch needs more funds, these will have to come from other branches of production.[295] Nor is he satisfied that consumers in the importing country gain, through the fall in price, only[296] $(p_b - p'_b)D_b$. For, he says, the quantity they now use has increased, say by an amount d; before the fall in price they would have to pay for this amount, $D_b + d$, a sum equal to $p_b(D_b + d)$, while they now pay only $p'_b(D_b + d)$. Their gain is therefore $(p_b - p'_b)(D_b + d)$. Such an argument may be as arbitrary as Cournot's but it really has helped to show the weakness in Cournot's calculation of real income.[297]

Cournot himself attempted in his *Principes*[298] to answer the main criticism of Hagen. Against Hagen's contention that, when an article is no longer produced or produced in a smaller quantity, the factors previously used for its production would find alternative employment in other branches, he observes that through his 'principle of compensation of demands' he had taken account, 'in the appreciation of average results, of the transfer of funds withdrawn from the demand of article A, to the demand of articles E, F, ...'.[299] But to the observation of Hagen that the increase in the production of a branch can come about only at the expense of other branches, he concedes that 'there may be circumstances when an industry will not be able thus to develop except at the expense of another'.[300]

R. de Fontenay in his review of the *Principes* goes much deeper in his critcism. He points out the very restricted way in which Cournot examined the problem; the changes in the social income are the very short-run and 'are far from taking account of the total phenomenon and the undefined effects of repercussion and reciprocity which are due to these first variations'.[301] Like Hagen, he wonders about the usefulness of measuring changes of the gross income; he feels that changes in net income and wages would be more useful to discuss.[302] But his main criticism is this: For the commodity M exported from country A to B, a commodity N of equal value has to be imported into

A from *B*. If *A* gains and *B* loses from the trade in commodity *M*, the contrary is true of commodity *N*. The error of Cournot, he writes,[303] 'is the result of the fact that, through a unilateral preoccupation and perhaps also through a notation which is at times complicated and incomplete, M. Cournot stressed too much the state of market *A* and the variations of the quantity and price of commodity *M*; while he dealt very summarily with this equal counter-value of commodity *N*, which he does not even designate and of which he does not denote algebraically either the demand or the price'.[304]

C. F. Bastable, in *The Theory of International Trade*,[305] finds fault with Cournot not only because of his results about the effect on social income, but also because he uses prices throughout his argument. He finds his results so 'unreal and impossible' that he implies that 'some disturbing cause must have influenced his judgment',[306] the disturbing cause being supposed to be Cournot's preoccupation with finding arguments in favour of protection.

For F. Y. Edgeworth, in the *Theory of International Values*,[307] it is Cournot's failure to account for the consumer's surplus in calculating the advantages drawn by consumers in the importing country (to which J. Bertrand had already drawn attention) which is the main weakness of his approach. The idea of consumer's surplus is also used in another way by A. Landry,[308] who shows that Cournot, not only failed to take into account the wider repercussions of changes in income, but also that he did not measure correctly the immediate advantages accruing to the nations from their imports and exports; for the prices, which Cournot uses, do not represent the utility derived. The fact that a country paid a certain price for its imports will mean that on the average it has derived greater utility from them than this price would indicate; while on the contrary the exports, through which it pays for these imports, will have a smaller utility for the nation because 'the mere fact that its members let foreigners take them at this price indicates that for them they have a smaller value in use'.[309]

H. E. Barrault develops further Fontenay's argument. Why should country *B*, he asks, not choose to export to *A* in payment for its import of *M*, a commodity on which it makes a profit equal or even superior to what *A* makes on the commodity *M*? In such a case, even under Cournot's definition of income, both countries may well find that their income has increased.[310]

J. W. Angell in *The Theory of International Prices* made the sole effort to rehabilitate Cournot's position in respect of the effects of international trade; he points out that Cournot was interested in the study of the effects of trade of a single commodity which is produced under conditions of increasing cost. But to justify Cournot's contention that there is a real loss to the importing country, he ignores the whole of Cournot's discussion on the principle of compensation of demands and substitutes in its place what he says is Cournot's 'unstated premise as to the probable loss from a displacement of domestic industry'[311] because of the lack of mobility of productive resources. But, as Viner has pointed out,[312] this was exactly exactly Hagen's argument, and Cournot, as we have already seen, 'expressly rejects this interpretation and claims that his method of computation gives full consideration to any income resulting from a transfer to other employment of the resources released from the production of *M*'.

From all this criticism one must carefully distinguish two separae issues. The first refers to the criticism of Cournot over his alleged measurement of the benefits from international trade. There is some confusion at this point; the second issue is that arising from Cournot's measurement of changes in income.

The confusion is due to Cournot's use of the term 'real changes in income'. We could interpret Cournot's argument in this way: if a change in money income is to be a real change, it must be accompanied by a change in the amount of goods over which the money income exercises command. Let us, therefore, assume, the argument continues, that there is, together with an increase in income equal to $p'_a D'_a - p_a D_a$, an increase in the price of only one good *A*, while prices of all other goods have remained constant. Now, therefore, an increased amount will have to be paid for the consumption of this good; if we deduct this amount from the total increase of the money income, the remainder will represent an increase in the command over goods, since there is an increase which is devoted to goods, other than *A*, the prices of which are assumed to remain unchanged.[313] His formula of 'real changes in income' is therefore an index of changes in quantities over which one has command and has nothing to do with measuring benefits, which is an entirely different thing. To accuse therefore Cournot that he did not measure correctly or fully the *benefits* from international trade is unjust; what he sought to do is, as he himself said in his title of the chapter, to study 'variations in the Social Income, resulting from the communication of markets'. A more valid criticism against him would be that he sought to base, on his conclusions about the effects on incomes, policy recommendations without seeking to enquire into the *benefits* from international trade arising from specialisation and better use of resources.[314]

But it is Cournot's attempt to measure changes in incomes in a system of partial equilibrium and, worse still, his attempt to prove that other prices and other incomes do remain unchanged, which is the root of the trouble.

Had he chosen to discuss the effects of international trade in a system of general equilibrium, he would not have assumed that it is only the price of the commodity studied which changes; the very basis of his calculations of the 'real changes in income', which is, as we saw, that other prices remain constant, would have vanished. Nor would he have been able to say that the exportation or importation of a commodity affects the money incomes of the producers of this commodity alone, and that this is reflected in the national income, other incomes and prices remaining unchanged. Even if he had dealt only in two commodities, he would have to concede that the exportation of the first commodity would mean the importation of the second; while prices of and incomes from the first commodity went up, the prices of and incomes from the second commodity in the same country would have gone down. There would be a flow of resources from production of the second commodity to the first; the obverse results would have been produced in the other country. The changed prices and incomes would again affect the domestic production and foreign trade of both countries, and the familiar movements of the Theory of Comparative Costs would have been set in motion.

9.10 COURNOT'S LATER ECONOMIC WORKS AND HIS VIEWS ON ECONOMIC POLICY

(i) The *Principes*

The *Principes de la théorie des richesses* appeared twenty-five years after the *Recherches*. The chief aim was to present again the ideas of the *Recherches*, but in a form more acceptable to the economists of his time. 'I would like to see today', he writes[315], 'if I have erred in my basic ideas or only in the form: and to this end I have taken up again my work of 1838 by correcting it, by developing it where the developments were missing, by completing it in those points which I had abstained from touching, and above all by *absolutely stripping it of the algebraic apparatus*.'

In the *Recherches*, however, Cournot's scope was restricted; he had treated only questions where mathematical analysis was applicable or which did not appear to him 'entirely cleared up already'.[316] The product was not a complete treatise on political economy but a selection of contributions to various specific topics. The aim of the *Principes* is the production of such 'a complete and dogmatic treatise on Political Economy'.[317]

The 198 pages of the *Recherches* without the mathematics and often reproduced verbatim[318] form the core of the 523 pages of the *Principes*. They are linked together and co-ordinated by sections which are of a descriptive, philosophic or historical character. This is in keeping with Cournot's conception of what he calls 'économie sociale' – 'the science of the economy of human societies',[319] whose scope includes considerations taken from the fields of politics, morals and philosophy,[320] and of which the pure theory of wealth forms only a part. 'But the theory of wealth', adds Cournot[321], 'is not to the 'économie sociale' in the relation of servant to mistress; she is rather in the relation of daughter to mother, and she is a daughter who, while advancing and developing, can never completely detach herself from her mother. To talk without figures of speech, the various chapters of the theory of wealth, which are susceptible of scientific treatment, cannot be co-ordinated, cannot be united, in those of its parts which are incapable of acquiring or have not yet acquired scientific form, except through considerations drawn from the "économie sociale".'

The book is divided into four sections devoted to wealth, money, the economic system and economic optimism.

The section on wealth includes Cournot's pure theory of price as already set out in the *Recherches*; there is also a discussion of the various kinds of wealth and a treatment of credit, capital and rent, essentially Ricardian in character. There is also a discussion of production where an entirely new idea, that of *economic equivalence*, is introduced. Two quantities of two factors are said to be equivalent if they produce the same amount of product; there is said then to exist indifference as to which amount will be employed. 'If an industrialist', writes Cournot[322], 'employs *indifferently m* units of commodity A or n units of commodity B, because he thus obtains the same product averaging the same expense, it will be warranted to say that m units of A is the economic equivalent of n units of B.'

Cournot thus arrived at the idea of the rate of substitution but did not proceed further than the assumption of a constant rate, as he would certainly have done, had it occurred to him to link his ideas of economic equivalence with his treatment of cost and revenue in the *Recherches*, to which we have already referred.

He proceeds, however, to state the equilibrium conditions of production under his constant rate; *the ratio of the prices of the two factors must be equal to their rate of substitution.* But under his assumption of a constant unchanging rate, it is an exceptional case where the ratio of prices happens to coincide with this rate, enabling thus both the factors to be used. If the ratio of prices is different from the constant rate, only one factor, the relatively cheaper, will be used throughout, despite their equivalence from the purely technological point of view.[323] *This is the very sperm of the general equilibrium theory of production* but Cournot's contribution has remained entirely unknown. Its only mention in the literature is in a review of the *Principes* in 1864 by R. de Fontenay who found it interesting but was not in a position to appreciate its significance.[324]

Cournot has suggested, in another significant contribution, the way that a table of quantities demanded and prices could be drawn up.

If the conditions, which could bring a shift in the demand curve, such as the population, tastes, distribution of wealth, the extent of the market etc., remain unchanged, but there are shifts in the supply curve through changes in costs, taxation etc., 'prices will change, and the corresponding variations in demand, provided they have been well recorded, will be able to serve in the construction of our empiric tables'.[325] But if there are shifts in the demand curve, 'construction of our tables will be rendered impossible, because they ought to express how demand changes in response to a change in price and not because of other causes'.[326]

The section on money contains Cournot's treatment of the changes in values and the theory of foreign exchange from the *Recherches* together with two chapters on the history of money and an examination of the conditions of production and value of precious metals and of paper money. Already in the *Recherches*, he had distinguished between periodic and secular variations in the value of various commodities.[327] To this now he adds a distinction between short-term and long-term variations: 'In the system of values, in the same way as in the movement of celestial bodies, we must distinguish disturbances which are transitory and accidental (like those of comets) or short-period inequalities, whose effects are compensated by the sole lapse of time, and those *secular* variations which proceed at a great slowness.'[328] He also discusses the way of measuring changes in the value of money by preparing *index numbers with the use of appropriate weights or 'co-efficients of importance'* as he calls them[329] and calls the fixed measure of value, which he had suggested in the *Recherches* by its proper name as 'monnaie de compte'.[330]

The section on the economic system is essentially a repetition of the *Recherches* sections on social income, international trade and taxation. Much play is made with what Cournot calls the 'Principle of Compensation of Demands'; to this principle we have already extensively referred in the section on international trade. It is however Cournot's discussion of Mill's ideas on international trade which is the novelty of the *Principes*.

(ii) The *Principes* and the theory of international values

John Stuart Mill's *Principles* appeared in 1848, ten years later than the publication of the *Recherches*. The analysis of international trade in the *Principles* follows, however, the same lines as those in the *Recherches*. The only essential difference is that the argument is conducted in non-mathematical terms and that the effects of such trade on prices and incomes are treated in a unified chapter.[331]

While, however, maintaining his own ideas, Cournot devotes a whole chapter[332] to the theory of international exchange, 'as given by J. Mill and Ricardo and as more recently developed by John Stuart Mill in his *Principles of Political Economy*',[333] a theory which he considers as 'ingenious, most novel and which appears to be supported by the authority of authors, who have acquired in these matters a just renown'.[334]

Cournot first gives a variation of Mill's classic example of England and Germany, where England has a comparative advantage in producing broadcloth and Germany linen.[335] He shows how each country will specialise when trade is established, and how the exchange ratio of the two commodities will, according to Mill, reach an equilibrium position where 'the demand on each side is precisely sufficient to carry off the supply on the other'.[336]

But he is not satisfied with Mill's answer to the criticism[337] that it was conceivable that, under his theory, more than one and even an infinity of equilibria of the ratio of exchange might exist. It will be remembered that Mill recognised this as a deficiency of his theory, and proposed to supplement it by taking into consideration not only 'the quantities demanded in each country of the imported commodities, but also the extent of the means of supplying that demand which are set at liberty in each country by the change in the direction of its industry'.[338] He would rather have Mill answer that such multiple equilibria are not a phenomenon peculiar to his theory; that 'general theories are not made for these exceptional and singular cases'; and that 'variations of the economic system, for the explanation of which theories are constructed, are usually contained within very strict limits so that there is no reason to admit the possibility of more maxima or of more than one situation of equilibrium in the interval of these limits'.[339]

Nor is he satisfied with the way Mill calculates the benefit from foreign trade. Mill had assumed that before trade 10 yards exchanged for 15 yards of linen in England and for 20 in Germany. If after trade, say, '10 yards of cloth exchange for 18 of linen, England will gain an advantage of 3 yards on every 15, Germany will save 2 out of every 20'.[340] This would mean an advantage of 20 per cent for England and 10 per cent for Germany.[341]

But, says Cournot,[342] one could calculate these percentages in another way. Germany obtains for 20 units of linen, $11\frac{1}{9}$ units of cloth instead of 10; 'this represents an advantage of $1\frac{1}{9}$ on 10 or of $11\frac{1}{9}$ per cent'.[343] England obtains 20 units of linen by giving $11\frac{1}{9}$ units of cloth instead of $13\frac{1}{3}$; 'this represents an economy of $2\frac{2}{9}$ on $13\frac{1}{3}$ or of $16\frac{2}{3}$ per cent'.[344] It appears, therefore, that 'with this second method of calculation, as plausible as the other',[345] exchange profits less England and more Germany.

This disparity of numerical results Cournot considers as 'a proof of the imperfection of the principles'[346] of Mill as opposed to his own numerical results, which are consistent no matter whether the 'real changes' in income are calculated from the point of view of revenue or of consumption.[347]

The chapter concludes with an attempt to justify his own method of approach as opposed to that of the authors of the theory of international exchange. 'They have departed from the principle of logic, which is generally true, that one must proceed from the simple to the complex and it has appeared obvious to them that, by first treating the case where exchange affects only two goods between two markets, they were dealing in an effective way with the simplest case. In this they were mistaken: because exchange, even when affecting only two goods, cannot take place without influencing, through its reaction, the whole of the economic system in both markets. It would, therefore, be impossible to appreciate the effects of these reactions, except in the case where one had recourse to a principle of compensation.'[348]

What this principle of compensation of demands is and to what unfortunate results its use led in the case of the evaluation of the effects of trade on income we have already seen. The theory of comparative cost being, even in the two-goods case, a theory of general equilibrium and thus embracing the whole economic system, was able to give more satisfactory results.

(iii) The *Revue Sommaire*

The last book of the *Principes* deals with questions of policy, which because of their importance we have chosen to examine in a separate section.

The appearance of the *Principes* had provoked a hostile review in the *Journal des Economistes*,[349] to which we have already referred in the section on international trade. There the reviewer made the remark: 'When one wants to criticise a science, one must be acquainted with its current state ... M. Cournot has stopped his watch at the time of Ricardo.'[350] This criticism appears to have particularly touched Cournot. It was this remark, as he himself admits,[351] which prompted him to attempt to present his views for a third time in the *Revue sommaire des doctrines economiques*, which is essentially a repetition, often word for word, of the arguments of his two previous works.

The only difference, apart from references to economic doctrines current at the time of writing and their critique and the decided rejection of Socialism, is a new recast of the same material. There are six sections now. The 'rural economy', where he discusses the question of rent; the 'industrial economy', which covers the discussion of wealth, production and credit; the section on money which is a repetition of the same section of the Principes; the section on 'prices and revenues', which lumps together his pure theory of price and the theory of social income and includes 'almost everything which', Cournot says[352], 'would justify ... our claims to originality'; finally the section on the 'State and Nationality', which is an exposition of his views on taxation, economic optimism and economic freedom, is followed by a section on the 'Social Question', which is essentially a criticism of Socialist theories.

It is thus evident that the outstanding work is the *Recherches*. The other works certainly help towards a better understanding of Cournot's thought; but how more rewarding would have been the result, if he had not chosen to drop the method of the *Recherches*, 'the original and fruitful side of his work'[353] in the vain attempt of attracting more attention from an indifferent public!

(iv) Cournot and economic policy

The last book of the *Principes de la théorie des richesses* deals, under the title *L'optimisme économique*, with the question of economic policy, which had scarcely been touched in the *Recherches*.

(a) The object of economic activity

Cournot, like the English classical economists,[354] believes that the final object of economic activity is human consumption. 'Wealth produced', he writes[355], 'must be consumed; without consumption economic production would have no aim and all economic activity would cease.'

Such consumption covers not only the present but also the future. 'Humanity', for whose benefit nature is exploited, consists 'of a series of generations which succeed one another in time.'[356] The necessity for provision for future consumption is stressed by Cournot not only in his advocacy of F. List's view of the need of creating productive power, as we shall see later, but also in his plea for a rational and regulated exploitation of resources which are subject to exhaustion. 'The obligation', he writes[357], 'of embracing the series of successive generations, for the purpose of defining economic optimism, becomes evident when we consider the utility to be derived from wealth which is exhausted by exploitation or the exhaustion of which depends on the method of exploitation.' How long the span of time in the future should be, cannot be definitely determined, for it depends on the point of view from which the question is approached. From the point of view of a family man it does not extend beyond the lifetime of his grandchildren, while from the point of view of nations, a view towards which Cournot leans, it may extend over several generations; even "five or six centuries" he observes[358], 'are only a moderate enough lapse of time in the duration of the life of nations'.

Cournot's consumption as the final end of economic activity includes not only that of the private individuals but also that of the state. 'All economic sacrifices,' he remarks[359], 'made with the purpose of maintaining the power of public authorities, both inside and outside, are economically justified' under all conditions. In addition to defence and the maintenance of law and order, the author of the *Principes*, following the English classical economists, includes the consumption of public 'institutions which have as their object the hygiene, morals and public instruction';[360] but he also includes that 'special intervention to achieve a given economic aim', about which more will be said later.

Cournot at the same time, while sympathetic to cosmopolitic ideas,[361] is primarily a nationalist[362] in questions of policy; the aim of economic activity is the provision of the needs of a particular state – and its subjects – considered as an entity in the international community. Hence his acceptance of the need for intervention by the state in the productive process to encourage the creation of productive forces within the nation,[363] in addition to the emphasis he lays on the need for national defence.[364,365]

(b) Cournot's paternalism

Cournot as we have seen is an utilitarian, but he can by no means be considered as an individualist utilitarian. It is true that he concedes that in an educated society it may happen that 'even coarse people have enough perspicacity to sort out what affects their proper interests, better than abler people who are strangers to these interests and who disperse their attention to many objects';[366] but there may be cases, he insists, where the majority of population are in such a condition 'as to make them deaf to the voice of their better interest' ('leur intérêt bien entendu').[367] There are cases, he remarks, where individual choice and taste cannot be relied upon for the definition of human happiness. 'Common sense', he writes[368], 'tells that the whims of fashion and vanity and the perversion of tastes among the people or the privileged classes can exert an influence on price in a way, which is as contrary to the natural order of things and as unfavourable as the arbitrary or systematic measures taken by the government', which are either unintentionally ill advised or which intentionally seek an aim which is purely egoistic.[369]

Cournot's paternalism is of the mild form, however; his veto over individual choice is when such choice transgresses what 'common sense' considers as useful,[370] but he refuses to visualise the economist as an arbiter of human destiny and the absolute controller of 'the goals of production and development'.[371] 'Is it better', he asks[372], 'to buy an increase of population at the price of more arduous labour or pay by a decline in population for more comfort, more leisure, more elegance and even (at least in certain cases) more morality in community life? ... Would the sacrifice of a large number of *lives* be too high a price to pay for the improvement in the conditions of *life*? The answer is the secret of God. The economist does not probe these mysteries, he does not at all rise to this height; he remains in the terrestrial regions.'[373]

Cournot having thus discarded the subjective measure of happiness as being of universal applicability, discards now also the measure imposed from outside. And the result is the impossibility of measuring it. 'How then can we define', he asks[374], 'economic improvement, when the definition would imply a comparison between heterogeneous things, which have no common measure, which cannot be measured ... and which in any case are not numerically comparable?' But if total human happiness cannot be measured, there can be no definite proof that a given policy maximises this happiness, which ideally should be its objective.[375]

These difficulties in measuring and comparing happiness have another result; no one could, according to Cournot, decide the optimum distribution of wealth.[376] 'And if the definition of "economic optimism",' he proceeds[377], 'from the point of view of production, depends on the law of demand and implies a previous definition of the best way of distribution of wealth, and if this last definition is impossible, it follows that it is impossible to define the *optimum* from both the point of view of production and from that of distribution.'[378]

The impossibility of defining 'absolute happiness' does not obviate from defining a 'relative happiness'. 'If there is a change in a part of the economic system, which is not of a nature to spread over the rest of the system, and if this change affects comparable things, we shall be able to declare a progress, an improvement.'[379] Thus Cournot considers that measures, which increase the population of a country without additional hardship to anyone or make life easier without affecting the population, are a good thing because they definitely increase happiness.[380] 'The difficulty cannot but arise when what favours the one, affects the other in an adverse way.'[381]

(c) The system of economic freedom

Cournot thus is definite that the aim is to maximise human happiness; but, as we have seen, when he seeks to define this optimum, he encounters difficulties. These difficulties do not, however, stop him from discussing the means for achieving this aim, for he chooses to ignore them. 'We refer now', he writes[382], 'to the principle of economic freedom, considered as the unique or one of the means of achieving the aim of economic optimism'; He proposes to discuss this no matter whether 'we have of this aim a clear and rational definition or whether our perception of this (aim) is confused'.[383]

Cournot is not generally in favour of economic freedom. It is true that 'it is quite possible to be an individualist utilitarian as regards ends and yet to be something quite other than individualist as regards means';[384] but it is very difficult for the opposite to happen. A non-individualist utilitarian as regards ends, like Cournot, cannot entirely trust that individualism *per se*, even within a proper framework, will be able to achieve in a satisfactory manner the aims set. But Cournot is not simply an *a priori* theoretician; he argues his case. As a matter of fact, Cournot reacts strongly against the 'Harmonielehre', the *a priori* belief in the existence of economic harmonies, which was prevalent amid certain quarters of thought of his time and his immediate past.[385] That there are harmonies in the moral sphere is accepted by Cournot. But, he adds[386], 'there is nothing in the harmonies of the moral order, from which one could conclude for or against harmonies of an economic order'. On the other hand, a certain harmony can be observed in natural phenomena, especially those involving living organisms. But economic society is not a living organism. 'It would be very difficult to accept,' he writes[387], 'and above all very difficult to prove that something analogous to the wonderful instinct of the animal, to the mysterious principle of evolution of the functions of life, operates within human societies (with a complicated, aged and increasingly artificial civilisation) and results in producing within the economic order, without direction or premeditation and without conscience, that perfect subordination of the parts to the whole (and) of the elementary organs to the complete organism.'

One cannot therefore accept that between the actions of individuals, freely pursuing their own interests, and the general interest there is 'an organic, instinctive or mysterious concert' [388]. If in fact such an accord exists, it is the result of a 'mechanical adjustment' and its 'existence should be proved by reasoning and the calculus',[389] a demonstration which our author claims had not that far been provided.

There are vivid passages in the *Principes*, where actions by individuals manifestly detrimental to the social interest are described.[390] Such actions, however, which are of a markedly antisocial character may be regulated by law and, of course, the most fervent apostles of economic freedom could very well have found a place for such regulations in the framework of law with which society was provided.[391] The important question is to see whether, under a regime of Economic Freedom,[392] there exists a form of market under which, a reconciliation of individual and social interests could automatically be achieved, the implication being that, if no such market form can be found, economic freedom cannot be accepted. Cournot rejects the market form of monopoly by referring to the results of his discussion on monopoly, where he had shown that a monopolist 'would rather lose a portion of the product than consent to a very large fall in price'.[393]

But he also rejects the market form of free competition.[394] Unlike the English classical economists who were mainly preoccupied with consumption, Cournot, though accepting consumption as the final aim, is preoccupied with the source of satisfying consumption i.e. production and especially with the need for promoting the productive forces of the nation.[395] Such arguments therefore as that the force of competition guides the motives of self-interest to produce what is needed by the consumers do not impress him. He is rather worried that unlimited competition may, under certain circumstances, harm the productive forces of the country. 'As under free competition,' he writes[396], 'each particular producer has no sensible influence on prices and total production, none of them can avert the unpleasant results' of their combined influence.

It is therefore possible that competition may be so acute as to push prices to such a low level 'as to bring about the discomfort of producers and vitiate the organs of production'.[397]

In such a case 'it does not only harm those immediately suffering, it becomes harmful to the whole social body, whatever apparent advantage it may for the moment give to the other classes of the society'.[398] Such free competition may, among other consequences,[399] bring about overproduction of consumer goods and commercial crises with the consequent waste of resources.[400]

(d) The methods of government intervention

Cournot, therefore, argues that no matter what the form of the market is, there is *in theory* some form of government intervention, which would assist in the better attainment of the aims of economic activity.

Such action on behalf of the government cannot be restricted 'to that general action which consists in the maintenance, through a good police, through good justice and through the maintenance of a sufficient public force, of freedom and the fidelity of engagements, and the safety of persons and properties'; nor to the creation of 'institutions which have as their aim the hygiene, the morals and public instruction'.[401]

In addition to the above there is place for 'special intervention to achieve a given economic aim'.[402]

The main forms of government intervention which Cournot has in mind are the following: The provision of public works, such as routes, canals, railways, ports, docks and so on.[403] Such services may be of indiscriminate benefit to the community; there are insurmountable obstacles to 'an ideal distribution of a purely economic expense among all those, whom this expense profits, in just proportion to the benefit they derive'.[404] A private individual who builds a road cannot charge all those, whom the opening of the route indirectly benefits; they 'can only be reached in their capacity as contributors to the State, when the State, recognising the necessities of the situation, undertakes itself the expenses of construction and maintenance or ensures a subsidy to those who undertake them'.[405]

There may, however, be other reasons for the state's filling the gap left by individual initiative. A project's advantages may take too long a time to become effective. 'A nation can sow to reap at the end of half a century but neither an individual, nor a Company can do this, whatever the relation between harvest and sowing.'[406] Uncertainty might be another reason for the individuals' shunning of projects which are considered essential. 'In the case of individual entrepreneurs, the perspective of large benefits must compensate for the uncertainty of success; and there is no way in which one could rely, in such a case, on competition among insurance companies to reduce the exaggerated premium,[407] necessary to insure against such uncertainty.'

The protection and direct encouragement of selected branches of the national industry are, however, the main forms of government intervention to which Cournot refers again and again.

An industry may be worthy of government intervention because it is necessary for the defence of the State or because it is one which brings honour to the nation by developing the Arts or the Sciences.[408] But beyond these, Government intervention must be extended in favour of infant industries. 'When a new industry has just been born (even that

which is destined to have the most vigorous growth) must it not at first
be sheltered and get acclimatized and all those employed by it, must
they not make their apprenticeship?'[409] 'Time is also needed to give a
new direction to the tastes, to the needs, to the habits of the
consumers, in such a way as to extend the market for the new product
as much as is required by the conditions of most economical
production.'[410] The extent of such protection and the time during
which it will last depend on the circumstances and cannot be 'the
object of a general discussion.'[411]

Cournot believes that for this form of 'encouragement given in a
purely economic aim, nobody doubts any more, in principle, the
utility of a temporary encouragement'.[412] But he, himself, is prepared
to go further, and allow the State to encourage and protect an industry
in a permanent way, if it considers that this is in the national interest.
He is not at all satisfied with the argument that this would have as a
result that 'the Government, by diverting capital from its natural
tendency,[413] makes necessarily a distribution less advantageous to
total production and to the wealth of the country'.[414] He points out
that the government encouragement will mean the diversion to the
chosen branch of not only capital but all other kinds of resources.
And since 'it has not been shown for either the capital or the other
productive resources, that the direction of the general interest should
necessarily co-incide with that of the resultant of individual forces',
why, he asks[415] 'should government encouragement not be that
additional force which would make the resultant of individual
interests coincide in direction with that of the general interest?'

The form of encouragement can simply be honorific rewards, which
do not cost anything or cost very little to taxpayers, like prizes, medals
and decorations.[416] But beyond this one must recognise to the State
'the right and the duty to distribute (within the limits of the resources
at its disposal) its protection and its encouragement, even in a
permanent way, in accordance with the way *which appears to it* the
most favourable to production'.[417]

There is another possible form of government intervention, on
which Cournot's stand is ambiguous, and which consists in 'directly
influencing the method of distribution of wealth'.[418] Cournot had, as
we have seen, been unable to define the optimum distribution of
wealth, but his stand here is that there has been in every society a
dominant idea of what this optimum should be and that Government
intervention has aimed at giving effect to this idea. The various laws
relating to succession and the acquisition of property are of major

importance in bringing about the desired redistribution,[419] progressive taxation on income or estate is another means by which 'Governments can influence in an efficacious, though slow, way the method of distribution of wealth',[420] if this is coupled with government spending favouring the working classes.

But Cournot is not prepared to accept measures leading to people ceasing to 'have as the principal objective of their offers the acquisition of private property and the creation of a fund of transmissible wealth';[421] for then he asks: 'What would become of the active stimulant of human effort, at all the steps of the social ladder?'

There are also other more far-reaching measures of government intervention which Cournot is prepared to contemplate like the conditional concession of soil to farmers to ensure its proper use or the compulsory acquisition of forests.[422] But there is an indispensable condition which must be met in all cases. This is that *'science will have clearly defined the aim and positively demonstrated the efficacy of the means'.*[423]

In practice, however, such demonstration and proof are not always possible. There are immense difficulties in the way 'of a just and complete evaluation of all economic effects, direct and indirect, which can result from the particular measure taken by the Government'.[424] Moreover, a protective measure leads to others and every industry clamours for protection. 'The more the protective system becomes complicated, the more difficult it becomes to appreciate its consequences and measure its effects.'[425] Under such circumstances it might be advisable to leave things to their natural course. 'In consequence, the maxim *laissez faire*, even if it does not have (as some would like) the value of an axiom or a theorem, must definitely be preferred in many cases, as an adage of practical wisdom.'[426] If one is not certain, the best thing is as it is often said of medicine, to leave nature act.

Cournot's approach is thus entirely pragmatic and as such contrasts sharply with that of the English classical economists, who believed that, given certain conditions, the system of Economic Freedom was definitely superior to any other.[427]

These are in broad outline Cournot's views on policy. But he was an extreme pessimist about the influence which economic arguments, such as his, could have on the actual conduct of policy. 'It must be recognized', he writes[428], 'that such questions as that of commercial liberty are not settled either by the arguments of scientific men or even by the wisdom of statesmen. A higher power drives nations in this direction or that, and when the day of a system is past, good reasons cannot restore its lost vitality any more than sophisms. The skill of statesmen, then, consists in tempering the ardour of innovation, without attempting an impossible struggle against the laws of providence. Possession of a sound theory may help in this labour of resistance to abrupt changes and assist in easing the transition from one system to another.'[429]

NOTES

1. The main source for Cournot's Biography is his *Souvenirs*, which were completed in 1859 but published only in 1913 by E.P. Bottinelli. The main biographies of Cournot are contained in H.L. Moore, 'Antoine Augustin Cournot' in *Revue de Métaphysique et de Morale* (Paris, May 1905, pp. 521–43) and 'The Personality of Cournot' in *Quarterly Journal of Economics* (1905, pp. 370 *et seq.*); Jean de la Harpe, 'De L'ordre et du hasard', *Neuchâtel* (1936, pp. 3 *et seq.*); L. Liard, 'Un géomètre philosophe' in *Revue des deux mondes* (Paris, July 1877, pp. 102 *et seq.*); T. Giacalone-Monaco, 'Nota Biografica e bibliografica su A.A. Cournot' in *Cournot nella economia e nella filosofia* (Padova, 1939, pp. 227 *et seq.*).
2. Cournot, *Souvenirs*, p. 35.
3. See Léon Walras, 'Cournot et l'économie mathématique' in *Gazette de Lausanne* (13 July 1905). Parts of this article are reproduced in La Harpe, op cit., pp. 143–5.
4. *Publication des mémoires militaires de Gouvion Saint-Cyr*; 4 vols (Paris Asselin, 1831). Cournot is the author of the introduction.
5. His theses for the doctorate were (a) *Mémoire sur le mouvement d'un corps rigide soutenu par un plan fixe* (Paris: Hachette, 1829) and (b) *De la figure des corps celestes*.
6. These were published chiefly in the *Bulletin des sciences mathématiques, astronomiques, physiques et chimiques* of Baron du Férussac between 1826 and 1831; other articles appear in the *Journal für die reine und angewandte Mathematik*, in the years 1830 and 1832; he later also contributed to Liouville's *Journal des mathématiques pures et appliquées*, 1838. While the authenticity of some of these articles, which Cournot signed with his full name, is undisputed, that of some others which were simply signed A.C. is disputed. See T. Giacalone-Monaco, op cit., p. 234.
7. These were *Eléments de mécanique de Rater et Lardner*, which were 'modified and completed' by Cournot (Paris, 1834) and *Traité d'astronomie de Herschel* (Paris, 1834). Both were translated from English.
8. Cournot, *Souvenirs*, Introduction, p. ix.
9. T. Giacalone-Monaco, op. cit. p. 231; La Harpe, op. cit. p. 31, also writes 'En politique il est ondoyant et fluent; il passe d'un camp à

l'autre certainement parce qu'il était trop intelligent pour faire un bon partisan: il y a toujours un arrière-fond de bêtise chez le "vrai partisan"! mais aussi par opportunisme et par crainte de nuire à sa tranquillité à laquelle il semble avoir tenu avec la même passion froide et consciente, qu'un Descartes.'

10. Cournot, *Traité élémentaire*, p. v. For an evaluation of Cournot's mathematical contributions see H. Poincaré, 'Cournot et les principes du calcul infinitésimal', in *Revue de Métaphysique* (1905) pp. 293 *et seq.* and Jean de La Harpe, 'Le rationalisme mathématique d'Antoine Augustin Cournot' in *Cournot nella Economia e nella filosofia* (Padova, 1939) pp. 3 *et seq.*

11. La Harpe, *De l'ordre et du hasard,* p. 20; H. Guitton, Preface to the *Recherches* (Camann-Lévy, 1974) pp. 12-13.

12. For criticism of Cournot's philosophic work see La Harpe, op. cit.; F. Mentré, *Cournot et la renaissance du probabilisme au XIXe siècle* (Paris, 1908); G. Milhaud, *Études sur Cournot* (Paris 1927); A. Darbon, *Le Concept du hasard dans la philosophie de Cournot* (Paris, 1911); J. Segond, *Cournot et la psychologie vitaliste* (Paris, 1911); E.P. Bottinelli, *Cournot métaphysicien de la connaissance* (Paris, 1913); R. Ruyer, *L'Humanité de l'avenir d'après Cournot* (Paris, 1930); various articles in the *Revue de Métaphysique et de Morale* (May 1905) by G. Milhaud, J. Tarde, C. Bouglé, F. Faure, A. Darlu, D. Parodi, F. Mentré, R. Audierne; the special volume: Amoroso *et al Cournot nella economia e nella filosofia* (Padova, 1939); and H. Guitton, op. cit., pp. 22-5.

13. La Harpe, *De l'ordre et du hasard*, p. 62.

14. Reichardt, op. cit., p. 6.

15. R. Roy, 'L'Oeuvre économique d'Augustin Cournot', in *Econometrica* (April 1939) p. 135.

16. La Harpe, op. cit., p. 63.

17. G. Lutfalla, pp. xiii–ix of the Introduction to the edition of the *Recherches* in the *Collection des économistes et des reformateurs sociaux de la France* (1938).

18. La Harpe, op. cit., p. 64.

19. Ibid., p. 64.

20. N.F. Canard *Principes d' économie politique* (Paris, 1801).

21. Cournot, *Researches into the Mathematical Principles of the Theory of Wealth*, trans. by N. T. Bacon (Macmillan) (1929) pp. 4–5. It is to this edition that we refer in all the coming chapters as *Researches*.

22. Cournot, *Researches*, p. 5.

23. Ibid., p. 48.

24. Ibid., p. 3.

25. Ibid., p. 2.

26. For as he says symbols and formulas 'are able to facilitate the exposition of problems, to render it more concise, to open the way to more extended developments, and to avoid the digression of vague argumentation'. Ibid., pp. 3–4.

27. Ibid., p. 4.

28. Ibid., p. 10. See also Aupetit, *'L'Oeuvre économique de Cournot'* in

Revue de Métaphysique et de Morale, (1905) p. 380.

29.   Ibid., p. 10.
30.   Ibid., p. 17.
31.   Ibid., p. 16. 'Political Economy fails to make progress by theory, towards its noble object of the improvement of the lot of mankind, either because the relations which it has to deal with are not reducible to fixed terms, or because these relations are much too complicated for our powers of combination and analysis.'
32.   Ibid., p. 49–50.
33.   See his equations in *Researches*, pp. 57, 120, and Fisher's 'Notes on Cournot's Mathematics', *Researches*, p. xv.
34.   Ibid., p. 51.
35.   Ibid., p. 10.
36.   Ibid., p. 9.
37.   Ibid., p. 17.
38.   Ibid., p. 17.
39.   Ibid., p. 24.
40.   Ibid., p. 24.
41.   Ibid., p. 22. Cournot's views on relative and absolute values are discussed by L. Walras in the 28th Lesson of the *Eléments d' économie politique pure*, 1st edn (1874) pp. 163–8 and in a letter to Cournot dated 20 March 1874, *Econometrica* (1935) pp. 122 *et seq*. Walras believes that while in theory one cannot accept the fixity of the value of a good because this would involve the fixity of all other values. In practice and in face of a great number of goods, such fixity may be accepted, changes in other values being insignificant.
42.   Ibid., p. 26.
43.   Cournot actually shows, ibid. p. 27, that a relation could be established to show how the monetary value of the article varied. Thus if p, p' are the values of an article in terms of the fixed modulus at two points of time, π, π' are the values of the monetary metal in terms of the modulus; the monetary value of the article will have varied in the ratio of

$$\frac{p}{\pi} \text{ to } \frac{p'}{\pi'}.$$

44.   Cournot uses the expression 'De la loi du débit' which is better translated as 'Law of Sales'. As however N. T. Bacon, Cournot's original translator into English, used the expression "Law of Demand", we have chosen to keep it. See also C.L. Fry and R.B. Ekelund, *'Cournot's Demand Theory: a Reassessment'*, in *History of Political Economy* (1971) p. 192.
45.   R. Roy, 'Cournot et l' école mathématique', *Econometrica* (1933) p. 17.
46.   *Researches*, p. 45.
47.   Ibid., p. 47.
48.   Cournot defines as the market 'the entire territory of which the parts are so united by the relations of unrestricted commerce that prices there take the same level throughout, with ease and rapidity'. Ibid., pp. 51–2n.

49. Ibid., p. 127, my underlining.
50. Ibid., p. 127.
51. Ibid., p. 47. It was Walras who later derived these individual demand curves. See Fisher, op. cit., *Quarterly Journal of Economics* (1898) p. 125.
52. *Researches*, pp. 47–8.
53. Ibid., p. 46.
54. Ibid., p. 46. E.g. diamonds
55. Ibid., p. 46.
56. Ibid., pp. 49–51.
57. Ibid., pp. 49–51.
58. Ibid., p. 50.
59. Ibid., p. 52.
60. Cournot's Fig. 1, reproduced at the end of *Researches*.
61. Ibid., pp. 52–3
62. Ibid., p. 53.
63. Ibid., p. 53. This is because from (2) above we get $-\dfrac{F(p)}{p} = F'(p)$ But $-\dfrac{F(p)}{p}$ is $\dfrac{nq}{0q}$ while $F'(p)$ is $\dfrac{nq}{qt}$. It follows therefore that $0q = qt$ and $0n = nt$.
64. Ibid., p. 54.
65. Ibid., pp. 53–4. This can be converted into traditional Marshallian elasticity of demand (Marshall, *Principles*, Math. Appendix, note III, p. 691), because by transfering the terms in (4) we get $\dfrac{\triangle D}{D} : \dfrac{\triangle p}{p} < 1$. The negative sign has already been taken into consideration by the assumption of Cournot that $\triangle + p$ leads to $D - \triangle D$.
66. Ibid., p. 54.
67. As we have seen, W. Whewell had used the concept of demand elasticity a little earlier than Cournot, but there is no indication that the latter was aware of Whewell's contribution.
68. *Researches*, pp. 54–5.
69. Ibid., p. 55.
70. Ibid., p. 57.
71. Ibid., p. 59. The italics are in the text. While therefore the absolute expense increases, the relative (or average) cost may decrease or increase.
72. Ibid., p. 59.
73. Ibid., p. 59.
74. Ibid., pp. 89–90.
75. Sometimes, in the economic literature, however, the terms increasing, decreasing or constant returns refer to the fact that the *average* cost curve, and not the *marginal* cost, is rising, falling or constant.
76. *Researches*, p. 59.
77. Ibid., p. 59.
78. Ibid., p. 60.
79. Ibid., p. 60.
80. Ibid., p. 60.

81. Cf. F. Bompaire, *Du principe de liberté économique dans l'oeuvre de Cournot et dans celle de l'Ecole de Lausanne* (Paris, 1931) p. 76; Roy, op. cit., 1933, p. 20.

82. *Researches*, p. 60.

83. *D* is in this case the tickets sold. Cf. *Researches*, p. 61.

84. Ibid., p. 91.

85. If the marginal cost $\varphi'_k(D_k)$ is decreasing *throughout*, however, the further production is increased the smaller becomes the marginal cost. Given free competition, such a hypothesis would mean 'that nothing would limit the production of the article', *Researches*, p. 91. It is not therefore strictly correct what is said by Edgeworth in his *Review of Cournot; Papers*, vol. III, p. 111, that 'equilibrium is not possible'. It is possible but only at zero price.

86. *Researches*, p. 91.

87. Ibid., p. 91.

88. Ibid., Fig. 6.

89. Ibid., p. 92.

90. Cournot has in his figure given his supply curves with their convex sides towards the axis *y*, but he adds later (p. 93) that 'the result of the construction would be the same if the curves turned their concave side towards this axis'.

91. *Researches*, p. 93. Cournot adds on the same page that the more inelastic is the demand curve, or as he says, the more *MN* approaches a straight line parallel to the abscissa, the more the increase in price will approximate the tax.

92. J.R. Hicks, 'Léon Walras'. *Econometrica*, vol. III (1934) pp. 339–40.

93. On the early theory of Monopoly see R. de Roover, 'Monopoly Theory before Adam Smith' in *Quarterly Journal of Economics* (1951) pp. 492–524, reproduced in R. de Roover's *Business, Banking and Economic Thought in Late Medieval and Early Modern Europe* (Univ. of Chicago, 1974) pp. 273–305.

94. Aristotle, *Politics* (Jowett trans. 1908) pp. 48–9.

95. Among others St. Thomas Aquinas, Albertus Magnus, Saint Bernadine of Siena, Molina, Lessius, Saint Antoninus Forciglioni, Joannes Maior, Soto, Medina, Binsfeld, Biel, etc.

96. N. Oresme, *Traictie de la première invention des monnoies* (1360).

97. C. Summenhart, *De Contractibus Licitis Atque Illicitis, Tractatus Conradi Summenhart, de Calvv.* (1500). See the Venice Edition of 1580, Tract. III Qu. LI.

98. Joannes Maior, Scotus, *Quartum Sententiarum* (1509), Dist. 15, Qu. 41.; D. Bañez, *Decisiones de Jure et Justitia* (1588) Qu. 77, art. 4.

99. Eg. Erasmus, Grotius and Jean Bodin.

100. J.J. Becher, *Politischer Diskurs von den eigentlichen Ursachen des Auffund Abnehmens der Städt, Länder und Republicken* (1668) pp. 26 et seq.

101. Among these John Wheeler, Sir Edwin Sandys, N. Brent, E. Misselden, J. Cary and G. Malynes. To the same category belongs K. Peutinger.

102. F. Galiani, 'Della Moneta' (1750) in Custodi, op. cit., vol. III, p. 47.

103. See Condorcet, *Mélanges d' Économie Politique* (1847) pp. 459 *et seq.*;

E.B. de Condillac, *Le Commerce et le gouvernement* (1776) pp. 227 *et seq.*

104. Eg. A. Smith, *Wealth of Nations* (1937 edn.) p. 61; Ricardo, *Principles of Political Economy and Taxation* (3rd edn, 1821) pp. 289 *et seq.*
105. Cournot, *Researches*, p. 56.
106. Ibid., pp. 82–3 and Cournot's Fig. 4.
107. Ibid., p. 84.
108. Ibid., p. 57.
109. Since (1) $\dfrac{\mathrm{d}pD}{\mathrm{d}p} = D + p\,\dfrac{\mathrm{d}D}{\mathrm{d}p}$ and (2) $\dfrac{\mathrm{d}\varphi(D)}{\mathrm{d}p} = \dfrac{\mathrm{d}\varphi(D)}{\mathrm{d}D} \cdot \dfrac{\mathrm{d}D}{\mathrm{d}p}$
110. Cournot's Fig. 5.
111. *Researches*, ch. VI, pp. 67–78.
112. C. Ellet, *An Essay on the Laws of Trade in Reference to the Works of Internal Improvement in the United States* (1839) p. 63 (There is a reprinted edition by A.M. Kelley, 1966).
113. J. Dupuit, '*De la mesure de l' utilité des travaux publics*', *Annales des Ponts et Chaussées* (1884) p. 375. See also *International Economic Papers*, no. 2 (1952) pp. 83–110.
114. C. Menger, *Grundsätze der Volkswirtschaftslebre* (1871) pp. 179 *et seq.*
115. Before Walras, M.G.F. Fauveau, in *Considérations mathématiques de l' impôt* (1854), had given a summary of Cournot's theory.
116. D. Lardner, *Railway Economy* (1850) pp. 287–92; R. Auspitz and R. Lieben, *Untersuchungen über die Theorie des Preises* (1889) pp. 361–71 also pp. 433 *et seq.* Here also belong such authors as M. Pantaleoni, E. Barone and L. Amoroso.
117. F.Y. Edgeworth, 'La teoria pura del monopolio,' *Giornale degli Economisti* (1897), pp. 13–31, 307–20 and 405–14, reproduced in *Papers Relating to Political Economy* (1925) Vol. I, pp. 111–95; H. Cunyghame, 'Some Improvements in Simple Geometrical Methods of Treating Exchange Value, Monopoly and Rent, *Economic Journal* (1892) p. 49. Other authors belonging to this category are A.L. Bowley, A. C. Pigou, K. Wicksell and F. Zeuthen.
118. A. Marshall, 'Graphic Representation by Aid of a Series of Hyperbolas of Some Economic Problems Having Reference to Monopolies, *Proceedings of the Cambridge Philosophical Society*, vol. II (1876) pp. 318–9.
119. Lardner, op. cit., p. 292, A Marshall, *Principles of Economics*, 8th edn p. X; S. Chapman, *Outlines of Political Economy* (1911) pp. 181–91 of the 1929 edn.
120. T.O. Yntema, 'The Influence of Dumping on Monopoly Price', *Journal of Political Economy* (1928) pp. 687–8.
121. E.H. Chamberlin, 'On the Origin of "Oligopoly" ', *Economic Journal* (June 1957) p. 214
122. Chamberlin, op. cit., pp. 213–14; E. Heckscher, *Mercantilism*, vol. I, p. 213; J. Schumpeter, *History of Economic Analysis* (1954) p. 305 n.
123. There were five editions of the *Meditazioni* during 1771. We refer to the third edition, when referring to an edition made in 1771.
124. Verri, op. cit. (1771) p. 21; Verri also dealt with the case of monopoly in an earlier work 'Riflessioni sulle leggi vincolanti principalmente nel

commercio de'grani', (1769), which is reproduced in P. Custodi,
   Scrittori Classici Italiani di Economia Politica, parte moderna, vol. XVI.
125. Verri, *Meditazioni* (1771) p. 21. The term 'universal commodity'
   denotes money.
126. See note 125.
127. Carli's annotation was made in 1771 and is reproduced in Custodi's
   Scrittori Classici, vol. XV, pp. 44–5.
128. Verri, *Meditazioni sulla Economia Politica*, in *Opere filosofiche del
   Conte Pietro Verri* (Paris, 1784) p. 202, to which we refer. Custodi, op.
   cit., vol. XV, pp. 44–5, gives also the second version.
129. Verri, op. cit. (1784) p. 202.
130. Cf. F. Zeuthen, *Problems of Monopoly and Economic Warfare* (1930)
   p. 29; R.F. Kahn, 'The Problem of Duopoly' in *Economic Journal*
   (1937) p. 4. J. Bertrand, *Théorie mathématique de la richesse sociale,
   par Léon Walras* (1883); 'Recherches *sur les principes mathématiques de
   la théorie des richesses par Augustin Cournot*, Paris, 1838', in *Journal
   des Savants* (1883) pp. 499–508. Bertrand, in reviewing the Cournot
   theory of oligopoly, described the Cournot oligopolists as proceeding
   through price adjustments, which is, of course, an inaccurate
   representation of Cournot's views.
131. Thus if $OD' > OD$ are the sales of the duopolist at two points of time
   where his price is $OP > OP'$ and there are no costs, Verri's condition is
   that $OP'(OD' - OD) > (OP - OP')$ OD or rectangle $DBCD' >$ rect.
   $PP'BA$. (Fig. 9.1n.)

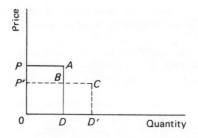

FIG. 9.1n

132. It is thus evident that whereas Carli would have the duopolists act
   through fear, Verri's version, motivated no doubt by Carli's criticism,
   seeks to base the explanation of their behaviour on more 'rational'
   grounds.
133. Verri, op. cit. (1784) p. 202.
134. That is, with reference to Fig. 9.1n, $(0P - 0P')0D$ is now smaller than
   in the case of duopoly, because $0D$ is smaller, and correspondingly a
   smaller extension of sales $0D' - 0D$ is needed to make rectangle
   $DBCD' >$ rectangle PP'BA.
135. Verri, *Meditazioni* (1784) p. 202.
136. Ibid., p. 202.
137. Ibid.

138. In Custodi, op. cit., vol. XVI, to which we refer.
139. Verri, *Riflessioni* p. 214.
140. Ibid., p. 214.
141. See esp. G. Ortes, 'Dell' economia nazionale' (1774), in Custodi, op. cit., parte moderna, vol. XXI–XXV.
142. In Custodi, op. cit. parte moderna, vol. XXIV, pp. 257–318.
143. Other interesting cases of a theory of economic conflict in terms of power are contained in, A.N. Isnard, *Traité des Richesses* (1781) vol. I, p. 4 and N.F. Canard, *Principes d' Économie Politique* (1801) pp. 29 *et seq.*, which we have already described.
144. Ortes, op. cit., p. 261. As is evident from the argument above Ortes may well be considered as a precursor of modern leadership arguments.
145. Ibid.
146. Ibid., p. 262.
147. Gioja, op. cit. (Milano, 1815) vol. III, p. 5.
148. Ibid., vol. III, p. 5.
149. Ibid., vol. III, p. 5.
150. O. Lange took a similar position in his *Price Flexibility and Employment*, p. 40, where he argues that the 'conventional price' is endowed with the halo of ethical norms and anyone who breaks away is penalised.
151. Gioja, op. cit., vol. III, p. 5.
152. Ibid., vol. III, p. 5.
153. Ibid., vol. III, p. 5.
154. Ibid., p. 5.
155. *Researches*, p. 79. This is therefore a case of simple oligopoly.
156. Ibid., p. 79. The words underlined are in italics in the text of Cournot.
157. Ibid., p. 80.
158. This is, therefore, equivalent to saying that each oligopolist assumes that the expectations of his rival about the market price will remain unchanged.
159. *Researches*, p. 80.
160. The oligopolist who fixes the market price automatically fixes the total quantity to be demanded, and as he assumes the rival's quantity as fixed and given, he thereby fixes the quantity which he himself will produce. But this *ex ante* price of his will be realised only if his assumptions about the rival's quantity, and therefore the rival's *ex ante* price, prove correct. If the expectations of neither seller prove to be correct, both *ex ante* prices will differ from the *ex post* market price.
161. *Researches*, p. 80 (my underlining).
162. But as already explained, the oligopolist may seek, instead of directly adjusting his quantity, to adjust the market price. The equation then, on the assumption of constant D_2, is

$$\frac{d(D_1 p)}{dp} = D_1 + p \frac{dD_1}{dD} \times \frac{dD}{dp} = D_1 + p \frac{1}{\dfrac{dD}{dD_1}} \times \frac{1}{\dfrac{dp}{dD}} = D_1 + \frac{p}{f'(D)} = 0$$

because when D_2 is constant

$$\frac{\mathrm{d}D}{\mathrm{d}D_1} = 1 \quad \text{and} \quad \frac{\mathrm{d}p}{\mathrm{d}D_1} = \frac{\mathrm{d}p}{\mathrm{d}D}$$

It can be seen that this result is exactly the same as that of equation (4) above. The same holds, when D_1 is given, for

$$\frac{\mathrm{d}(D_2 p)}{\mathrm{d}p} = D_2 + \frac{p}{\mathrm{f}'(D)} = 0 \quad \text{which is the same as (5)}$$

163. *Researches*, p. 82.
164. Equations (4a) and (5a) may be written as a sum in the form

$$2\mathrm{f}(D) + (D_1 + D_2)\mathrm{f}'(D) = 2\mathrm{f}(D) + D\frac{\mathrm{d}p}{\mathrm{d}D} = 2p + D\frac{\mathrm{d}p}{\mathrm{d}D} = 0$$

Multiplying this by

$$\frac{\mathrm{d}D}{\mathrm{d}p}$$

we can transform it into equation (6).
165. *Researches*, p. 81 and Fig. 2. These curves will be called by later authors 'reaction curves'. Cf. E. Schneider, *Reine Theorie monopolistischer Wirtschaftsformen* (1938) p. 142.
166. *Researches*, p. 81. The words underlined are in italics in Cournot's text.
167. See note 166.
168. For a discussion of stability in dynamic terms before Cournot see the first chapters of this work.
169. *Researches*, pp. 81–2 and Fig. 3.
170. Ibid., p. 82. This can be proved easily, because when $D_1 = 0$, equation (4a) above, which plots $m_1 n_1$, reduces to

    a) $p = \mathrm{f}(D_2) = 0$

while equation (5a) reduces to

    b) $\mathrm{f}(D_2) + D_2\mathrm{f}'(D_2) = 0$

In the first case, D_2 corresponds to a price equal to zero; in the second case, it corresponds to a price which would make pD_2 a maximum, since (b) is the condition for this maximum. In the first case, therefore, D_2 will be greater than in the second case and $om_1 > om_2$. By a similar demonstration it is proved that $on_2 > on_1$.
171. *Researches*, p. 82.
172. Ibid., p. 83. The words underlined are in italics in Cournot's text. The above argument can be easily demonstrated by means of Fig. 9.2n. The

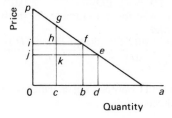

FIG. 9.2n

maximum revenue is given by a quantity *ob*, equal to half of *oa*. If one were to set his quantity at half of *ob*, equal to *oc* and the other actually produced *ob*, they would find that this would prove ultimately the best they could have done. But if (1) offers *oc*, (2) is tempted to offer what will maximise his revenue in the next period; this is half *ca* and is therefore equal to *cd* which is greater than *cb*. This, with given *oc*, would give a price *oj* and (1) would see his hopes frustrated as his revenue would be *ojkc*, which is smaller than the expected *oihc*.

173.   See note 172.

174. $-\dfrac{F(p)}{F'(p)}$ is positive, since $F_{(p)} \geqslant 0$ and $F'(p)$, because of the nature of the demand, is negative. Fig. 9.6 is Cournot's Fig. 4, slightly amended. See also Researches p. 84.

175.   Ibid., p. 85.

176.   Ibid., pp. 85–6. If the marginal costs are equal, it can be seen from (11) that there will be no difference in the equilibrium quantities of the producers.

177.   Ibid., pp. 84 *et seq.*

178.   Because $3f(D) + (D_1 + D_2 + D_3)f'(D)$ can be multiplied by $\dfrac{dD}{dp} =$

$\dfrac{1}{f'(D)}$ and since we have $p = f(D)$, (12) can be transformed into (13) above.

179.   This is an adaptation of Cournot's Fig. 4.

180.   This is of course evident from equation (13b) the solution of which gives
$$p = \frac{1}{n}\left(-\frac{F(p)}{F'(p)}\right) \text{ where } -\frac{F(p)}{F'(p)} \text{ is as}$$
already explained positive. The greater *n* is, the smaller is *p* and as *n* tends to infinity, *p* tends to become equal to zero.

181.   *Researches*, p. 85.

182.   Ibid., p. 85.

183. $f'(D)$ in the first equation of (15) is equal to $\dfrac{df(D)}{dD_1}$, in the second equation to $\dfrac{df(D)}{dD_2}$ and so on. The above summation is based on the fact that
$$\frac{df(D)}{dD_1} = \frac{df(D)}{dD_2} = \ldots = \frac{df(D)}{dD}$$
This can be easily proved for, for example, for the first, D_2, D_3 etc. are assumed constant and
$$\frac{df(D)}{dD_1} = \frac{df(D)}{dD} \times \frac{dD}{dD_1} = \frac{df(D)}{dD} \times \frac{d(D_1 + D_2 + \ldots D_n)}{dD_1} = \frac{df(D)}{dD} = \frac{dp}{dD}$$

184.   *Researches*, p. 86

185.   Ibid., pp. 87 *et seq.* and Cournot's Fig. 5, which we reproduce (Fig. 9.8) with slight amendments.

186.   Ibid., pp. 86–7.

187.   Ibid., pp. 87–9.

188.   Ellet, *Laws of Trade* (1839) p. 26.

189.   Ibid., p. 59. A similar diagram is also given ibid., p. 25. The diagram

has been slightly amended in its notation.

190. Ellet, op. cit., pp. 58–9.
191. Ibid., p. 59.
192. Ibid., p. 60.
193. Ibid., p. 73.
194. Ibid., p. 39.
195. Ibid., p. 74.
196. E. g. E.H. Chamberlin, *The Theory of Monopolistic Competition*, 7th edn (1960) pp. 30–55; W.J. Fellner, *Competition Among the Few* (1960) pp. 55–119; E. Schneider, *Einführung in die Wirtschaftstheorie*, IV Teil (1962) pp. 348–79.
197. By R.D. Theocharis, 'On the Stability of the Cournot Solution on the Oligopoly Problem', *Review of Economic Studies* (1960) pp. 133–4; also R.D. Theocharis, *'Some Dynamic Aspects of the Oligopoly Problem'*, *Jahrbücher für Nationalökonomie und Statistik* (1965) pp. 354–64.
198. Mainly by Koji Okuguchi, F.M. Fisher, M. McManus and R.E. Quant, F.H. Hahn, R.L. Bishop, C.R. Frank, J. Hadar, R. Sato, K. Nagatani, etc. mainly in the *Review of Economic Studies*.

    For a masterly exposition and full bibliography see K. Okuguchi, *Expectations and Stability in Oligopoly Models*, (Springer–Verlag, 1976).
199. Chapter IX of the *Recherches*, where this subject is discussed has the title 'Of the Mutual Relations of Producers'.
200. See for example F. Zeuthen's definition of bilateral monopoly in his *Problems of Monopoly and Economic Warfare* (1930, p. 5) pp. 63 *et seq.*
201. Thus when E. Schneider, op. cit., pp. 60 *et seq.* describes a variation of the Cournot case, where there is a monopolist of one factor while the other factors are not subject to monopoly, but where there is at the same time a monopoly of the final product to which the factors contribute, he is describing a genuine case of bilateral monopoly.
202. Formulations in terms of a theory of bilateral monopoly, may be found in Verri's *Meditazioni* (1771) p. 22; in Ortes, *Calcolo sopra il valore delle opinione Umane*, in Custodi, op. cit p.m., vol. XXIV, p. 261 and in canard, op. cit., pp. 28 *et seq.*
203. *Researches*, p. 99. It is assumed that these factors are copper and zinc, the alloy of which is used to make brass.
204. Thus $D_1 = m_1 D = m_1 F(p) = m_1 F(m_1 p_1 + m_2 p_2)$. Similarly for D_2. Ibid., p. 100.
205. As $F(m_1 p_1 + m_2 p_2) = F(p)$, we shall have when we add the equations of (6) $2F(p) + pF'(p) = 0$. Dividing by 2, we get equation (8).
206. *Researches*, p. 103. The figure is a variation of Cournot's Fig. 4.
207. Ibid., p. 103.
208. Ibid., pp. 101–2, Cournot's Figs. 7 and 8. There may however be an exceptional case where

    $F(p) = \dfrac{a}{b + p^2}$. This function gives as the two reaction curves 'two conjugate hyperbolas of which the limbs $m_1 n_1$ and $m_2 n_2$ have a common asymptote and cannot meet'. (See Fig. 9.3n) Researches, p. 104 and

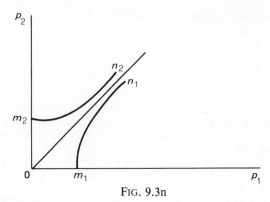

Fig. 9.3n

Fig. 9.

209. Ibid., p. 102.
210. Ibid., pp. 103–4.
211. Ibid., p. 105.
212. See equations (3) and (4), p. 174.
213. Since given equation (13a) the right hand side of (14) is equal with the left hand side of (14a).
214. *Researches*, pp. 106–7.
215. Ibid., p. 104.
216. Ibid., pp. 104–5.
217. This is Fig. 10 of the *Researches*, with slight alterations. Line h_1h_2 is plotted from equation (15) so that

$$\text{when } p_1 = 0,\, p_2 = \frac{\pi}{m_2} \qquad \text{and}$$

$$\text{when } p_2 = 0,\, p_1 = \frac{\pi}{m_1}$$

218. Ibid., p. 105.
219. Ibid., p. 105.
220. The remaining pages of ch. IX of the *Researches* are given to a discussion of price determination when the factors are sold under conditions of free competition.
221. Ellet, *Laws of Trade*, pp. 73 *et seq.*
222. Ibid., p. 70. The maximising toll would be equal to half of OP in Fig. 9.4n below. OP is the toll at which the quantity is zero and the commodity is therefore, excluded from the line.
223. Ibid., p. 79. The argument is the same as that used by Chamberlin, in *The Theory of Monopolistic Competition* (1949, p. 33 *et seq.*) to demonstrate the approach towards equilibrium of the duopolists. Thus at toll p, equal to OP, no quantity is transported. The first company fixes the toll at $\frac{p}{2}$ equal to OH; the second firm, considering OH as given, fixes the toll at HG, which is half OH and so on until equilibrium is reached at a toll $\frac{p}{3}$ each (Fig. 9.4n).
224. F.Y. Edgeworth, 'The Pure Theory of Monopoly', op. cit., vol. I, pp. 121 *et seq.*

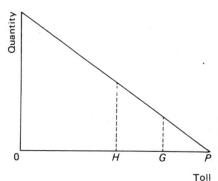

FIG. 9.4n

225. H.L. Moore, 'Paradoxes of Competition', *Quarterly Journal of Economics*, pp. 227–8; A. Marshall, *Principles*, pp. 493–5.
226. A.L. Bowley, *The Mathematical Groundwork of Economics*, (1924) p. 61; K. Wicksell, 'Selected papers on Economic Theory', op. cit., p. 221; F. Zeuthen, *Problems or Monopoly and Economic Warfare*, 1930, pp. 63 *et seq.* Other authors dealing with the problem include: E. Schneider, *Reine Theorie monopolistischer Wirtschaftsformen* (1932) pp. 50–1 and H. von Stackelberg, *Marktform und Gleichgewicht* (1934) pp. 58–9.
227. *Researches*, p. 127.
228. Ibid., p. 128.
229. Ibid., p. 150. The distinction between the two terms is that social income refers to the income of a society as opposed to the income over 'the whole extent of national territory'.
230. Ibid., p. 128.
231. Irving Fisher, 'Cournot and Mathematical Economics', in *Quarterly Journal of Economics* (Jan. 1898) p. 130.
232. Fisher, ibid., pp. 130–1. Fisher would, some years later in *The Nature of Capital and Income* (1906, p. 101), define the income of a community as 'the total flow of services from all its instruments' to combine with services from durable goods not the consumers' goods themselves, but their services.
233. *Researches*, p. 128.
234. Ibid., pp. 129–30. The demand curve is assumed elastic and when, therefore

$$p_o < p_1 \qquad p_o D_o > p_1 D_1$$

235. Ibid., p. 130.
236. Ibid., p. 133.
237. Ibid., p. 133.
238. V. Pareto, 'Di un errore del Cournot nel trattare l'economia politica colla matematica', in *Giornale degli Economisti* (Jan. 1892) pp. 1–14; see also Fisher, op. cit. (1898) p. 132.
239. Pareto, ibid., pp. 3 *et seq.*
240. Ibid., p. 5. It can be seen that if p_0, p_1, p_2 are taken sufficiently close together, the rectangle *EFGB* would be identified with the triangle under the curve. This is what Fisher, op. cit (1898, p. 132), means when he says that if Cournot had reached the conception of consumers' rent

he would have avoided this difficulty. The loss of consumers' surplus when a price changes to p_1 from p_0 would be ABp_0p_1 and the 'real diminution' would be then, not simply the rectangle $p_0(D_0 - D_1)$ or AED_0D_1, but the trapezoid ABD_0D_1. See Fisher, op. cit., p. 132 n.

241. Pareto, op. cit., p. 5.

242. Ibid., p. 5.

243. Ibid., p. 5.

244. *Researches*, p. 131.

245. Edgeworth, 'Cournot', in Palgrave's *Dictionary of Political Economy* (1925) p. 446.

246. *Researches*, p. 55.

247. Ibid., ch. III.

248. Ibid., p. 29.

249. Ibid., p. 30.

250. In general c_{ik} means 'the amount of silver given at (k) in exchange for a weight of silver expressed by 1 and payable at (i)'; Ibid., pp. 40-1.

251. Ibid., p. 32.

252. Ibid., p. 33. The system (4) may be reduced thus: Since $\dfrac{1}{c_{12}} = c_{21}$ and $c_{32}c_{21} = c_{31}$, we have for the second equation of the system $(m_{21} + m_{23})$ $\dfrac{1}{c_{12}} = (m_{12}c_{12} + m_{32}c_{32})\dfrac{1}{c_{12}}$, which gives $(m_{21} + m_{23})c_{21} = m_{12} + m_{32}c_{31}$; and also since $\dfrac{1}{c_{13}} = c_{31}$ and $c_{23}c_{31} = c_{21}$, the third equation of (4) becomes $(m_{31} + m_{32})c_{31} = m_{13} + m_{23}c_{21}$. These two equations can be solved simultaneously to find the values of c_{21} and c_{31}, from which the value of c_{32} can be found. See Ibid., pp. 33-4.

253. A.N. Isnard, *Traité des richesses* (1781); J. Lang, '*Grundlinien der Politischen Arithmetik*' (1811).

254. 'Mon père', (writes L. Walras in his article 'Cournot et l'économie mathématique' in the *Gazette de Lausanne*, 13 July 1905), 'économiste lui aussi, avait été le camarade de Cournot a l'Ecole Normale de Paris, licencié en 1822 par l'abbé de Frayssinous, et avait sans doute reçu l'hommage de cet opuscule que je trouvai dans sa bibliothèque et que je lus en 1853-1854 durant ma troisième année de mathématiques.'

255. The reduced by system is $(m_{21} + m_{23})c_{21} = m_{12} + m_{32}c_{31}$
$(m_{31} + m_{32})c_{31} = m_{13} + m_{23}c_{21}$
But equations one and two in the system (4), and consequently the first equation of the reduced system, are no longer true since they express that centres (1) and (2) balance their accounts without transfer of metal. The equation $(m_{31} + m_{32})c_{31} = m_{13} + m_{23}\gamma_{21}$ gives the value c_{31} and since γ_{21} is known, the value $c_{32} = c_{31} \times c_{12}$ may be found from $c_{12} = \dfrac{1}{\gamma_{21}}$. *Researches*, pp. 35-6.

256. Ibid., p. 41.

257. Ibid., pp. 42-3.

258. Thus the two chapters of the *Recherches* where international trade problems are discussed have the titles 'Of the Communication of Markets' (ch. X) and 'Of Variations in the Social income, Resulting from the Communication of Markets' (ch. XII).

259. J. St. Mill, *Principles of Political Economy*, book III, ch. XVII, §1, p. 575 (edn of 1926).
260. E. Barone, *Grundzüge der Theoretischen Nationalökonomie* (1927) pp. 101 *et seq*. See also R. Schüller, *Schutzzoll und Freihandel*, pp. 58 *et seq.*, and also G. von Haberler, *The Theory of International Trade*, (1950) pp. 170 *et seq.*, for similar treatment. Haberler, though mentioning Barone and Schüller, does not mention that the original formulator of this line of approach was Cournot.
261. Haberler, op. cit., pp. 169–70.
262. Ibid., pp. 169–70.
263. *Researches*, p. 117.
264. All these results may be illustrated by Barone's diagrams (Fig. 9.5n) op. cit., p. 101 *et seq.*, for the simplest case where $e = 0$.

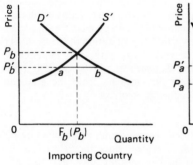 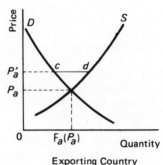

FIG. 9.5n

After communication, not only must $p'_a = p'_b$ but also the equality $ab = cd$ or $F_b(p'_b) - W_b(p'_b) = W_a(p'_a) - F_a(p'_a)$, which is a form of equation (4), must be established in equilibrium. It is immediately obvious that $p'_a > p_a$, $F_a(p'_a) < F_a(p_a)$ and $W_a(p'_a) > W_a(p_a)$ while the opposite holds for the importing country.

265. This will become clear if we use the arithmetical example, which Cournot gives in the *Principes* pp. 314–15 (see Table 9.1n).

TABLE 9.1n

	Country A			Country B			Total production
	Production	Exports	Consumption	Production	Imports	Consumption	
Before trade	10,000	—	10,000	10,000	—	10,000	20,000
After trade	11,000	2,500	8,500	8,000	2,500	10,500	19,000

Such a result is, Cournot points out, improbable 'for it implies that a fall in price, adequate to reduce from 10,000 to 8,000 (or by a fifth) production in market B, does not raise consumption except from 10,000 to 10,500 (or by a twentieth) in the same market. *Principes*, p. 315.

266. *Researches*, pp. 120–1. Transposing equation (4) we get and it must be

$$\frac{F'_a(p_a)}{W'_a(p_a)} > \frac{F'_b(p_b)}{W'_b(p_b)}$$

remembered that both $F'_a(p_a)$ and $F'_b(p_b)$, being gradients of demand curves, are negative. In absolute terms therefore the ratio of the importing country should be greater than that of the exporting, if production is to increase after trade.

Elasticity of demand in the exporting country must not therefore be very *inelastic*, as Edgeworth ('Theory of International Values', *Econ. Journal*, 1894, p. 625) maintains, if total production is to be reduced after communication; for price rises in the exporting market and inelasticity in demand means, ceteris paribus, a higher quantity than elasticity. It seems to me that Edgeworth's erroneous results are due to his misinterpretation of equation (4) as being a condition for a reduced total quantity. Nor is Edgeworth's interpretation of Cournot's gradients in terms of elasticities a very hapy one, for as R.G.D. Allen (*Mathematical Analysis for Economists*, 1949, p. 255) points out, though 'tempting to estimate the elasticity from the gradient of the demand curve' such a procedure is incorrect.

267. *Researches*, pp. 121–2.

268. Ibid., p. 122.

269. Ibid., p. 122, equation (6). The correct result is obtained by putting in this equation $\epsilon = 0$, which is evident since the effect δ of the tax u should vanish when $u = 0$. The mistake was first pointed out by Edgeworth, op. cit., *Econ. Journal* (1894) p. 627, who mentions that it had also been discovered independently by A. Berry and C. P. Sanger. Berry also discovered the mistake in the inequality on p. 158 of the *Researches* (Art. 90). See also Fisher, 'Cournot and Mathematical Economics' in *Quarterly Journal of Economics* 1898) p. 129 and 'Notes on Cournot', ibid., n 50 *et seq.*

270. See Edgeworth, op. cit., p. 627.

271. *Researches*, ch. XII.

272. Ibid., pp. 151–2.

273. Ibid., pp. 152 *et seq.* All these results may be shown in Figure 9.6n.

The increase in the income of producers is equal to the area cabfeh. What the principle of compensation purports to show is that this increase plus the amount released by consumers of M, who no longer buy it, cannot be devoted to the demand of other commodities, for it is exactly counterbalanced by the amount expended on imports, of equal value to exports (area *dibf*) plus the extra amount needed by those who continue to buy M domestically at the increased price. In other words, that the areas

cabfeh + dghe = dibf + caig which is immediately obvious.

274. It is the income in toto which, Cournot maintains, remains unchanged. The income of individual producers may change but these secondary effects will on the average compensate for one another.

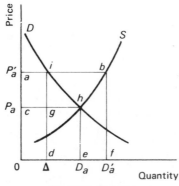

Exporting Country

FIG. 9.6n

275. J. Viner, *Studies in the Theory of International Trade* (1937) appears to have misunderstood Cournot's reasoning on this point. After giving equations parallel to (5), (6), (7) and (8) above in the case of the importing market, he remarks on p. 587: 'It would seem that so far *there is no net change in the national money income,* since the loss to producers of M is offset by a corresponding gain to the rest of the community.' But Cournot, by virtue of a process of reasoning which no one has satisfactorily explained, calls this sum $p_b D_b - p'_b D'_b$ 'the nominal reduction in national income'; and Viner adds in a footnote 'The only explanation I can offer ... is that Cournot held that since the change in the price of *M* and in the money income of producers of *M* would affect the price and the incomes of producers of *any other one commodity only to a negligible extent,* it was permissible to assume that the prices and the incomes of producers in country B of other commodities than M would remain unaltered', which would be equivalent to saying that one could ignore water spread from a tank 'thinly over a great area', no matter how large the original amount of water in the tank was. [My underlining.]

But Cournot never said that there would be no net change in the national income; his argument is that there *will be no net change in toto in the income of producers other than those of M.*

Nor is his argument that the effects from the change in the income of *M* will be spread thinly over the whole area and that one could therefore ignore the whole amount 'of water originally in the tank'; that was his reason for ignoring individual variations in the incomes within the group of producers other than *M*; in Cournot's argument, the water, no matter how large its original amount was, once released would have no effect on the neighbouring area for exactly counterbalancing forces would appear; the only net result would be the 'empty tank'.

276. *Researches*, p. 151.
277. The effect, that is, of trade on social income.
278. It is however interesting to note that, in a letter to Walras, Cournot considers this principle as a postulate, which could be admitted on the

basis of the 'Law of large numbers', a proposition which Walras accepted, pointing out at the same time that this would lead "to the way which leads to numerical applications". See this correspondence in *Econometrica* (1935) pp. 119–27, esp. pp. 120, 123 and in *Economie Appliquée* (1952) pp. 5–33.

279. *Researches*, p. 153.

280. Since $D'_a > D_a$ and $D'_a - \triangle = E > D_a - \triangle$

281. *Researches*, p. 154, explains the result $p'_aE - p_a(D_a - \triangle)$ in another way. 'This exportation', he writes, 'has placed market A in the enjoyment of commodities of foreign origin of which the value is p'_aE. In exchange it has dispossessed it of the quantity $D_a - \triangle$ of commodity M, of which the value was $p_a(D_a - \triangle)$; the profit is $p'_aE - p_a(D_a - \triangle)'$.

282. Ibid., p. 156. It must be noted that in Cournot's notation $\triangle$ is the consumption of M in market A after trade, and $D'_b + E$ the consumption of M in B after communication.

283. Cournot arrives at the same result through 'direct considerations'. The quantity $D_b - D'_b$ ceases to be produced and producers in B lose $p_b(D_b - D'_b)$; but this loss is partly compensated 'by the advantage to home consumers' equal to $(p_b - p'_b)(D_b - D'_b)$, who 'are able to procure for the price p'_b the same quantity which they formerly paid p_b for'. The net result is $p'_b(D_b - D'_b)$. See ibid., p. 157.

284. 'The only direct advantage of foreign commerce consists in the imports. A country obtains things which it either could not have produced at all, or which it must have produced at a greater expense of capital and labour than the cost of things which it exports to pay for them.' Mill, op. cit., pp. 578–9 (1926).

285. *Researches*, p. 154.

286. Ibid., p. 156. It is after quoting this passage from Cournot, that J. Bertrand, in *Journal des Savants* (1883, p. 504) makes the following hard-hitting comment: 'Let us suppose, for example, that the price of woollen cloth drops by half in the nation which is declared impoverished; those who used to wear in winter cotton clothes will be able to replace them by woollen clothes, and by thus making *a use of their income more to their liking*, will be able to diminish mortality. This is an advantage, Cournot recognises it; but, being unable to evaluate it in his formulae, he simply forewarns that he will not take it into account. Do we have the right not to reproach him of anything?' These advantages were actually measured by J. Dupuit in 1844 through the use of the concept of 'relative utility' or what is today known as 'consumer's surplus'.

287. Ibid., p. 156.

288. Ibid., p. 157. On the following pages Cournot discusses the question of allocation of profits from the business of transportation of the commodity. These profits are, in equilibrium, equal to $(p'_b - p'_a)E$; if transportation is carried on uniquely by the exporting country its income is further increased by this amount; if it is carried on uniquely by the importing country, the real diminution of its income $p'_b(D_b - D'_b)$ is, Cournot says, more than compensated by $(p'_b - p'_a)E$. The net result is $p'_b(D_b - D'_b) - (p'_b - p'_a)E = p'_aE - p'_b[E - (D_b -$

$D'_b)]$. From this, Cournot derives (p. 158) that $p'_aE < p'_b[E - (D_b - D'_b)]$ since he says $p'_a < p'_b$ and $E < E - (D_b - D'_b)$. But, in actual fact, since according to his premises, $D_b - D'_b > 0$, we get $E > E - (D_b - D'_b)$. It is, therefore, by no means certain that profits from transportation will exceed the diminution in income. See also Fisher's Preface, *Researches*, p. XI, and Edgeworth, op. cit., *Econ. Journal* (1894) p. 627. The results, therefore, in Researches, pp. 159–60, do not necessarily follows from Cournot's premises.

289. *Researches,* p. 161.
290. Ibid., p. 161.
291. Ibid., p. 162.
292. Ibid., pp. 162–3.
293. Konigsberg (1844) pp. 30–1.
294. Ibid.
295. He thus assumes not only perfect mobility of resources but also that they are fully employed.
296. *Researches*, p. 156.
297. Thus while Cournot maintains that the gain to the consumers is equal to the rectangle *EAFC*, Hagen says that it is equal to the rectangle *EFBD* (see Fig. 9.7n). If the concept of consumer's surplus had been utilised it would have been found that the gain would have been the intermediate area EFDA Fig. 9.7n. See also Edgeworth, op. cit. (1894) p. 630.

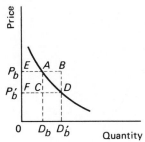

FIG. 9.7n

298. *Principes*, pp. 329 *et seq.*
299. Ibid., p. 330 and p. 303.
300. Ibid., p. 331.
301. R. de Fontenay, 'Principes de la théorie des richesses', *Journal des Economistes*, vol. 43 (Aug. 1864) p. 239.
302. Ibid., p. 242.
303. Ibid., p. 240.
304. Fontenay, op. cit., p. 240. In an obvious reference to what Cournot wrote in his *Researches*, p. 161, which we have mentioned above, Fontenay writes on p. 240 n 1, that it is evident from Art. 91 of the *Researches* that a friendly critic had drawn Cournot's attention to this fact before the publication of the *Recherches* and he adds 'Comment se fait-il que malgré cela, il l'ait reproduite sans aucune modification dans l'ouvrage de 1863?'

305. Dublin 1887, Appendix C, pp. 172–4.
306. Bastable, op. cit., p. 173. Fisher, on the other hand, op. cit. (1898) p. 129 believes all is due to Cournot's mistake.
307. *Economic Journal* (1894) p. 628. On p. 629 in answer to Bastable's criticism of Cournot that he carried on his discussion by using money as measure, whose value can be altered by changes in the terms of trade, Edgeworth says that it could be tenable 'that Cournot means to restrict his theory to small disturbances of trade, the effects of which on the level of money may be neglected'.
308. *Manuel d'économique* (1908) p. 839.
309. Landry, op. cit., p. 839.
310. H. E. Barrault, 'Les Doctrines de Cournot sur le Commerce International' in *Revue d'Histoire des Doctrines Économiques et Sociales* (1912) p. 112.
311. Angell, *The Theory of International Prices* (1926) p. 244.
312. Viner, op. cit., p. 587 n.
313. There is, however, a mistake in Cournot's actual calculations, if he really intends the above interpretation. For from the nominal increase, $p'_a D'_a - p_a D_a$ he deducts the amount which consumers had to pay in excess for the *diminished* quantity of A, i.e. $(p'_a - p_a)\triangle$; if the remainder were to be a true index of changes in the goods, which a money income commands, one should deduct the amount which consumers had to pay in excess, if they were to buy the *same* quantity of A, i.e. one should deduct $(p'_a - p_a)Da$; the remainder would then be, in the case of the exporting country, $p'_a(D'_a - D_a)$ or equal to rectangle $deD'_a D_a$, and not the figure $abcD_a D'_a e$, which is the result of Cournot's calculation (Fig. 9.8n).

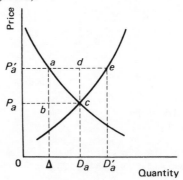

FIG. 9.8n

314. See especially, *Principes*, pp. 468 *et seq.*
315. Cournot, *Principes de la théorie des richesses* (1863) p. 11 [My underlining.] We refer to this book as *Principes*.
316. *Researches*, p. 5.
317. Ibid., p. 5.
318. Cf e.g. *Recherches* (1838) p. 1 and *Principes*, p. 1, *Recherches*, p. 3 and *Principes* p. 2, *Recherches*, P. 53 and *Principes* p. 97, *Recherches* p. 146 and *Principes* p. 263, etc.

319. *Principes*, p. 18.
320. E. Depitre, 'Note sur les oeuvres économiques d'Augustin Cournot', in *Revue d'Histoire des Doctrines Économiques* et Sociales (1908) p. 192.
321. *Principes*, pp. 20–1.
322. *Principes*, p. 60; my underlining.
323. '*Et les prix de chaque unité seront précisément en raison, de leur valeur économique*. Si le rapport du prix etait autre, *l'équivalence, quant à la force productrice, subsisterait toujours*: seulement il faudrait que l'un des modes de production fut provisoirement delaissé par l'industrie, ou exclu du cercle de la production économique.' *Principes*, pp. 60–1. [My underlining] Of course, under conditions of constancy, the marginal rate of substitution is identified with Cournot's rate.
324. 'Une conception un peu trop sommairement esquissée mais remarquable.' R. de Fontenay, op. cit., p. 245.
325. *Principes*, p. 100.
326. Ibid.
327. *Researches*, p. 25.
328. *Principes*, p. 149.
329. Ibid., p. 151.
330. Ibid., pp. 157 *et seq.*
331. Ibid., book III, ch. IV.
332. Ibid., Book III, ch. VI, pp. 338 *et seq.*
333. *Principes*, p. 337.
334. Ibid., p. 337.
335. Mill, op. cit., p. 584 *et seq.* (1926); *Principes*, pp. 338 *et seq.* Cournot actually uses the same numbers as Mill, but refers to countries M and N and goods A and B.
336. Mill, op. cit., p. 586.
337. Advanced chiefly by W. Thornton. Cf. Mill, op. cit., pp. 596 *et seq.*
338. Mill, op. cit., p. 597. The result was that Mill formulated the law of international values as follows: Under the assumption of a demand exactly in proportion to the cheapness, 'the whole of the commodities which the two countries can respectively make for exportation, with the *labour and capital thrown out* of employment by importation, will exchange against one another'. Mill, op. cit. p. 600. It is interesting to note that Cournot refers to Mill's theorem, immediately previous to the above, which speaks only of *capital* thrown out; he thinks that not only capital but also labour and even productive resources when limited, in fact every limited factor of production thrown out of employment by importation, must be included, if it is the comparative scarcity of this particular factor which determines the level of the quantity of goods to be produced for exportation. *Principes*, pp. 342–4.
339. Ibid., p. 341.
340. Mill, op. cit., p. 585.
341. *Principes*, p. 344.
342. Ibid., p. 345.
343. Ibid., p. 345.
344. Ibid., p. 345.
345. Ibid., p. 345.
346. Ibid., p. 346. Of course, as we have seen, little meaning can be found in

Cournot's calculations of real changes in income.

347. Ibid., p. 346.
348. Ibid., pp. 349–50.
349. R. De Fontenay, op. cit., 1864.
350. Ibid., p. 247.
351. *Revue Sommaire* (1877) p. 111.
352. Ibid., p. 161.
353. L. Walras, 'Compte rendu des 'Principes de la théorie des Richesses' ' in *Indépendant de la Moselle* (13 July 1863)
354. L. C. Robbins, *The Theory of Economic Policy in English Classical Political Economy* (1952) pp. 7 *et seq.*
355. *Principes*, p. 56.
356. Ibid., p. 412.
357. Ibid., p. 413. It is in this context that Cournot (ibid., p. 482) insists that the Government must positively encourage savings 'with which there will be formed in the long run the great capitals' which are so necessary for the superiority of the productive forces of a nation.
358. Ibid., p. 413.
359. Ibid., p. 502.
360. *Principes*, p. 448.
361. See especially *Principes*, book IV, ch. VI.
362. Thus in *Principes*, pp. 492–3 he writes 'the formation of great national units must be considered as economic progress, despite the increasing charges imposed on the people by the expenses of a more complicated administration, the maintenance of big armies, and the taste for great enterprises which are the natural consequences of an increase in power'. And he adds: 'Today economic interests (like political interests) need a flag to cover them, which will make them respected in the world; and this flag can only be that of a great nation.'
363. These forces are, chiefly, industry and the labour force, the 'force vitale' as he calls it. 'Nothing necessarily limits (for each particular nation) the wealth and revenue which have their principal source in labour and industry; new products can indefinitely be exchanged one against another, provided that a suitable direction is given to the various branches of production and provided that one finds in the immense commercial world on the one hand markets always open to the national industry and on the other hand, through purchases of raw materials and foodstuffs produced abroad, means for feeding the industrial activity and the increase in the industrial population generated therefrom.' *Principes*, p. 287. The influence of List is obvious. Cf. F. List, *The National System of Political Economy* (1841).
364. See e.g. *Principes*, pp. 438, 492–3, 503.
365. But though he believes that, for his time at least, the aim of economic activity is consumption by the citizens of each state, he argues that there exist cosmopolitic tendencies towards the merger of interests of 'nations having the same general system of civilisation'. Cournot, ibid., p. 500.
366. *Principes*, p. 428.
367. Ibid., p. 427.
368. Ibid., p. 420.

369. Ibid., p. 420, where he adds, 'Only the cultivators of the poppy and the merchants of opium find good the fact that the Chinese have the taste to poison themselves with opium'.
370. Which, of course, in Cournot's estimation, includes the need for protecting and encouraging, at least temporarily the nation's productive forces.
371. Robbins, op. cit., p. 182.
372. *Principes*, pp. 414–15.
373. Ibid., 414–15.
374. Ibid., pp. 514–15.
375. This is the meaning in which Cournot uses the term 'optimisme economique'; it is the search for a policy which will lead to optimum results in terms of happiness.
376. *Principes*, p. 418.
377. Ibid., p. 418.
378. For the same reason Cournot rejects the money value of goods as representing the happiness which their consumption involves; for the 'money value depends on the law of demand, which depends (as already seen) on the method of distribution of wealth and on the tastes of the consumers'. *Principes*, p. 419.
379. Ibid., p. 422.
380. Ibid., p. 423.
381. Ibid., p. 423.
382. Ibid., p. 427.
383. Ibid., p. 427.
384. Robbins, op. cit., p. 186.
385. Like F. Bastiat, *Les Harmonies économiques* (1850) and C. Dunoyer, *De la liberté du travail* (1845).
386. *Principes*, p. 429.
387. Ibid., pp. 429–30.
388. Ibid., p. 430.
389. Ibid., p. 430.
390. Such as the burning down of forests for the purpose of obtaining potassium (*Principes*, pp. 430–1) or the egoistic tendencies of capital (Ibid., p. 438).
391. Such might very well be Smith's control of the price of monopolised bread. See Robbins, op. cit., p. 58.
392. Cournot's definition of economic freedom implies simply 'freedom from state interference', once a proper framework has been provided and could be applied to discussion of any market form. 'Economic freedom' in English classical economics had the special meaning of freedom from state interference as long as competition was free. See Robbins op. cit., pp. 57 *et seq.*
393. *Principes*. p. 275 and also p. 107.
394. Cournot refers, of course, to the competition of producers. As regards consumers, he implicitly assumes, throughout the discussion, that there is free competition, and also, with the reservations noted above, freedom in their choice of final goods.
395. This is a difference we have already noticed in the theory of inter-

national trade and accounts for the widely different results which they and Cournot get.

396. *Principes*, p. 437.
397. Ibid., p. 437.
398. Ibid., p. 437.
399. Such as the deterioration in the quality of the products. *Ibid.,* p. 437.
400. Ibid., p. 437, where, in an aside, he adds that the inevitable result of all these is that all those affected will seek by 'association, discipline and regulation' to hedge against the uncertainties of free competition.
401. Ibid., p. 448.
402. Ibid., p. 449. The necessity for the provision of such works by the state was also accepted by the English classical economists. Robbins. op. cit. p. 55 *et seq.*
403. See note 411.
404. *Principes*, p. 450.
405. Ibid., pp. 451–2.
406. Ibid. p. 452. But Cournot points also to the fact that the State may get involved in reckless and unprofitable enterprises, which become a permanent charge to the public.
407. Ibid., p. 452.
408. Ibid., p. 455.
409. Ibid., p. 456.
410. Ibid., p. 457.
411. Ibid., p. 457.
412. Ibid., p. 456.
413. Which is to seek the greatest profit. Ibid., p. 458.
414. Ibid., p. 458.
415. Ibid., p. 458.
416. Ibid., p. 459.
417. Ibid., p. 460; my underlining.
418. Ibid., p. 463.
419. Ibid., p. 464.
420. Ibid., p. 464.
421. Ibid., p. 464.
422. Ibid., p. 443.
423. Ibid., p. 444; my underlining.
424. Ibid., p. 461.
425. Ibid., p. 461.
426. Ibid., p. 462.
427. See Robbins, op. cit., pp. 11 *et seq.*
428. *Researches*, p. 171.
429. A similar statement is to be found in the concluding paragraphs of the *Principes*, p. 522.

Bibliography

I. A BIBLIOGRAPHY OF MATHEMATICAL ECONOMICS BEFORE COURNOT[1]

Aristotle, *Nicomachean Ethics*, book v, 1131b, 1133a, b.

Beccaria, Cesare, 'Tentativo analitico sui contrabbandi!: Estratto dal foglio periodico intitolato', *Il Caffè*, vol. I (Brescia, 1764); reproduced in Custodi, P., *Scrittori Classici Italiani di Economia Politica*, parte moderna, vol. XII (Milano, 1804) pp. 235–41.

See also W.J. Baumol and S.M. Goldfeld, 'Precursors in Mathematical Economics: an Anthology' (LSE, 1968) pp. 149–50; there is also a French translation by G.H. Bousquet, in *Revue Economique*, no. 5, 1960, pp. 817–20.

[F.J.]

____, 'Del disordine e dei rimedi delle monete (1762)' reproduced in Custodi, *Scrittori Classici Italiani di Economia Politica*, parte moderna, vol. XII (Milano, 1804).

Bernoulli, Daniel, 'Specimen theoriae novae de mensura sortis', *Commentarii academiae scientiarum imperialis Petropolitanae*, vol. V (1738) pp. 175–92. Translated by A. Pringsheim: 'Die Grundlage der modernen Werthlehre. Versuch einer neuen Theorie der Wertbestimmung von Glücksfällen' (Leipzig, 1896). There is also an English translation by L. Sommer in the *Econometrica*, vol. XXII (1954) pp. 23–36.

1. There exist two bibliographies on this subject:
    (a) The bibliography in W. S. Jevons, *The Theory of Political Economy*, 2nd edn (1879) Appendix I, pp. 301–2 and 310. Works included in this appendix are marked [J.] in our bibliography. Works not included in this edition but included in Appendix V, pp. 322–6, of the 4th edn of *The Theory* of Jevons (1924), are marked [Je.].
    (b) The 'Bibliography of Mathematical Economics from Ceva to Cournot', prepared by Irving Fisher and included in the English translation of Cournot's *Recherches* by N.T. Bacon (1929 edn, pp. 173–6). Works mentioned by Fisher are marked [F.]. Works not mentioned by either bear no mark.

See also W.J. Baumol and S.M. Goldfeld, op. cit., pp. 15–26. [F. Je.]

Bosellini, Carlo, 'Progressi delle scienze economiche', *Giornale Arcadico di Scienze, Lettere ed Arti*, vol. xxix (Roma, 1826) p. 72.

Buffon, Georges Louis Leclerc, Count of, 'Éssai d'arithmétique morale (1777), in *Œuvres philosophiques* (1954) p. 469.

Buquoy, Georg von, 'Die Theorie der Nationalwirthschaft, nach einem neuen Plane und nach mehreren eigenen Ansichten dargestellt' (Leipzig, 1815). [F.J.]

Cagnazzi, *Elementi di Economia Politica* (Naples, 1813) pp. 217–19.

Canard, N-F, *Éssai sur la circulation de l'impôt* (Paris, 1801).

——, *Principes d' économie politique* (Paris 1801).

See also W.J. Baumol and S.M. Goldfeld, op. cit., pp. 157–60.

(F.J.)

Cazaux, L. F. G. de, 'Élémens d'économie privée et publique; ou Science de la valeur des choses et de la richesse des individus et des nations (Paris and Toulouse, 1825) pp. 20 *et seq.*, 84. [F.Je.]

Ceva, Giovanni, 'De re numaria, quoad fieri potuit geometrice tractata, ad illustrissimos et excellentissimos dominos Praesidem Quaestoresque hujus arciducalis Caesarei Magistratus Mantuae' (Mantova, 1711); reproduced in Eugenio Masé-Dari, *Un precursore della econometria*, Modena (1935) pp. 37–59.

Also, in a French translation by G.H. Bousquet and J. Roussier in *Revue d' histoire économique et sociale* (1958) pp. 140–69. [F.Je.]

Condorcet, M. J. A. Caritat, marquis de, *Vie de Monsieur Turgot* (London, 1786) pp. 158–66. [F.Je.]

De Peñalver, Lopez, 'Reflexiones sobre la variacion del precio del trigo' (Madrid, 1812); reproduced by F. Estape in *Anales de Economia 1953–55*, pp. 207–52. Extracts in French have been published by G.H. Bousquet in 'Lopez de Peñalver: Reflexions sur les variations du prix du Blé (une étude économétrique de 1812)', *Revue d' Histoire Économique et Sociale* (1961) pp. 496–509.

Du Bois-Aymé, 'Examen de quelques questions d'économie politique, et notamment de l'ouvrage de M. Ferrier intitulé: du Gouvernement' (Paris, 1823) pp. 71–7, 102–4.

Duleau, Notes in Barnabé, Brisson, 'Éssai sur le système général de navigation intérieure de la France' (1829) pp. ii and xiii n, 160–1.

[J.]

Du Pont de Nemours, Pierre Samuel. 'Des courbes Politiques (1774), in Carl Knies (ed.), *Carl Friedrichs von Baden brieflicher Verkehr mit Mirabeau und Du Pont*, vol. ii (Heidelberg, 1892) pp. 289 *et seq*. Also translated with an introduction by H. W. Spiegel under the title *On Economic Curves* (Baltimore, 1955).

Du Villard de Durand, J.H.T., *Recherches sur les rentes, les emprunts et les remboursements* (Paris and Geneva, 1787) pp. 1–22. See also, W.J. Baumol and S.M. Goldfeld, op. cit., pp. 153–4.

'E.R.' 'An Essay on Some General Principles of Political Economy, on Taxes upon Raw Produce and on Commutation of Tithes' (London, 1822).

Ferroni, Pietro, 'Esame di alcuni passi delle Meditazioni sulla Economia Politica del Conte Pietro Verri. Memoria del Matematico Dott. Pietro Ferroni letta nella Società de' Georgofili di Firenze il di 2 Marzo 1796, reproduced in Custodi, P., op. cit., parte moderna, vol. xvii, pp. 384–99.

Forbonnais, François Véron de, *Élémens du commerce* (1st edn, Paris, 1754, 2nd edn, 1766) vol. ii, pp. 113 *et seq.*, 128–9. [F.Je.]

Frisi, Paolo, Note dell' editore, in the sixth edition of P. Verri, *Meditazioni sulla Economia Politica* (Livorno, 1772) pp. 37–9, 43, 84, 92, 97–8, 112, 130, 134, 152, 155–6, 168–9, 198, 232 and 237 *et seq*; reproduced also in M. Fasiani, 'F. Fuoco: Applicazione dell' Algebra all' Economia Politica' (Genova, 1937).

Fuoco, Francesco, *Saggi Economici*, 2 vols (Pisa, 1825–7). [F.J.]

Gale, Samuel, *An Essay on the Nature and Principles of Public Credit* (London, 1784) esp. pp. 23–5.

Garnier, Germain, *Abrégé élémentaire des principes de l' économie politique* (Paris, 1796; new edn 1846) pp. 195–6.

Gioja, Melchiorre, 'Discussione economica sul dipartimento d' Olona' (1803); republished in his *Opere Minori* (Lugano, 1835) vol. xiv, esp. pp. 176–7.

____, *Nuovo Prospetto delle Scienze Economiche*, 6 vols (Milano, 1815–17) vol. i, p. 43; vol. iii, pp. 7–35; vol. vi, pp. 316 *et seq.*

Hermann, Friedrich, *Staatswirthschaftliche Untersuchungen* (München, 1832) pp. 80 *et seq.*, 103, 133, 168n, 187n, 190n. [Je.]

Hutcheson, Francis, *An Inquiry into the Original of Our Ideas of Beauty and Virtue* (London, 1720). [J.]

____, *An Essay on the Nature and Conduct of the Passions and Affections, with Illustrations on the Moral Sense* (London, 1728). [J.]

Isnard, Achylle-Nicolas, *Traité des richesses* 2 vols (London and Lausanne, 1781). See also, W.J. Baumol and S.M. Goldfeld, op. cit., pp. 255–70.

Kröncke, Claus. *Versuch einer Theorie des Fuhrwerks mit Anwen-*

dung auf den Strassenbau (Giessen, 1802). [F.J.]

——, *Das Steuerwesen nach seiner Natur und seinen Wirkungen untersucht* (Darmstadt and Giessen, 1804). [F.J.]

——, *Anleitung zur Regulirung der Steuer* (1810) [F.Je.]

Lang, Joseph, *Über den obersten Grundsatz der politischen Ökonomie* (Riga, 1809). [F.J.]

——, *Grundlinien der Politischen Arithmetik* (Charkow, 1811). See also, W.J. Baumol and S.M. Goldfeld, op. cit., pp. 260–6. [F.Je.]

Laplace, Pierre Simon de., *Théorie analytique des probabilités* (1812) pp. 187, 432–3.

——, 'Éssai philosophique sur les probabilités' (1814) p. 21.

Lloyd, Henry, 'An Essay on the Theory of Money' (London, 1771); summarised by P. Frisi in Verri's *Meditazioni*, 6th edn (1772) pp. 237 *et seq.* [F.J.]

Lubé, D.G. 'An Argument Against the Gold Standard with an Examination of the Principles of the Modern economists' (London, 1832). [F.J.]

Mariotte, Edmé, 'Éssai de logique', *Œuvres de M. Mariotte*, vol. I (Leide, 1717) pp. 609–701, esp. pp. 629, 665–8. [F.Je.]

Ortes, Giammaria, 'Calcolo sopra il valore delle opinioni umane' (Venice, 1757); reproduced in Custodi, op. cit., parte moderna, vol. XXIV, pp. 270 *et seq.*

——, 'Errori popolari intorno all' Economia Nazionale (1771); reproduced in Custodi, op. cit., parte moderna, vol. XXV, pp. 10 *et seq.*

——, 'Annotazioni dell' autore del libro degli 'Errori popolari sull' Economia Nazionale' (1771); reproduced in Custodi, op. cit., parte moderna, vol. XXV, pp.2 35 *et seq.*

——, 'Dell' Economia Nazionale', (1774); reproduced in Custodi, op. cit., parte moderna, vol. XXII, pp. 44 *et seq.*, 365–6.

Poisson, Siméon-Denis, *Recherches sur la probabilité des jugements*, (1837) p. 72.

Rau, K.H, 'Grundsätze der Volkswirthschaftslehre (Leipzig and Heidelberg, 1826). [F.Je.]

Ressi, Adeodato. *Dell' Economia della Specie Umana* (1st edn, 1807) vol. III (1819) p. 248.

Say, J. B., *Cours complet d'économie politique pratique* vol. II (Paris, 1828) pp. 321 et seq. esp. pp. 334–5.

Silio, Guglielmo, 'Saggio su l' influenza dell analisi nelle Scienze Politiche ed Economiche applicata ai contrabbandi', *Nuova*

Raccolta di Opuscoli di Autori Siciliani, vol. v (Palermo, 1792) pp. 91–173. [F.J.]

Simonde, J.C.L., 'De la richesse commerciale ou principes d'économie politique appliqués à la Législation du Commerce'. Genève, vol. I (1803) pp. 104–8 and 215–16. [F.Je]

Spinelli, Trojano, 'Riflessioni politiche sopra alcuni punti della scienza della moneta' (Naples, 1750).

Thompson, Thomas Perronet, 'The Instrument of Exchange', *Westminster Review*, vol. I (1824) pp. 171–205 reprinted separately in 1830 and 1842. [F.J.]

———, 'An Exposition of Fallacies on Rent, Tithes, etc. Containing an Examination of Mr Ricardo's Theory of Profit (London, 1826) pp. 30, 39–40. [F.Je.]

———, 'Postscript to the Article on the Instrument of Exchange, *Westminster Review*, vol. XII, (1830) pp. 525–33. [F.Je.]

Thünen, J. H. von, *Der isolirte Staat in Beziehung auf Landwirthschaft und Nationalökonomie*, vol. I (Hamburg, 1826). [F.J.]

Turner, Samuel, *A letter addressed to the Right Hon. Robert Peel with reference to the Expediency of the resumption of cash payments at the period fixed by law* (London, 1819).

———, 'Considerations upon the Agriculture, Commerce and Manufactures of the British Empire' (London, 1822) pp. 34–7.

Vaccolini, Domenico, 'Elogio di Luigi Valeriani Molinari' (Lugo, 1829) pp. 12 *et seq.*

Valeriani Molinari, Luigi, 'Del prezzo delle cose tutte mercatabili' (Bologna, 1806).

———,'Operette concernenti quella parte del gius delle genti e pubblico che dicesi pubblica economia (Bologna, 1815) pp. 24–7.

———, 'Apologia della formola $p = \dfrac{i}{0}$, trattandosi del come si determini il prezzo delle cose tutte mercatabili, contro ciò che ne dice il celebre autore del' *Nuovo Prospetto delle Scienze Economiche* (Bologna, 1816). [F.Je.]

———, 'Discorso apologetico in cui si sostiene recarsi invano pel celebre autore del *Nuovo Prospetto delle Scienze Economiche* contro l' Apologia della formola $p = \dfrac{i}{0}$, trattandosi del come si determinini il prezzo delle cose tutte mercatabili, ciò che il medesimo ha scritto nel', vol. II, pp. 114–17, 141–6, e nel IV, pag. 214–19, 244–63 dell' opera suddetta (Bologna, 1817). [F.Je.]

———, 'Contro la sentenza del celebre Inglese Giuspubblicista-

Economico Adam Smith che l' unità monetaria moneta di conto traggesi nella colta Europa dall' argento piuttosto per particolari consuetudini che per universali cagioni' (Bologna, 1821) pp. 5–12 in Valeriani's *Ricerche Critiche ed Economiche*, vol. I (Bologna, 1819–21).

———, *Saggi di Erotemi*, (Bologna, 1825) pp. 115–36, 160 *et seq*.

Vasco, Giambattista, 'Saggio Politico della Moneta' (1772); reproduced in Custodi, op. cit., parte moderna, vol. XXXIII, pp. 109–15 n.

See also W.J. Baumol and S.M. Goldfeld, op. cit., pp. 250–2.

Venturi, G. B., (Probably) 'Meditazioni sulla Economia Politica, Edizione sesta accresciuta dall' Autore' (Livorno, 1772) nella Stamperia dell' Enciclopedia in ottavo in *'Nuovo Giornale de' Letterati d' Italia'*, vol. III, Modena (1773) pp. 228–83.

Waldegrave, James, Excerpt from a Letter in P.R. de Montmort, *Essay d' analyse sur les jeux de hazard,* 2nd edn (Paris, 1713) pp. 409–12.

See also, W.J. Baumol and S.M. Goldfeld, op. cit., pp. 7–9.

Whewell, William, 'Mathematical Exposition of Some Doctrines of Political Economy (1829) in *Cambridge Philosophical Transactions,* vol. III (1830) pp. 191–229.   [F.J.]

Whewell, William, 'Mathematical Exposition of some of the leading doctrines in Mr Ricardo's Principles of Political Economy and Taxation (1831) in *Cambridge Philosophical Transactions*, vol. IV (1833) pp. 155–98.   [F.J.]

Note. W.S. Jevons in his bibliography includes the following works, which we have not included above:

Condillac, Étienne Bonnot de, *Le commerce et le gouvernement,* (Paris, 1776).

Lang, Joseph, *Historische Entwickelung der Deutschen Steuerverfassung* (Riga, 1793).

Walras, Auguste, *De la nature de la richesse et de l'origine de la Valeur* (Paris, 1831).

II. A BIBLIOGRAPHY OF COURNOT'S WORKS

1. *Recherches sur les principes mathématiques de la théorie des richesses* (Paris: Hachette, 1838).

   The English translation bears the title: *Researches into the Mathematical Principles of the Theory of Wealth*, trans. by N.T.

Bacon, 1897. There also exist Italian and German translations of this work.

2. *Traité élémentaire de la théorie des fonctions et du calcul infinitésimal,* 2 vols (Paris: Hachette, 1841; 2nd edn 1857). There exists a German translation of this work.

3. *Exposition de la théorie des chances et des probabilités* (Paris: Hachette, 1843).
   There exists a German translation of this work.

4. *De l' origine et des limites de la correspondance entre l' algèbre et la géométrie* (Paris: Hachette, 1847).

5. *Éssai sur les fondements de nos connaissances et sur les caractères de la critique philosophique,* 2 vols (Paris: Hachette, 1851; 2nd 1912; 3rd edn in one vol. 1922).

6. *Traité de l' enchaînement des idées fondamentales dans les sciences et dans l' histoire,* 2 vols (Paris: Hachette, 1861; later editions in 1911 and 1922).

7. *Principes de la théorie des richesses* (Paris: Hachette, 1863).

8. *Des Institutions d' instruction publique en France* (Paris; Hachette, 1864).

9. *Considérations sur la marche des idées et des événements dans les temps modernes,* 2 vols (Paris; Hachette, 1872; new edition, 1934).

10. *Matérialisme, vitalisme, rationalisme: études sur l' emploi des données de la science en philosophie* (Paris, Hachette, 1875; new edn 1923).

11. *Revue sommaire des doctrines économiques* (Paris; Hachette, 1877).

12. *Souvenirs (1760–1860).* Written in 1859 and published with an Introduction by E.P. Bottinelli (Paris; Hachette, 1913).

Other publications and translations:

a. *Mémoires militaires du maréchal Gouvion Saint-Cyr,* 4 vols (Paris: Asselin, 1831).

b. *Éléments de mécanique de Rater et de Lardner,* trans. by A. Cournot (Paris, 1834). (Contains a chapter by Cournot 'De la mesure des forces du travail des machines'.)

c. *Traité d' astronomie de Herschel*; trans. by A. Cournot (Paris: Paulin, 1834, 2nd edn. 1836). (Contains a section by Cournot: 'Application de la théorie des chances à la série des orbites des comètes dans l' espace').

d. Annotated translation of *Lettres d' Euler à une princesse d'*

Allemagne sur divers sujets de physique et de philosophie (Paris: Hachette, 1842).

e. Various articles in *Dictionnaire des sciences philosophiques* of A. Franck (Paris: Hachette, 1843–52).

f. Various articles in: *Bulletin des Sciences Mathématiques, Astronomiques, Physiques et Chimiques of Baron de Férussac*, 1826–1831; *Journal des Mathématiques Pures et Appliquées of Liouville*, 1838; *Journal für die reine und angewandte Mathematik*, 1830 and 1832.

Doctoral theses

a. *Mémoire sur le mouvement d' un corps rigide soutenu par un plan fixe* (Paris: Hachette, 1829). (Principal Thesis).

b. 'De la figure des corps celestes' (1829) (Complementary Thesis).

Correspondence with Léon Walras

a. Léon Walras et sa correspondance avec Augustin Cournot et Stanley Jevons, (Avec une note d'Etienne Antonelli), *Econometrica*, vol. III (1935) pp. 119–27.

b. 'Walras L. et Cournot A. – Correspondance complète' (Avec une introduction et des notes par William Jaffé), *Économie Appliquée*, vol. V (1952) pp. 5–33.

III A SELECTED BIBLIOGRAPHY ON COURNOT

Amoroso, L., 'Teoria matematica del programma economico' *Cournot nella economia e nellafilosofia*, (Padova, 1939) pp. 123–44.

_____, *Lezioni di economia matematica* (Bologna, 1921).

Angell, J.W., *The Theory of International Prices* (1926) pp. 239 *et seq*.

Antonelli, E., 'Léon Walras et sa corréspondance avec Augustin Cournot et Stanley Jevons, avec une note', *Econometrica* (1935) vol. III, pp. 119–27.

Audierne, R., 'Note sur la classification des connaissances humaines dans Comte et dans Cournot', *Revue de Métaphysique et de Morale* (1905).

Aupetit, A., 'L' oeuvre économique de Cournot', *Revue de Métaphysique et de Morale* (1905) pp. 377–93.

Barrault, H.E., 'Les doctrines de Cournot sur le Commerce International', *Revue d' Histoire des Doctrines Économiques et Sociales* (1912) pp. 110–24.

Bastable, C.F., *The Theory of International Trade* (1887) esp. pp. 172–4.

Bertrand, J., 'Théorie mathématique de la richesse sociale, par Léon Walras (1883); 'Recherches sur les Principes mathématiques de la Théorie des Richesses par Augustin Cournot (Paris, 1838) in *Journal des Savants* (1883) pp. 499–508; reproduced in the 1938 edition of *Recherches, Collection des Économistes* (Paris) pp. 233–50.

Bompaire, F., 'Du principe de Liberté économique dans l' oeuvre de Cournot et dans nelle de l' école de Lausanne' (Paris, 1931).

____, 'L' économie mathématique d' aprèsl' oeuvre comparée de ses représentants les plus typiques: A. Cournot, L. Walras et V. Pareto', in *Revue d' Économie Politique* (Paris, July–Aug. 1932).

Bordin, A., 'Le teorie economiche di A. Cournot e l' ordinamento corporativo', in *Cournot nella economia e nella filosofia* (Padova, 1939) pp. 181–226.

Bottinelli, E.P., *Cournot métaphysicien de la connaissance* (Paris, 1913).

____, Introduction and notes to Cournot's *Souvenirs* (Paris, 1913).

Bouglé, G., 'Les rapports de l' histoire et de la science sociale d' après Cournot', *Revenue de Métaphysique et de Morale* (1905).

Darbon, A., *Le concept du hasard dans la philosophie de Cournot.* (Paris, 1911).

Darlu, A., 'Quelques vues de Cournot sur la politique' *Revue de Métaphysique et de Morale* (1905).

Depitre, E., 'Note sur les oeuvres économiques d' Augustin Cournot', *Revue d' Histoire des Doctrines Économiques et Sociales* (1908) pp. 187–96.

Dmitriev, V.K., *Economic Essays on Value, Competition and Utility* (Original text published in Moscow, 1902; Trans. from the 1904 edn by D. Fry and edited by D.M. Nuti, 1974). See the second essay on 'The Theory of Competition of Augustine Cournot', ibid., pp. 97–178.
There is also a french translation under the title: *Éssais économiques* (Paris: Centre National de la Recherche Scientifique, 1968).

Edgeworth, F. Y., 'Cournot', in Palgrave's *Dictionary of Political Economy*. (1925) pp. 445–6.

____, *Papers Relating to Political Economy*, vols I–III. Also 'The Pure Theory of International Values', *Economic Journal* (1894) esp. pp. 628–9; reproduced in *Papers etc.*, vol. II, pp. 3–60.

Faure, F., 'Les idées de Cournot sur la statistique', *Revue de Métaphysique et de Morale* (1905) pp. 395–411.

Fauveau, M.G., 'Considérations Mathématiques sur la Théorie de la Valeur', *Journal des Économistes* (1867) pp. 31–40.

Fisher, I., 'Cournot and mathematical Economics', *Quarterly Journal of Economics* (1898) pp. 119–38.

——, 'Notes on Cournot's mathematics', *A. Cournot: Researches into the Mathematical Principles of the Theory of Wealth*, Trans. by N. T. Bacon, (1929) pp. xiii–xxiv.

See also in *Quarterly Journal of Economics*, (1898) pp. 238–44.

——, 'Cournot forty years ago,' *Econometrica* (1938) pp. 198–202.

Fontenay, R. de; 'Principes de la Théorie des richesses', *Journal des Économistes* (1864) pp. 231–51.

Fry, C.L. and Ekelund R.B., 'Cournot's Demand Theory: a Reassessment', *History of Political Economy* (1971) pp. 190–7.

Giacalone-Monaco, T., 'A proposito del centenario delle *Recherches* di A.A. Cournot', *Bolletino dell' Associazione degli antichi studenti 'Primo Lanzoni' del R. Instituto superiore di Economia e Commercio* (Venezia, 1938).

Also, in *La Vita Italiana* (Mar. 1938).

——, 'Antonio Agostino Cournot a Roma', *La Vita Italiana* (Roma, May 1938).

——, 'Nota biografica e bibliografica su A.A. Cournot', in Amoroso et al., *Cournot nella economia e nella filosofia,* (Padova, 1939) pp. 227 *et seq.*

Gide, C., 'La Théorie de l' Economie Politique de S. Jevons', *Journal des Economistes*, (1884) p. 190.

Guitton, H., 'Cournot et Pareto' in *Cahiers de l' I.S.E.A.* Cahiers franco-italiens (1963).

——, 'Cournot', *Encyclopedia of the Social Sciences* (1968).

——, Preface to the *Recherches sur les principes mathématiques de la théorie des Richesses.* (Paris: Calmann-Levy. 1974) pp. 7–25.

Hagen, C.H., 'Die Nothwendigkeit der Handelsfreiheit für das Nationaleinkommen, mathematisch nachgewiesen' (1844) pp. 30–1.

Hecht, L., *A. Cournot und L. Walras* (Heidelberg, 1930).

Knight F.H., Introduction to Carl Menger's *Principles of Economics* (1950).

La Harpe, J. de la., *De l' ordre et du hasard* (Neuchâtel, 1936).

——, 'Le rationalisme mathématique d' Antoine-Augustin Cournot', *Cournot nella Economia e nella filosofia* (Padova, 1939) pp. 1–26.

Landry, A., *Manuel d' Économie Politique* (1908) p. 839.

Lanzillo, A., ' "Caso" o vitalismo' *Cournot nella economia e nella filosofia* (Padova, 1939) pp. 59–84.

Liard, L., 'Un géomètre philosophe' *Revue des deux mondes* (Paris, 1877) pp. 102 *et seq.*

Lutfalla, G., Introduction to the edition of the *Recherches*, in the *Collection des économistes et des réformateurs sociaux de la France* (1938) pp. v-xxv.

Mentré, F., 'Les racines historiques du probabilisme rationnel de Cournot', *Revue de Métaphysique et de Morale* (1905).

——, *Cournot et la rennaissance du probabilisme au XIX siècle* (Paris, 1908).

Milhaud, G., 'Note sur la raison chez Cournot', *Revue de Métaphysique et de Morale* (1905).

——, *Études sur Cournot* (Paris, 1927).

Moore, H.L., 'The Personality of Antoine Augustin Cournot', *Quarterly Journal of Economics* (1905) pp. 370–99.

——, 'Antoine-Augustin Cournot', *Revue de Métaphysique et de Morale* (1905) pp. 521–43.

Nichol, A.J., 'A Re-appraisal of Cournot's Theory of Duopoly Price', *Journal of Political Economy* (1934), pp. 80–105.
Journal of Political Economy (1934), pp. 80–105.

——, 'Tragedies in the life of Cournot', *Econometrica* (1938) pp. 193–7.

Pareto, V. 'Di un errore del Cournot nel trattare l' Economia politica colla matematica', *Giornale degli Economisti* (1892) pp. 1–14.

Parodi, D., 'Le criticisme de Cournot', *Revue de Métaphysique de Morale* (1905) pp. 461–84.

Pietri-Tonelli, A. de., 'Generalizzazioni via via più larghe della soluzione data da Cournot al problema economico particolare dello scambio dei beni economici, fro i soggetti economici di spazi economici elementari diversi, in un tempo economico elementare', *Cournot nella economia e nella filosofia* (Padova, 1939) pp. 145–80.

Poincaré, H., 'Cournot et les principes du calcul infinitésimal' *Revue de Métaphysique et de Morale* (1905) pp. 293–306.

Reichardt, H., *Augustin Cournot: Sein Beitrag zur exakten Wirtschaftswissenschaft* (1954).

Rhodes, G.F., 'A Note Interpreting Cournot's Economics by His General Epistemology, *History of Political Economy* (1978) pp. 315–21.

Roy, R., 'Cournot et la Thèorie des Richesses', *Revue d' Économie*

Politique (1938) pp. 1547–60.

____, 'Cournot et la Théorie Mathématique des Richesses', Amoroso, *Cournot nella economia e nella filosofia* (1939) pp. 85–96.

____, 'Cournot et l' école mathématique', *Econometrica* (1933) pp. 13–22.

____, 'L' oeuvre économique d' Augustin Cournot', *Econometrica* (1939) pp. 134–44.

Ruyer, R., *L' humanité de l' avenir d' après Cournot* (Paris 1930).

Segond, J., *Cournot et la phychologie vitaliste* (Paris, 1911).

Scherer, E., 'Cournot', *Journal des Économistes* (1877) p. 304.

Sonnenschein, H., 'The Dual of Duopoly Is Complementary Monopoly: or Two of Cournot's Theories Are One', *Journal of Political Economy* (1968) pp. 316–18.

Tarde, G., 'L' accident et le rationnel en Histoire d' après Cournot', *Revue de Métaphysique et de Morale* (1905) pp. 319–47.

Viner, J., *Studies in the Theory of International Trade* (1937) pp. 586 *et seq.*

Walras, L., 'Cournot et l' économie mathématique's *Gazette de Lausanne* (13 July 1905). Fractions of this article are reproduced in de la Harpe, op. cit., pp. 143–5.

____, 'Principes d' une théorie mathématique de l' échange'. Memoir read before the 'Académie des sciences morales et politiques' on the 16 and 23 August 1873. Published in April 1874 in the *Journal des Économistes*.

____, 'Compte rendu des "Principes de la thèorie des richesses, *Indépendant de la Moselle* (13 July 1863), reproduced in the 1938 edn of the *Recherches* (*Collection des Économistes* 1938, pp. 22–32).

____, *Correspondence and Related Papers*, ed. W. Jaffé (1965) vol. 2.

IV OTHER BIBLIOGRAPHY

Allix, F. 'Un précurseur de l'école mathématique: Nicolas-François Canard,' *Revue d'Histoire Économique et Sociale* (Paris, 1920) pp. 38–67.

Antonelli, G. B., *Sulla Teoria Matematica della Economia Politica* (1886).

Calsoyas C.D., 'The Mathematical Theory of Monopoly in 1839: Charles Ellet jr', *Journal of Political Economy* (1950) pp. 162–70.

Chamberlin E.H., *The Theory of Monopolistic Competition* (1933).

____, 'On the Origin of Oligopoly', *Economic Journal* (1957) pp. 211–18.

Clark C., 'Von Thünen's Isolated State', *Oxford Economic Papers* (1967) pp. 370–7.

Dupuit, A.J.E., 'De la mesure de l' utilité des travaux publics', *Annales des Ponts et Chaussées*, vol. XIII (1844) pp. 332–75; trans. in *International Economic Papers*, no. 2 (1952) pp. 83–110.

____, 'De l' influence des péages sur l'utilité des voies de communication', *Annales des Ponts et Chaussées*, vol. XVII (1849) pp. 170–248; trans. in part in *International Economic Papers*, no. 11 (1962) pp. 7–31.

____, 'Péages' in *Dictionnaire de l' Economie Politique* (Coquelin et Guillaumin, 1852) pp. 341 *et seq.*

____, 'De l' utilité et de sa mesure', *Journal des Economistes* (1853) pp. 1–27.

Ekelund R.B., 'Jules Dupuit and the Early Theory of Marginal Cost Pricing', *Journal of Political Economy* (1968) pp. 462–71.

____, 'A Note on Jules Dupuit and Neoclassical Monopoly Theory', *Southern Economic Journal* (1969) pp. 257–62.

____, 'Price Discrimination and Product Differentiation in Economic Theory: an Early Analysis', *Quarterly Journal of Economics* (1970) pp. 268–78.

Ekelund R.B. and Gramm W.P., 'Early French Contributions to Marshallian Demand Theory', *Southern Economic Journal* (1970) pp. 277–86.

Ekelund R.B., and Hooks D.L., 'Joint Demand, Discriminating Two Parts Tariffs and Location Theory: an Early American Contribution', *Western Economic Journal* (1972) pp. 84–94.

Ellet, C., 'An Essay on the Laws of Trade in reference to the Works of Internal Improvement in the United States' (1839).

____, 'The Laws of Trade Applied to the Determination of the Most Advantageous Fare for Passengers on Railroads' (1840).

Fasiani, Mauro, "F. Fuoco: Applicazione dell' Algebra all' Economia Politica." Con note e appendici di Mauro Fasiani (Genova, 1937).

Fellner, W.J., *Competition Among the Few* (1949).

Gangemi, L. *Svolgimento del pensiero Economico* (1932).

Heertje A. and Hirschfeld R., 'Quelques Remarques sur la Dynamisation de la Théorie de l' Oligopole, *Économie Appliquée*, tome XVI (1963) pp. 33–41.

Horner, Francis, 'Canard: Principes d' Économie Politique', *Edin-*

burgh Review, no. II (1803) pp. 431–50.

Houghton R.W., 'A Note on the Early History of Consumers' Surplus', *Economica* (1958) pp. 49–57.

Jean-Faure, André, *Giammaria Ortes: un Vénitien du Settecento* (1934).

Leigh A.H., 'Von Thünen's Theory of Distribution and the Advent of Marginal Analysis', *Journal of Political Economy* (1946) pp. 481–502.

Le Trosne, Guillaume François, *De l'ordre Social* (Paris, 1777) p. 320, n 2.

Lewis L.G.D., *Charles Ellet Jr.: The Engineer as Individualist, 1810 1862* (Univ. of Illinois, 1968).

Loria, A, 'Teoria del Valore', *Archivio Giuridico* (Bologna, 1882).

Machlup F., *Economics of Sellers' Competition* (Baltimore, 1952).

Marescotti, Angelo, *Sulla Economia Sociale* (1856),

Masé-Dari, E, *Un precursore della Econometria* (1935).

Montanari, A. *La matematica applicata all' Economia Politica da Cesare Beccaria, Guglielmo Silio, Luigi Molinari Valeriani e Antonio Soialoja* (1892).

_____, *Contributo alla storia della teoria del valore* (1889).

Moore H.L., 'Von Thünen's Theory of Natural Wages', *Quarterly Journal of Economics* (1895) pp. 291–304 and 388–408.

Moret, Jacques, *L'emploi des mathématiques en économie politique* (1915).

Nicolini, F., 'Un antico economista matematico' *Giornale degli Economisti e Annali di Economia* (1878) pp. 11–23.

Okuguchi K., *Expectations and Stability in Oligopoly Models* (Springer-Verlag, 1976).

Ott A.E., *Einführung in die dynamische Wirtschaftstheorie, (Vandenhoech und Ruprecht)* (Göttingen, 1963).

Pecchio, Giuseppe, *Histoire de l'Économie Politique en Italie* (1830).

Robertson, R.M., 'Mathematical Economics before Cournot', *Journal of Political Economy* (1949) pp. 523–36.

Rossi, Giovanni, *La matematica applicata alla teoria della ricchezza sociale* (1889).

Schneider E., 'Johann Heinrich von Thünen', *Econometrica* (1934) pp. 1–12.

Spiegel, H.W., *Pierre Samuel Du Pont de Nemours 'On Economic Curves'* (1955).

Stigler G.J., 'The Development of Utility Theory', *Journal of Politi-*

cal Economy (1950) pp. 307–27 and 373–96.

Valeri, A. *Pietro Verri* (1937).

Weinberger O., *Mathematishe Volkswirtschaftslehre* (Stuttgart, 1930).

Index

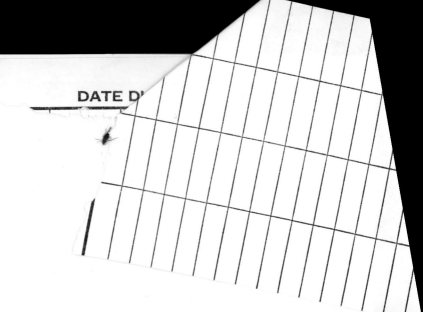

DATE D